W9-CES-376

GOLDA is a
fascinating and vividly written biography of
Golda Meir, a remarkable woman whose life
has been closely interwoven with the creation
of Israel.

This book is both the dramatic story of one
of the great human beings of our time and a
carefully researched history of a nation that
has faced a constant struggle for survival over
centuries.

For this edition Miss Mann has added a new
chapter recounting recent events, including
preparations for the celebration of the 25th
anniversary of the founding of Israel.

Golda

The Life of
Israel's Prime Minister

by
Peggy Mann

Updated Edition

WASHINGTON SQUARE PRESS
POCKET BOOKS • NEW YORK

GOLDA: The Life of Israel's Prime Minister

Coward, McCann edition published 1972

WASHINGTON SQUARE PRESS edition published May, 1973

3rd printing.........................April, 1974

Ł

Published by
POCKET BOOKS, a division of Simon & Schuster, Inc.,
630 Fifth Avenue, New York, N.Y.

WASHINGTON SQUARE PRESS editions are distributed
in the U.S. by Simon & Schuster, Inc., 630 Fifth Avenue,
New York, N.Y. 10020, and in Canada by Simon & Schuster of Canada, Ltd., Markham, Ontario, Canada.

Standard Book Number: 671-48132-0.
Library of Congress Catalog Card Number: 70-132591.
This WASHINGTON SQUARE PRESS edition is published by ar-
rangement with Coward, McCann & Geoghegan, Inc. Copyright, ©,
1971, 1973, by Peggy Mann. All rights reserved. This book, or por-
tions thereof, may not be reproduced by any means without permission of the original publisher: Coward, McCann & Geoghegan, Inc.,
200 Madison Avenue, New York, N.Y. 10016.
Cover art by David Harris.
Printed in the U.S.A.

Acknowledgments

My deep appreciation to Golda Meir for the time she gave to this book. My thanks also to Mrs. Meir's sister, Clara Stern; her son, Menachem Meir; her daughter-in-law, Ayalah Meir; her personal assistant, Lou Kaddar; her lifelong friend Regina Medzini; and Nahum Eshkol for their invaluable assistance. I would also like to thank for their help in information gathering or checking the manuscript Theodore Adams, Yakov Aviad, Ehud Avriel, Moshe Ben-David, Ezra Dannin, Simcha Dinitz, Judith Epstein, Ruth Gruber, William Houlton, Edna Mann, Lilly Nesher, Daniel Pinkas, Amit Silman, Esther Togman, and Mort Yarmon. And my thanks to my editor Margaret Frith for her talented cooperation every chapter of the way.

Of the numerous books, articles and documents used in researching this biography, the author would like to note the two which were invaluable: The autobiography, *Zikhroynes* ("Memories"), written by Golda Meir's older sister, Shana Korngold, Tel Aviv, 1968, and *Golda Meir: Israel's Leader,* by Marie Syrkin, a close friend of Mrs. Meir for many years. The personal letters quoted in this book were excerpted from those in Dr. Syrkin's biography, published by G. P. Putnam's Sons, New York, 1969.

Golda

Chapter 1

They were squatting in the alley, building a high castle of mud.

One of the children looked up sharply, a five-year-old girl named Golda. "Be quiet!" she said. She had heard the sound of horses' hoofs, muffled by mud.

But the others kept on chattering and laughing loudly.

The Cossacks came then, rounding the corner at full gallop. With wild screams and laughter they charged straight at the children who stared, frozen, unable to move.

Slashing at the air with swords, sabers, whips, the Cossacks jumped their horses over the huddled bodies and charged on down the street, their cries trailing behind them: "Death to the Jews!"

Golda ran into the house, sobbing with terror. "Mama." She bolted the heavy door. *"Mama!"*

But no one was home except little Tzipka, who sat on the floor playing with some stones.

Mama was never at home any more, not since they'd moved here to Pinsk.

Golda went to the window and stood looking out. She did not want her sister to see her cry.

She hated it here in this city of Pinsk, this city of swamps and muddy streets. Streets where playing children could be trampled to death in the afternoon.

There had been no Cossacks in Kiev.

Fervently she wished they'd never moved. Things had

been better in Kiev, with Papa working and Mama always at home.

"Papa," she whispered, "why did you have to go away?"

In Kiev she had never felt afraid.

Maybe once—but that was all.

Once, when she was four years old, she'd watched her father hammering planks over the front door. When she asked why, Papa had said something about a pogrom.

And Golda had asked, "What is a pogrom?"

"Sometimes," Papa said, "people get drunk and run through the streets shouting, 'Death to the Jews.' They break into homes where Jews live. To rob. To—" He shrugged and said no more.

But she understood the unspoken words. *"Why,* Papa? Why would they do those things?"

"Why? Goldie, people have been asking that question for two thousand years. They've never been given the answer."

All that night she had been afraid; she slept very little. But the next morning her father had taken the planks away. There was no pogrom after all. Yet, the question *why* remained deep in Golda's mind.

And why should a Jew not be paid for his work? She had asked this question too—until her mother told her not to mention it any more, for it only made Papa feel bad.

Because he was a fine carpenter, Papa always had plenty of work in Kiev. Orders even came in from aristocrats and royalty. But when it was time to pay for the work the customers often refused. Because Moshe Mabovitch was a Jew. And who bothered to pay Jews?

Then, one day, Papa's chance came.

He'd won the contract to supply desks and chairs for a new school. The bids had been submitted by numbers only; no name. No one knew that the contract had been given to a Jewish carpenter.

Papa was elated. With this one job he would earn enough to set himself up in his own shop. His children would have milk to drink every day and meat once a week. He could at last become somebody: Moshe Mabovitch the Cabinetmaker.

He had borrowed money to buy the materials he needed and to hire additional carpenters. He worked all day and late every night and the job was finished before the deadline. "Everything exactly to specifications," Papa had exclaimed with pride. "Except I used a better grade of wood than they asked for. After all, this is a new school. If they're pleased, they may have a lot more work for me."

He hired three horses and carts to deliver the load. The family stood by the doorway to wave good-bye. Papa was a very handsome man, and he sat tall with the reins in his hands. He was singing softly.

He came home, broken.

When he walked in his face looked gray. He sat down in a chair.

No one said, "What happened?" Everyone was afraid to ask.

After a while Papa spoke. His voice was flat. "The superintendent liked my work. He nodded and smiled as he examined the desks and chairs. He was obviously very satisfied. Then he asked my name. I said, 'Moshe Mabovitch, Excellency.' The superintendent frowned. *Mabovitch?* he said. Then he told me, 'I'm afraid this work is not at all what we want. You're disqualified.' "

Mama gasped.

Papa looked at her. "Don't worry, Bluma. The superintendent is doing me a great honor. He is keeping the desks and chairs. The only thing is—I will not be paid."

"Why not?" Golda exclaimed. "You worked so hard!"

Papa nodded. "That doesn't matter, Goldie. The only thing which seems to matter is that Mabovitch is a Jewish name."

He said very little after that. And he worked very little. Mostly he just sat in a chair reading a book or staring out the window.

Then came the night of Shavuot.

Usually they had only bread, potatoes, and beans for dinner. But on holidays there was always something special. And on this night of Shavuot there was also dried fish. It should have been a festive dinner. But Papa's depression seemed to have reached inside each one of them.

Papa broke a piece of bread and ate it. Then he said "how can we go on like this? To live always without hope?"

Mama did not answer.

Papa broke a piece of bread and ate it. Then he said in a quiet voice, "I can't stand this any more. I am leaving Russia. I am going to America."

Papa had sold most of their belongings plus his carpentry tools, which brought in enough money to get him to the United States. There Jews were paid like anyone else. Papa would soon save enough to send them tickets so they could join him.

Meanwhile, Mama, with her three daughters, had returned to her hometown of Pinsk.

She had to. She was no longer allowed to remain in Kiev for with Moshe gone the family lost its government dispensation to live outside the Pale of Settlement—the sections of Russia set aside for the Jews.

It was sometimes possible for a Jew with special—and needed—talents to take a government examination which, if he passed, enabled him and his wife and children to live outside the Pale. Papa had taken such an examination. He had succeeded. Consequently, the Jew Mabovitch, his wife Bluma, and his first-born child, Shana, had been given a dispensation to live in Kiev, the capital city of the Ukraine.

Golda had been born there, on May 3, 1898, in the tenth year of the parents' marriage. (Bluma had actually borne five children between Shana and Golda—one girl and four boys. They all had died.)

Tzipka, too, had been born in Kiev, in 1902—the year before Papa went away and Mama moved back to the Pale.

When they first got to Pinsk they had all crowded in with Bluma's father, an old man they called *Zayde,* or Grandpa. Then, since they had no money at all, Mama started baking bread and peddling it door to door, while

Zayde looked after Golda and Tzipka. *Zayde* worked too; he owned a small tavern. But he could keep an eye on the children as they played outside in the alley or in the room where *Zayde* lived behind the tavern. Shana went to school —and to numerous meetings which she refused to talk about.

Finally, Bluma earned enough money to move her family into two small rooms. Golda and Tzipka slept in the kitchen, the walls of which were black with soot from the stove. Mama and Shana shared the tiny back room. The house was next door to the police station, and during the nights they were often startled awake by the screams of prisoners being beaten.

That was the worst part of living in Pinsk, the terrible sounds of screaming in the nighttime.

They'd had only one short letter from Papa, reporting that he had tried his luck first in New York City. But, when he finally found a job, it paid only three dollars a week. He would never make enough money to send for his family at that rate of pay. So HIAS—the Hebrew Immigrant Aid Society—had given him a ticket to Milwaukee, Wisconsin, in the hope that his skill as a carpenter might earn him more in the Midwestern city which was not overpopulated with penniless immigrants willing to work for next to nothing.

He had found a job as a railroad carpenter. But Papa had not mentioned how much he was making. Or when he would send the tickets so they could join him.

"I want my Mama!"

Golda turned away from the window. Little Tzipka had stopped playing with her stones. She was standing up, looking cross.

"Mama's out," Golda said. "Selling bread."

"I want my Papa," Tzipka demanded.

"Papa's gone away."

Tzipka's lower lip trembled.

"Don't cry!" Golda said quickly. "Here!" She took Tzipka's pacifier from the shelf, a lump of sugar tied in a clean cloth.

Tzipka started to suck intently on her sugar.

"I'll play with you," Golda said, "till Mama gets home." She squatted by the pile of stones and began setting them out in a pattern. "Let's make a boat," she said. "A boat that can take us to Milwaukee."

A few days later on a Saturday afternoon Golda was curled up in her favorite spot, the warming shelf above the stove. The house was quiet; everyone was at synagogue. Suddenly the door opened. Her older sister, Shana, came in, followed by ten others.

Golda was about to climb down from the shelf, but something about the behavior of the group made her draw back in silence. Everyone seemed tense, upset. Shana bolted the door. Two men stood by the window as if on guard duty.

The rest spoke quietly. They sat on the floor.

Shana set the samovar on the table. "If the police break in," she said, "we're having a Sabbath tea party!"

Presently someone announced, "Shamai will now report."

At the risk of being seen, Golda peeped out over the edge of the shelf. She'd heard *Zayde* teasing Shana about a young man named Shamai.

He stood up by the kitchen table. He was certainly handsome. He wore his hair long to his shoulders. Golda watched him, entranced. Shana was fifteen. Many girls married at fifteen. Perhaps this Shamai would soon become a member of their family. Then she heard him say the word pogrom—and she started to listen.

He was reporting on a pogrom which had just taken place in a city called Kishinev. Rumors had been spread about a Christian servant girl who was murdered by her Jewish master.

"However," Shamai said, "what happened was this: the girl took poison and died. The Jewish family she worked for did everything possible to save her life. Nevertheless, printed handbills were circulated through the streets, granting permission to inflict 'bloody punishment'—as they put it—on fifty thousand Jews of Kishinev during the Easter holiday.

"Some of you may have read reports," Shamai went on. "But I have spoken to a man who was there. A man who saw."

He paused for a moment. "It started at noontime, when the Easter churchbells began to ring. A large crowd of townspeople broke into Jewish homes and shops, stealing or destroying everything in sight. The police did nothing. They stood by, watching. So, by nightfall, the looters turned into murderers, fell upon Jews with knives and clubs, torturing them, killing them. Only once did the police interfere. A group of Jews were trying to defend themselves—with sticks. So the police stepped in to disarm the Jews."

Cries of horror broke out in the gathered group. Golda felt fury burning within her. She too wanted to cry out. But she said nothing.

Shamai raised his hand for silence. "Wait. Hear the rest. All that night and all the next day it went on. Some Jews had nails driven into their heads. Some had their eyes put out. Children were thrown from garret windows, dashed to pieces on the street below. Women were raped, after which their stomachs were ripped open, their breasts cut off. Still the police did nothing. Nor did the city officials. Or the so-called intelligentsia. Students. Doctors. Lawyers. Priests. They walked leisurely along the streets, watching the show."

He paused. A taut stillness stretched through the room.

"At last," Shamai went on, "at six that evening troops finally appeared. The crowds fled. The pogrom was over." He paused again. "*That* pogrom," he said.

After the stark silence there came such a swell of sound that it seemed the walls of the kitchen must burst apart.

"*Quiet!*" Shamai cried out. The word slashed through the air like a whip. The group responded at once. "Don't forget," he warned, "the police are right next door."

They spoke then with intensity, but softly. Golda understood little of what they were saying. She understood one thing only. In the city of Kishinev Jewish children like herself had been thrown out of windows. Jewish women like her mother had been murdered—left to die with stomachs slit open like animals. Jews who had wronged no one had been tortured and killed. Why? *Why?*

When the others had gone, Golda climbed down from her place on the warming shelf. She ran to Shana, clung to her. She did not cry. The horror within her was so deep it seemed to have frozen her tears.

"So you heard," Shana kept saying as she stroked Golda's hair. "I didn't know . . . I didn't realize you were up there."

She tried then, by way of comforting Golda, to explain. "We're *doing* something about it. Don't you understand? That's what our secret meetings are for. But you must never tell anyone about these meetings. Never!"

"What—would happen?" Golda asked in a tight, small voice.

"When the police catch a member of our group," Shana said, "he is flogged with a whip. The lucky ones are released—after a night of torture. Some are sent to Siberia to a slave labor camp. Some are killed."

Golda looked up at her sister. "I'll never tell," she said. "Even if they put out my eyes and slit my stomach, I'll never tell."

Shana began to weep. She took Golda onto her lap and held her, hugging her. "I wish that you hadn't heard," she said over and over again.

Golda liked sitting there with her sister's arms tight around her. It made her feel safe. Shana would protect her.

Presently she asked, "How will you stop the pogroms?"

"Stop them?"

Golda nodded.

"Oh," Shana said. "Well—" she spoke slowly. "Some in our group, like Shamai, feel if the Czar is overthrown, then Jews will have a chance. Others think the only way we'll ever have freedom, equality, is if we have our own country. Just as Russians do. Or Frenchmen. Or Americans."

"That's a good idea," Golda said.

Shana laughed a little. But her laughter sounded like someone starting to cry. "It's not a very original idea, Goldie. You said it yourself last Passover."

"I did?"

"You said, 'L'shanah ha-baah bi Yerushalayim'—Next year in Jerusalem. You said it along with millions of Jews all over the world."

"Oh," said Golda. "I thought I was only saying a prayer."

Shana nodded. "For hundreds of years, perhaps, that's all it was. A prayer. Now it's something much more. Now it's—a plan. A movement. Called Political Zionism. A year before you were born, Goldie, there was a meeting in Switzerland. Delegates came from almost every country in which Jews live. And together they formed this new movement. 'To establish,' she recited, 'to establish for the Jewish people a publicly recognized, legally secured home in Palestine. Jerusalem," she added, "is the capital city of Palestine. Jerusalem, founded by the Jewish king named David, three thousand years ago."

"Oh," said Golda, not understanding very much of what her sister was saying. "Well," she added, "tomorrow I'm not going to eat anything either!"

"What?" said Shana.

"At the end of the meeting you all said you'd fast tomorrow, didn't you? For the dead Jews of Kishinev."

Shana nodded. "I suppose that was the only thing we did agree on."

"Well, I'm fasting too!" Golda said.

The next day she ate no breakfast. No lunch.

Zayde tried to explain that it would not help the dead Jews of Kishinev if a five-year-old girl went hungry all day long.

"Maybe it won't do any good," said Golda. "But at least it's doing something!"

And she refused to eat or to drink even a mouthful of water until the sun had set that evening.

Chapter 2

For three long years the family lived with fear.

Now when the night quiet was split by the sounds of screaming from the police station next door, Golda would lie in bed rigid with terror. Perhaps they were flogging, torturing, her sister Shana.

Over and over, Bluma Mabovitch pleaded with her eldest daughter to stop attending the dangerous secret meetings. But Shana paid no attention. Finally, in desperation, Bluma disowned her rebellious daughter, locked her out of the house. So Shana went to live with her aunt. But the aunt soon became terrorized. What if Shana should be arrested in *her* home? So *she* locked Shana out—whereupon Bluma took the girl back again.

Zayde had another theory about Shana's secret meetings. "She's running around with those fool rebels for one reason only. His name is Shamai Korngold. And until that young man pays her some attention, we'll all live in danger."

Such remarks about Shamai made Shana so furious that she would slam out of the house. And when she returned she often refused to speak to *Zayde* for days.

Golda frequently found herself wondering whether all the secret meetings her sister attended would ever result in anything. The pogroms and the savage raids of the Cossacks became more frequent along Russia's western border in the territory where Jews were permitted to settle. The Czar sent a special contingent of Cossacks to Pinsk to put

10

down the revolutionaries. They often galloped through the streets at twilight, for it was then that the young people began to gather, after work. Sometimes the Cossacks came quietly, their horses' hoofs muffled by the mud, for they did not want their quarry to flee. Suddenly then the street would explode with wild shouts, raucous laughter—and the screams of Jews who had been struck down by whips and sabers.

By now Golda had heard—and overheard—many impassioned Zionist speeches. The name Theodor Herzl was sometimes mentioned. It seemed he was having meetings with the Sultan of Turkey, the Kaiser of Germany, the Prime Minister of England; trying to persuade them that the Jews would be safe only if they had once again their own homeland in Palestine.

This man named Herzl wrote papers, raised money, had meetings, established federations of Zionists in many faraway lands. It was he, in fact, who had organized the First Zionist Congress in Switzerland, two years before Golda was born. Shana had even shown her a newspaper picture of Herzl. He was handsome, with black hair and a heavy black beard. But somehow, even though she had seen his picture, Golda could not make herself believe that he really existed. He sounded more like some hero in a storybook.

She did believe that Palestine existed; with its capital city, Jerusalem. But if Jews had been saying, "Next year in Jerusalem" for eighteen hundred years, what hope could there be that she, Goldie Mabovitch from Pinsk, Russia, would ever really *get* there?

Consequently, all her hopes fastened around a single magic word: Milwaukee. She often whispered it over and over like an incantation when she went to bed: "Mil . . . wau . . . kee . . ."

But when would Papa ever earn enough money to buy the boat tickets?

She had by now even forgotten what he looked like. Sometimes she would stand in front of the photograph on Mama's shelf, staring at the face of the handsome, bearded man with ears which stuck out a little. "Papa," she would whisper, "have you forgotten us too?"

Then, late one Wednesday afternoon in the spring of 1906, *Zayde* came into the small room behind his tavern where Golda and Tzipka were playing. He was smiling, which was not unusual. He often smiled. He sat down and pulled Golda onto his lap, which *was* unusual. It was also somewhat unpleasant, for the old man always smelled strongly of onions. This was understandable since *Zayde* ate only black bread and onions dipped in salt, except on the Sabbath when he added a little fish or meat.

"Well, girl, you are going!" he announced, breathing heavily into Golda's face.

"Going where?" Golda said, trying politely to remove herself from *Zayde*'s lap.

The old man tightened his arms around her. "How shall I get on without my little Goldie? And," he added, "my pretty Tzipka."

"Where are we going, *Zayde?*" Golda said again.

His answer seemed to explode in her ears. "To America."

Golda stared at him.

"Yes," said *Zayde*, "I never thought I'd live to see the day, but your Papa has finally sent the boat tickets. Your mother wants me to bring you home at once."

Golda let out a yell, so loud that Tzipka, frightened, began to cry.

Golda scrambled off her grandfather's lap and hugged her little sister. "For once you have nothing to cry about, Tzip. *We're going to Milwaukee!*"

The actual parting, when it came, was far less joyous than Golda had anticipated.

Shana did not want to leave at all. Everyone knew why, but said nothing. If Shamai had shown even the mildest interest in her, she might well have remained in Pinsk, living with her aunt or grandfather until—hopefully— Shamai proposed. But Shamai seemed genuinely delighted

when Shana informed him she was going to the United
States.

Bluma, of course, was excited. She would soon be seeing
her husband again. But to rip up the roots of forty years,
to make a new life as a stranger in an unknown land—it
was not easy.

Even Golda felt unexpected depths of sadness when she
said good-bye to her friends and relatives. And when she
clung to *Zayde* at the railroad station, the old man's oniony
smell seemed somehow almost beautiful.

They had to leave the country illegally, for Moshe had
not sent enough money to purchase government passports.

"It's just as well," Bluma said. "Your father's motto
always was 'Stay away from the authorities.' "

A string of agents replaced the authorities. Each had to
be paid in advance.

On the first evening, the family—hot, dirty, and exhausted—reached a city where an old woman met them at
the station. "Are you—the people?" She took them to her
home where, Bluma had been told, they would find a hot
meal and beds for the night.

Instead, a seedy-looking man came panting in to announce: "The police have just discovered that Jews are
attempting to cross the border. Without papers. We must
bribe them all. You must give us more money, Mrs. Mabovitch. Then we'll leave at once. I have a wagon waiting.
We'll go through the forest."

Bluma Mabovitch was not a tall woman. But when she
stood up and crossed her hefty arms over her ample bo-
som, she could be an imposing figure indeed. "We have
paid," she announced, "all we're going to pay! You promised we would cross the border by train. And so we will.
If not, we return to Pinsk tonight. And you, sir, can return
our money!"

Early the next morning the Mabovitches crossed the
border—by train.

They had been supplied with passports of persons long
deceased. Bluma had to pass for a girl of twenty. Eighteen-
year-old Shana wore her hair loose and tried to look
twelve. Eight-year-old Golda's papers declared she was

five. And little Tzipka crossed the border with a total stranger whom she had been directed to call Mama.

The passport examination went by without incident. But when they finally got off the train in Galicia, Poland, the Mabovitches discovered that all their luggage had been stolen.

Along with dozens of other passengers, they were crowded into a wooden hut. A few filthy blankets had been thrown as bedding on the dirt floor. There was no room to stretch out, so Bluma sat, holding her smallest child in her lap. Tzipka began to sob, "I want to go home. I want to go home."

"We are going home," Bluma promised, stroking the little girl's hair. "To a new home. With Papa."

They were, however, a long time getting there. After two days of waiting in the wooden hut, a train finally came. After another two days of traveling, sitting up all the way, they reached the port of Antwerp, Belgium. There they were taken to the Immigration Home, where they had their first warm meal since leaving Pinsk. And their first wash.

Bluma removed a few of the coins she had sewn into her clothes and ventured out to buy some underwear and sweaters for the girls. With this they would have to make do till they got to Milwaukee.

Two days later the name Mabovitch was finally called out in the dining hall of the Immigration Home. They would sail the next morning on a ship bound for Quebec, Canada—if they passed the medical examination. They lined up in fear. Many passengers had, they knew, already been rejected—for such inconsequential items as hair lice or bad eyes.

But the four Mabovitch females were told to board the ship.

They had a cabin in steerage class—a dank and airless room, so small that the stocky Bluma could barely turn around. "Well," she announced, "there would never be room in here for us *and* our baggage. We're lucky it was stolen."

The seas were rough all the way. At times they were

sure the ship would capsize. Passengers staggered up from below, weak and pale, to stand retching by the ship's railing. It seemed that Goldie Mabovitch was the only one aboard who was not seasick. Indeed, she was always hungry. At mealtimes each of the steerage passengers who wanted to partake of the unpalatable food stood by the door of his cabin with a cup and small plate. Then a crew member would come along and slop out some stew or gruel and tepid tea. Golda usually had second helpings.

Finally after fourteen days, the ship reached Quebec.

It was a long hot train trip from Quebec to Milwaukee. Golda's excitement was dampened by total exhaustion. It had been a month since they kissed *Zayde* good-bye at the railroad station in Pinsk. A month of difficult and almost constant travel.

She was fast alseep when the train pulled into the Milwaukee station.

"Wake up!" Mama was shaking her shoulder. "Comb your hair. We're here!"

Perhaps it was because they all felt suddenly strange and somehow afraid, perhaps that is why they took so long getting ready. When they finally left the train there were only a few people waiting by the tracks. One of them was a tall, spare-looking, handsome man who was staring at them.

Bluma took a hesitant step toward him. "Girls, it's your—Papa," she said softly.

Papa? This man, Golda felt, was a total stranger. He looked nothing like the photograph Mama kept on the bedroom shelf. This man had no beard, no black suit. And he looked young. Much younger than Mama.

The man walked toward them slowly. "Hello, Bluma," he said in a formal manner. "Shana. Golda. And is this big girl my baby?" He stooped and lifted Tzipka into his arms. Only with her did he seem relaxed. "You don't remember your Papa, do you? You were only eighteen months when I went away."

"I want to get down," Tzipka said in quite a loud voice.

He put her down, and she hid behind Mama's long black skirts.

"Where's all your baggage?" the man asked.

So Mama started telling him how it had been stolen, and Golda chimed in with some details of the trip, and as they started to walk toward the station doors Tzipka held his hand—and they began to be a family again.

Papa had not, after all, found a place for them to live. He took them to a room he had rented in the apartment of a Polish-Jewish family named Badner. Golda looked at it in some dismay. After all the stories she had told Tzipka about the wonders of Milwaukee, America, here they were, five of them, crowded into one room. At least back in Pinsk they'd had two rooms.

But the wonders of Milwaukee, America, soon became amply evident.

Mrs. Badner came in, smiling, to announce that dinner was ready. She had prepared a banquet for them, starting with gefilte fish and ending with fresh-baked pastries. As they sat down to eat, Mama said, rather embarrassed, "Don't mind how we look, Mrs. Badner. All our things were stolen."

At which point Papa announced, "By tomorrow, Mrs. Badner, you won't recognize these four ladies. I'm taking them to Schusters to buy some new clothes."

Schusters Department Store, Golda decided, was a sample of heaven built on the earth. There were racks and counters and shelves filled with *hundreds* of different dresses, in all sizes, hats, shoes, stockings, underwear, coats, hair ribbons. . . . Papa picked out an entire outfit for each of them.

Shana, who had been unusually quiet since she arrived in Milwaukee, said, "I don't want a hat, Papa. I never wear hats."

Papa turned on her rather sharply. "In America, young lady, you will dress like everyone else! I don't want people pointing you out as a greenhorn from Pinsk!"

Golda and Tzipka, however, were thrilled at each of

Papa's purchases. And when everything had been wrapped and paid for, they did not want to leave. "Let's spend all day in this store," Golda suggested. "Just wandering around!"

In her new American outfit Bluma promptly regained her confidence, and the following morning she set out to find the family a place to live.

The Badner apartment was in a section of Milwaukee inhabited primarily by Jews from Eastern Europe. It was a section with a common language: Yiddish. Since Yiddish was also the Mabovitches' family language, Bluma soon found herself feeling quite at home.

After a few days she was able to announce, "Well, I've come across the perfect place! A little grocery store on the corner of Sixth and Walnut streets. And behind the shop there's an apartment with *five* rooms!"

"Forget it!" said Papa. "I do not plan to spend my days haggling with housewives over the price of dill pickles."

"Well," said Mama, "I do. Besides, I've already given a down payment on the property."

"And just where did you get the money?"

"I borrowed it," said Bluma. "From a German money-lender.

They moved in the following morning.

The house and shop were thick with dirt and grime. Even so, the place seemed to Golda and Tzipka a private paradise. Behind the small, dark shop, a doorway led to a small, dark kitchen. Off the kitchen was a small, dark bedroom—the parents' room. Upstairs there were three more rooms—the living room, with a pot-bellied "parlor stove," and two bedrooms. Shana would have her own room, for the first time in her life. Golda and Tzipka would share the single bed in the remaining room. The house also had a basement and a backyard containing a clothesline and weeds.

Golda decided that her favorite feature was the icebox. Back in Pinsk refrigeration had consisted of a hole in the ground with a piece of ice in it, covered with straw. "And since we're going into the grocery business," Mama exclaimed, "this icebox will always be filled! You girls will never go hungry again."

Shana was specially intrigued by the water which ran into the kitchen sink—merely by the turn of a handle. Back home in Pinsk water had to be pumped from a well, a difficult job, often impossible in winter when the well water froze. She was also pleased by the gaslights which gave far brighter illumination than the smelly oil lamps used in Pinsk.

Tzipka's special delight was the flush toilet in the backyard outhouse. She stood entranced, pulling the long rusty chain, watching the water gurgle loudly down the toilet bowl.

Mama's heart obviously lay in the small, musty shop. "I started working in my father's shop when I was six years old," she said. "It's in my blood."

They spent several days scrubbing the place clean. Papa made shelves and a long table for the shop. "And that," he announced to Bluma, "is my total contribution. If you want this store, you'll have to run it yourself."

"And what," said Mama, "will you be doing?"

"I will be a building contractor."

Bluma did not know exactly what a building contractor was. But it sounded rather splendid. So she kissed him proudly. "That will be fine," she said.

Actually, Mama had expected that Shana would work full time in the grocery shop. But Shana, like Papa, had only disdain for the store. "If I'd wanted to work in a *kreml,** I could have stayed in Pinsk," she declared. She consequently got a factory job. Which left eight-year-old Golda to assist Mama in the store.

At six every morning Mama went out to the wholesale markets to buy fresh fruits, vegetables, and bread. Golda opened the shop. She enjoyed it, standing on a box behind the counter—so her head would show above the shelf—taking orders, then measuring out one-eighth of a pound of butter, a cup of sugar, six rolls, and putting everything

---

* Small, dingy, hole-in-the-wall type of shop.

into separate paper bags. Somehow the ladies who came in to shop seemed ashamed to haggle over prices with a child. So Golda managed to do fairly well. Even so, since all of their customers seemed to be constantly short of cash, Bluma found herself having to make repeated trips to the East Side to visit the German moneylender.

The children, however, did not know this. Nor did Papa, who retained his part-time job as a railroad carpenter while waiting for his business as a building contractor to develop.

The months passed by quickly enough and soon the city of Milwaukee was celebrating summer's official end with a splendid Labor Day parade.

As a union member Papa was entitled to march. He was always a meticulous dresser. His suit—no matter how old and worn—was always perfectly pressed and spotless. And for the parade he bought himself a brand-new straw hat.

"Papa," Golda exclaimed, "you'll be the handsomest marcher in Milwaukee!"

She and Tzipka, of course, wore their new Schusters dresses—starched so stiffly that the skirts stood up by themselves. Their hair ribbons were huge. So were their smiles as they stood on the edge of the sidewalk listening to the far-off martial music and waiting for Papa and the parade to come into view.

Mounted policemen lined the street to hold back the crowds. Suddenly a police horse reared in front of Tzipka.

"Cossacks!" the child screamed and fell down in a dead faint.

The terrors of Pinsk had not been forgotten.

They were never forgotten.

Indeed, they helped to shape the life of Golda Mabovitch, the girl who grew up to become Prime Minister of Israel.

Chapter 3

It was September, the first day of school—the *free* public school, a splendid three-story brick building on Fourth Street. Golda still could scarcely believe it. In Pinsk the only school she had been to was run by a sleepy old rabbi who taught his class the Hebrew letters and a smattering of Jewish history. Bluma had, furthermore, discouraged Golda from going since the rabbi had to be paid. What, she frequently inquired, did girls need with an education?

But here in America it was expected that girls as well as boys be sent to school. Indeed, it was even required by law!

Golda looked up at Mr. Finn, the principal, as she held tightly to Tzipka's hand.

"What's your name?" the principal asked.

"Golda, sir."

He nodded. "Golda. . . . Well, that's all right. You can keep that name."

"And what's *your* name?"

"Tzipka, sir."

"Tzipka?" Mr. Finn frowned. "What kind of a name is *that?* We'll call you—" he thought for a moment, "Clara!"

And Clara she became, from that moment on, to everyone outside her family.

Mr. Finn turned back to Golda. "What's your last name?"

She told him.

20

"How do you spell it?" asked Mr. Finn.

"M-a-b-o-w-e-h-z."

"That's a strange spelling. Are you sure?"

She nodded. "Yes, sir. That's what the sign says over my mama's grocery store."

It was, indeed, what the sign said, for this was the English spelling the sign painter had determined on as translation for the name Mabovitch.

"M-a-b-o-w-e-h-z," said Mr. Finn, writing down the name on a form.

And this was the spelling the family retained through the years.

Then Mr. Finn discovered that the newly named Clara was only four years old. "Bring her home," he told Golda. "She can't come back till she's five."

"But I can't bring her home," Golda exclaimed. "Mama's busy running the store. She *needs* Tzipka out of the house."

Mr. Finn shrugged. "If we took her, she'd be the youngest in the class. And then she'd have to do kindergarten all over again next year."

"That's all right," Golda said. "She'll *love* that. Won't you, Tzip?" And she gave Tzipka a little shove.

Unlike Golda, Tzipka had not learned very much English during the summer. She did not know what her sister and this tall man were talking about. She looked up at Golda, who was nodding at her strenuously. So Tzipka nodded too.

As it turned out, she hated kindergarten. She was a creative child. During the summer she and Golda had put on plays in the basement; they had fashioned kites out of newspaper; they had sewn their own rag dolls. But in kindergarten nothing of the sort was done. And after her short lifetime of freedom, Tzipka found school both regimented and boring. They had, for example, coloring books. But they could not select their own colors. The teacher directed: "The sky, blue; the barn, red." And if the crayon went over the heavy black line, she spoke to them severely. In between "lessons" each child had to sit in absolute silence, hands folded before him on the table.

One day as they walked home, Tzipka told Golda in eloquent Yiddish, "Well, I am certainly not going back next year to do those same stupid things all over again!"

"It'll get better," Golda promised. "Wait till you get to the second grade where *I* am. It's wonderful!"

As the years went on, Tzipka did find school more enjoyable. But it was difficult following Golda who, it turned out, was a brilliant and conscientious student, making 95 or more in each subject.

One night as they lay in bed, Tzipka announced, "It's a wonder I don't hate you, Goldie. Every teacher I've had says to me, 'You sure aren't like your sister Golda!' " Then she paused. "And they don't even know you work in the store till ten at night. And all day Sunday. How do you do it, Goldie? And get all your homework done besides?"

There was no answer. Perhaps Golda was already asleep. Or perhaps she had no answer.

"Well . . . excuse my back," Tzipka said, as she turned toward the wall. It was a special politeness the sisters had; each would excuse herself when she turned over in the narrow bed.

("When Shana gets married," Mama often said, "you girls won't have to sleep together any more. In the meantime, thank goodness you're both skinny!")

Not only was Golda the smartest child in the class, she was also, without doubt, one of the most popular. In addition, inspired perhaps by her sister Shana, her social consciousness developed early.

Although school was free, schoolbooks were not, and some of Golda's classmates were too poor to buy books. When she was ten Golda decided to do something about this. She hung up hand-lettered posters announcing a public meeting run by the American Young Sisters Society. She had made up the name. It sounded, she felt, impressive.

The hall was well filled. Word had spread that a fourth

grade girl had organized the meeting and would be its chairman. She proved an able one. In loud, clear words she explained how important it was that *all* children be able to have school books. "We called this meeting," she concluded, "because we knew if you understood the problem you would help."

Many purses were opened that night and a substantial sum of money was collected for the needy students of the Fourth Street School.

This was not to be the last fund-raising meeting at which Golda spoke. Indeed, thirty-five years later, when the new country called Israel was about to be born, its leader, David Ben-Gurion, would proclaim: "Some day when our history is written it will be said that there was a Jewish woman who raised the money which made this nation possible."

The Jewish woman he referred to was Golda.

Chapter 4

A letter came one day from Pinsk which seemed to transform Shana.

It was from her aunt who reported that Shamai had been arrested. His wealthy grandfather had, however, bribed the police, who released him. Shamai had fled the country and was now working in a cigarette factory in New York City. The thoughtful aunt even set down his address.

Shana promptly wrote to him suggesting that he come to Milwaukee.

One week later he arrived.

Golda accompanied her sister to the railroad station. Wide-eyed, she watched as Shana and Shamai ran to each other, embraced, and kissed.

Later, Shana confided to Golda that this was the first time he had ever kissed her. "Maybe," she added softly, almost to herself, "maybe here in Milwaukee he will begin to notice me a little."

He did.

Shamai had been lonely in New York City. He knew no English. He had no friends, no profession. Life had been difficult indeed.

Perhaps that was why he suddenly found Shana Mabovitch so attractive. Or perhaps it was because she was, in fact, a highly attractive young girl who shared his background and beliefs, and who adored him.

Bluma Mabovitch, however, looked with something less than delight at the arrival of the young man from Pinsk. She had been determined that Shana should marry well—a man who could give her an easier life than she, Bluma, had thus far known. But *this* young man, Shamai, was hopeless!

Shana reported one day with pride that Shamai's wealthy grandfather had offered to give the boy all his money if Shamai would promise to pray three times a day and go to Palestine. Shamai had replied that he was not interested in Palestine. And he never prayed at all. Whereupon, the grandfather cut him off without a cent. The young man's high-handed behavior in this crucial matter so incensed the practical Bluma that she forbade Shamai to come into her house again. Whereupon, Shana moved out.

She had, in fact, moved out several times before after heated arguments with her mother, most of them about the fact that Shana refused to help in the store. But always, after a short time, Shana moved back again. She had last come home after she injured her finger on a factory sewing machine. The finger became infected. The entire hand swelled.

Bluma had welcomed her recalcitrant daughter with the caustic words: "When it hurts, everybody runs home!"

But this time Shana did not "run home."

She began spitting blood.

The doctor insisted that she stop work at once and go to a sanitarium in Denver, Colorado. Fortunately, this was feasible. Wealthy Jews supported a number of sanitariums in Denver, which were free for those who could not afford to pay.

Since the stubborn mother and daughter had still not made up, and since in family matters Papa abided by his wife's directives, it was only Golda and Shamai who saw Shana off at the station.

"I'll write you every day," Shamai vowed, as he held her in his arms.

"You won't!" Shana wept. "You'll forget all about me. I know."

But he did not forget. Indeed, some months later he moved to Denver to be with Shana, taking the only job he could get—washing dishes in a sanitarium.

Slowly, Shana recovered and was finally dismissed from the sanitarium. But the doctors advised her to remain in the dry climate of Denver. She took a job in another hospital, setting tables, sweeping, working in the bakery. Shamai, meanwhile, expanded his activities. In addition to dishwashing in the daytime, he worked for a dry cleaner at night. And, on the side, he studied accounting and book-keeping.

Then, again, Shana started spitting blood and was hos-pitalized once more.

One evening when Shamai came to visit he said, quite casually, "When you see the doctor tomorrow ask him when you'll be well enough to get married."

Shana felt her heart exploding into her head. But she managed merely to nod. "I'll ask him," she said.

When she put the crucial question to her doctor, he frowned and pulled at his stubby beard. "When will you be well enough to marry? I'm afraid, my child, that the answer is never."

When Shamai heard this verdict he merely shrugged.

"So who says we have to live a very long life?" he said. "We'll live a little less. And we'll be happy."

When she was dismissed from the hospital, Shana and Shamai were married. The bride was twenty years old. A year later she gave birth to a baby girl, a beautiful child with blond curly hair. They named her Judith.

Shana and her mother had made up. Shamai had opened his own dry cleaning establishment in Denver. Life was at last, and for the first time, truly happy for Shana.

Then, suddenly, came a startling letter from her sister Goldie in Milwaukee.

Unlike Shana, Golda had always gotten along well with her mother. There was only one thing they ever had serious conflicts about—word battles which often ended with Golda in tears: the child objected to opening the store while Bluma went off to the wholesale market. She objected because this made her late for school. Mama usually ended her side of the argument with a sharp retort in Yiddish: *"West sein a rebbetzin mit a tog speter!"* (You'll be a learned lady a day later!")

Nor did she think anything of keeping Golda home to mind the store all day long. Bluma was, it seemed, a fertile woman. Although she gave birth to no more babies, she had frequent miscarriages, each of which left her indisposed for several weeks. Since Papa was involved with his highly unprofitable business as a building contractor and little Tzipka was notably inefficient as a saleslady, this left only Goldie to mind the store.

One day, however, a truant officer came to the shop. He was a severe-looking man with piercing eyes and a heavy black mustache. He informed Mama that the law required every child under fourteen years of age to attend school regularly, which her daughter Golda was not doing.

Frightened, Mama promised that in the future Goldie would be to school on time.

And, for a while, she was. Mama got up even earlier— at 5 A.M.—so that she could go to the wholesale market and be back to open the store before it was time for Golda to leave for school. Then Bluma worked in the store until

10 at night, also doing the cooking, the baking, the washing, the ironing, and the cleaning for the family.

Not surprisingly, after her next miscarriage she was too exhausted to make any kind of recovery and lay in bed for weeks. Once more Golda worked in the shop as soon as she got home from school every day and all day Sunday. On Saturdays, she and Regina Hamburger—her best friend since the second grade—worked at the Boston Department Store from 9 A.M. till 9 P.M. They wrapped packages and made deliveries. The pay was one dollar a day.

When Golda graduated as valedictorian of her class, her mother was elated. Now the girl could work full time in the grocery store. Even in America girls were not expected to go to *high* school!

Golda, however, expected to go. And after some tearful arguments, her parents agreed. Papa had, for once, sided with her—albeit rather faintly. Perhaps he felt guilty that he, the breadwinner, actually earned so little. He was a wise, gentle, and scholarly man, but not cut out for business. He was, as Mama frequently exclaimed, "too trusting." Once, for example, he went to the wholesale market for her and bought some apples. As he walked home, the juice of the rotten apples leaked through his string bag, leaving a trail behind him. The apples on top of the bag were red and rosy. Papa had never thought of looking at the apples the wholesale fruitman had put on the bottom.

The same faults held true in his contracting business. He could not compete against the sharp, shrewd tricks practiced by his competitors. Consequently, through the years, Golda's letters to Shana frequently included such phrases as *I can tell you that Pa does not work yet*. And again, some months later, *Papa still isn't working*.

Golda wrote regularly; matter-of-fact letters, keeping Shana abreast of conditions at home. Never once, however, had she sounded particularly bitter or aggrieved—until the letter she wrote during her first term at North Division High School.

In this letter she exploded with fury.

She had decided to become a teacher because—as she explained to Shana—such a profession was "intellectually and socially useful." Mama, however, had found out that married women were not permitted to teach in the local schools. "You want to be an old maid?" she had screamed at Golda. *"That's* what you're studying for?"

Papa now sided strongly with Mama. Either Golda must quit school and go to work like other sensible girls her age, or she must transfer to a business school to be trained in subjects which would help her get a job and, who knows, a husband too.

This was not, however, the final blow. The section of Golda's letter in which the words fairly shook with anger concerned a Mr. Goodstein, *"an old man! Twice my age!"*

Mr. Goodstein was in real estate. Mr. Goodstein was well to do. Mr. Goodstein came regularly into the grocery store for, it seemed, he had fallen in love with Golda. He had, furthermore, asked Mama for permission to make Goldie his wife.

Mama had demurred a little. "But she's so young. Only fourteen."

Mr. Goodstein considerately said that he would be willing to wait a few years. Whereupon Mama had agreed that this would be a most suitable match. And had so informed Golda.

When she read her sister's outraged letter, Shana too was furious. Bluma had tried the same tricks with her—foisting her off on some man *Mama* felt was "suitable."

Shana showed the letter to Shamai. They discussed the matter at some length. Then he sat down and wrote a letter to Golda.

. . . *No, Goldie, I say that you shouldn't stop school. You are too young to work; you have good chances to become something. My advice is that you should get ready and come to us. We are not rich either, but you will have good chances here to study. We will do all we can for you.*

At the end Shana added several sentences: *First, you'll have all the opportunities to study; second, you'll have plenty to eat; third, you'll have the necessary clothes that a person ought to have.*

The letter was dated November 15, 1912. It was a letter that dramatically changed Golda's life.

Chapter 5

Some weeks later, at four in the morning, Golda tied a rope around her packed suitcase and carefully lowered it out the window. Her friend Regina was waiting below in a dark alley on the side of the grocery store. Regina untied the suitcase and crept off with it. Presently, she boarded a trolley car, rode to the railway station, and checked the valise at the baggage department.

Golda meanwhile went back to bed.

She got up at the usual time. Dressed in the usual way. Ate her breakfast. Called good-bye to her parents. And left. But she did not, as usual, walk the fourteen blocks to school. Instead, she went to the railway station.

The train was late. And as Golda sat on the hard wooden bench in the waiting room she became more and more nervous. She had written a postcard asking her parents' forgiveness for the pain she was causing them. *I'm going to live with Shana,* she had concluded, *so I can study.* She had planned to be on the train speeding toward Denver by the time the morning mail was delivered. It had never entered her head that the train might be late.

Anxiously, she kept looking down the track for the tardy train. And when she sat on the waiting room bench her eyes were fastened on the door. She fully expected the furious Bluma to fly in at any moment to repossess her and haul her back home.

Finally, however, the train came. Bluma didn't. And

Goldie Mabovitch mounted the iron stairway, excited—
and scared.

"Why you're—grown up!" Shana exclaimed when she
met her sister at the station. "And you're beautiful."

Goldie's slender figure had filled out. Her auburn hair
was pulled back loosely and worn in a single thick braid
over her shoulder. Her blue-gray eyes seemed somehow
larger and deeper. Her nose was straight, a little long, but
it "fitted" the strength of her face. She had Mama's firm
jaw and mouth. Yet, when she smiled, her eyes crinkled
and the firm, almost stern, look was replaced by a joyful
sweetness.

On the way to Shana's house she chatted with excitement about her trip and how she had raised the money for
her fare. Much of it had been saved from English lessons
she gave to immigrants at ten cents an hour. Suddenly in
the midst of a sentence she stopped and looked at Shana.
"I wonder how Mama and Pa are feeling right now," she
said.

She was soon to find out.

A letter full of recriminations arrived from Tzipka. She
felt that her sister had deserted her, and she took great
pains to describe her parents' anguish. Mama, she reported, had read Golda's postcard and burst into sobs.
Then she had run straight to Regina Hamburger's mother.
When Regina came home for lunch, she confessed to the
role she had played. Whereupon, Mrs. Hamburger had
smacked Regina across the face. And Bluma started sobbing once more. (While all this was going on, Golda realized guiltily, she herself had been sitting right there in the
railroad station waiting for the train.)

Then came a letter from Regina reporting on neighborhood speculation about Golda's secret flight. *I hope I won't
hurt your feelings, but everybody thought you had eloped
with an Italian. How they got the idea I can't get at. . . .
Now, dear Goldie, don't get angry at me for writing this
but I can't help it, you asked . . . I burned with anger and
resentment, but what could I do?*

At first the pattern of life in Denver was little different from that in Milwaukee. She went to high school, and after school she worked each day in the store. This time the sign over the store read: SAM KORNGOLD: DRY CLEANERS. It was her brother-in-law's shop; Shamai had been Americanized to Sam.

She'd had some experience with dry cleaning, for every Sunday morning she and Tzipka had taken a can of naphtha gas into the backyard and proceeded to clean their dresses and Papa's suits. (The naphtha gas was highly inflammable and the can might well have exploded in the hot sun. But, fortunately, this never occurred.)

When "Sam's" dry cleaning shop closed at seven o'clock, Golda went home and helped her sister prepare dinner, after which Shamai went off to his night job as a janitor. And Golda did her homework at the kitchen table.

Several times a week, in the evenings and on Sunday afternoon, friends of the Korngolds dropped in for tea and conversation. Or perhaps the more accurate word was—arguments.

There was a veritable colony of East European intellectuals who, like Shana, had been dismissed from the hospital with the stipulation that they remain in Denver until they were completely cured. In some cases the consumptive was too weak to fend for himself, so a healthy member of the family moved to Denver to look after the sick one. One such was a young man named Morris Myerson. He had come to Denver to care for his consumptive sister. As the fifteen-year-old Goldie sat on the sidelines listening to the vehement debates between anarchists, Socialists, Marxists, Zionists, she was impressed by the quiet yet forceful wisdom of this young man.

She did not remain listening on the sidelines for long. Many of the Korngolds' visitors were bachelors. And Golda soon found herself the center of a social whirl. There were far more invitations to lectures, concerts, and meetings than there were nights in the week. Golda, hugely enjoying the ardent attention of so many attractive young men, took to going out practically every night. And coming home very late.

All of which scandalized the rather straitlaced Shana.

When—toward the end of her first year in Denver—several of the young men proposed marriage, Golda suddenly saw herself in a new light. She was no longer a schoolgirl to be dictated to, bossed about. She was a woman, quite capable of making her own decisions about her own life. Consequently, after one particularly vehement fight with Shana about the late hours she was keeping, Golda announced, "Very well! I'll *leave!*" And she stalked out of the house.

If Golda was stubborn, Shana was equally so, and neither made the least move to patch up the quarrel.

Since Golda had no money to live on she had to quit school and work full time. She found herself a small room and a job in a laundry which specialized in lace curtains. For twelve hours a day, six days a week, she stood stretching curtains onto wooden frames, pinning them in place. Her fingers bled with pinpricks.

Finally she found an easier job, selling fabrics in a department store. The days were long and dreary, but the nights came alive with excitement.

Each of the young men she went out with had his own special attractions. Each was deeply involved with life, and with his own political philosophy. Golda suddenly found herself fascinated by politics, and each of her ardent suitors tried to win her as a disciple.

The political philosophy which seemed to make most sense to her—which, in fact, stirred her deeply—was Zionism. Jews—who had been persecuted for centuries, driven from one country to another, tortured and killed without reason—Jews *must* have some place on this earth where they could live without fear. Some land where they could rule their own destiny. Some land where they could be free.

Jews had been free once; had ruled their own destiny for some 2,000 years in the land the Bible called Canaan, a land the Roman conquerors had renamed Palestine—a name they had fashioned from the word Philistines, the dreaded ancient enemies of the Jews.

The Bible was filled with passages stating that God had given this land to the Jews. Twenty centuries before the birth of Christ God had promised this land to the first Hebrew, Abraham: *"And I will give to thee, and to thy seed after thee . . . all the land of Canaan, for an everlasting possession."**

Goldie Mabovitch was not notably religious. But whether the Bible was regarded as the direct words of God or the legends, philosophies, and historical reports set down by a series of ancient scribes, the indisputable fact was that Jews had lived in Palestine centuries longer than any other peoples. Indeed, many thousands of Jewish families had managed to survive in Palestine through all the centuries of oppressors who had conquered the country since the Romans razed Jerusalem to the ground in 70 A.D.

It seemed obvious to Golda that the course Jews must follow lay in reclamation of their Promised Land. Eagerly, she read reports in magazines such as *The Young Maccabean* or *New Judea*—reports about the Jews who were returning to the Holy Land.

They came illegally, for Palestine had been ruled by the Ottoman Turks since the 16th century. And the Turks did not welcome Jews. Still, they came. Most of them from pogrom-ridden Eastern Europe—idealistic young scholars, tailors, shopkeepers. And most of them penniless. It took some two years to make the journey, because they had to walk most of the way. They had started coming in the 1880's. And by 1914 over 115,000 Jews had made their way back to Palestine.

Golda spent many hours on the street corners shaking a small blue and white box marked JEWISH NATIONAL FUND. This organization raised money to buy land in Palestine, most of it rocky, eroded hillsides or malarial marshes— the only land the Turkish and Arab landowners would sell them, at exorbitant prices.

Often as she stood on the street corner asking for donations or as she participated in a heated debate on Zionism,

* Genesis 12:7.

Golda wondered uneasily what she was doing *here*. Should she not actually follow her beliefs across the seas? Should she not be working on the land bought by the Jewish National Fund? Should she not be helping to reclaim the homeland?

But somehow Denver, Colorado, seemed a very long way from Palestine. Perhaps, one day in the future. . . . In the meantime, well, she was only sixteen years old. And in the meantime—it seemed she was falling in love.

Morris Myerson was not notably handsome. He wore steel-rimmed spectacles. And his hair was rather thin. *But* —as Golda wrote Regina, her only confidante in this secret matter—*he has a beautiful soul!*

Morris, also an immigrant from Russia, was only a few years older than she. But he seemed to Golda eminently wise. He was different from the other young men she dated. He did not seem particularly interested in politics or "causes." His interest lay in the arts: music, poetry, painting. And he opened exciting new worlds for Golda.

On their first date he took her to a public concert in the park. It was a week after Golda had stalked out of her sister's house—wearing only the blouse and skirt she had on. She was too proud to return for her clothes, and she had not yet made sufficient money to increase her wardrobe. However, she wanted to wear something special for her date with Morris. So she bought herself a new straw hat in Woolworth's. "Be careful it don't rain on you, dear," the saleslady had said, "or you'll end up red all over."

During the concert Golda, in her becoming red hat, was far more concerned about the ominous looking skies than she was about the music. But when the concert was over she and Morris walked hand in hand through the park. He analyzed for her in clear but eloquent words the symphony they had just heard.

When he had finished, Golda exclaimed, "Oh, now I wish I could hear that music all over again!"

And, rather shyly, Morris said, "There's a concert downtown next Saturday night. If you'd like, I'll get tickets."

He had very little money, a common condition among the young men Golda dated in Denver. They took any sort of job which came along. Morris was a sign painter—when he could get work. Perhaps, Golda reflected, he would one day be a real painter. He was obviously artistic. He would often cut beautiful reproductions from magazines, frame them himself, and present them to her. And whenever he collected a few extra pennies he bought her flowers.

Because his occupation as sign painter did not keep him very occupied, Morris spent many hours at the public library. He seemed to know a good deal about every subject, and to Golda—who had left high school after the second year—his erudition was a constant amazement.

She found herself seeing less and less of the other young men, more and more of Morris Myerson. Then one evening Morris told her that he loved her and wanted to marry her. Golda replied soberly that she too was in love, but since she had just turned sixteen she was too young yet to marry.

Late that night, in a state of euphoria, she wrote off to Regina, who answered promptly, congratulating Golda on her "blissful happiness."

Then another letter came. From Papa. She had not heard from him since she left home. Although she had resumed correspondence with her mother, Bluma often informed her that Papa did not even want the name Goldie mentioned in his house.

Golda had not, of course, told her mother that she had left school and was working full time in a department store. But evidently Bluma had now found out.

The letter from Papa Mabovitch was a surprising one. If Golda would only come home, he promised, she could finish high school. Furthermore, she could then go on to Milwaukee Normal School for Teachers.

Golda knew that she wanted to marry Morris Myerson. But she wanted to have a career as well, and to this Morris had no objection. She must at least graduate from high school; then, perhaps, when she went to teachers' college, they could be married.

Morris, still the sole support of his consumptive sister, had to remain in Denver. But he promised to come straight to Milwaukee as soon as his sister recovered.

Meanwhile, Golda returned to Milwaukee alone.

Chapter 6

"Who *is* this man who keeps writing you letters from Denver?" Bluma asked the question frequently.

But Golda would merely shrug and say, "Oh, just— somebody."

So they took to calling him Mr. Somebody.

Whenever a letter arrived from this mysterious Mr. Somebody, Golda would run off with it to her room. And when she emerged it was usually with a soft and secret smile.

The letters kept coming, two and three times a week. Finally, Bluma decided she could stand the suspense no longer. Two more had just arrived from *him*. Golda was still in school. Carefully, Bluma steamed the envelopes open. But to no avail. The letters were written in English. She could barely understand a word. The handwriting was neat and beautiful. But what did the letters *say*?

Twelve-year-old Tzipka was in her room, doing her homework. Bluma marched in. "Read these to me!" she demanded.

Tzipka glanced at the letters, then looked up horrified. "Mama, these are *private*. They're written to Goldie!" She handed the letters back.

"Look," said Bluma. "I'm a mother. I have a responsibility to know what kind of a man my child is carrying on with. It's my duty! *Read the letters!*" And she handed them back to Tzipka.

"But I'm a Camp Fire Girl!" Tzipka exclaimed tearfully. "I have to keep my honor bright!"

"My duty," Bluma proclaimed, "is more important than your honor. Now"—her voice rose ominously—"*Read! In Yiddish!*"

So, Tzipka read, omitting however the very personal opening paragraph. *"Are you still worrying about me and the meaning of the strain of sadness you discern in my letters . . . ? My sadness is . . . only part of that universal sadness that is bound to permeate every person endowed with the least bit of sensibility and clarity of vision. Can any thinking person be altogether happy and satisfied? Therefore, don't worry. Be the same happy smiling Goldie you were heretofore!*"

Tzipka looked up. "Is that enough, Mama?"

"What rubbish!" Bluma announced. Then she said, her voice somewhat softer, "It sounds the sort of thing your father might have written to me when he was young. Read more!"

"Well," said Tzipka, "here he writes, *I have repeatedly asked you not to contradict me on the question of your beauty . . . you pop up every now and then with these same timid and self-deprecating remarks which I cannot bear . . .*"

Then Tzipka handed the letters back. "Now that's enough, Mama. You've done your—duty! You can see he sounds very nice. I won't translate another word."

Bluma nodded. She put the letters in their envelopes, stuck down the flaps. And said no more about them.

Tzipka however felt weighed down by guilt. Late that night she crept into Golda's room and confessed.

Golda was furious.

And the following day honor-bright Tzipka found herself in double trouble. Golda wouldn't speak to her because she had read the letters. And Mama wouldn't speak to her because she had told.

Thereafter, no more of Morris' letters came to the house. Upon Golda's suggestion they were sent instead to Regina's home.

Golda was still in high school when the First World War broke out in Europe. And with the war came dire reports of increased pogroms. The Jewish Pale of Settlement lay, unfortunately, in the very territory where Russian and German-Austrian armies clashed most often in violent battle. When the White Russian Army fled in retreat they slaughtered Jews in that section for being German sympathizers. When the Russians swept back and Germans fled from the same section, *they* murdered Jews for being Russian spies.

The White Russian armies—including the savage Ukrainian Cossacks—and their bitter opponents, the Germans, seemed to agree on one tenet only: anti-Semitism. And they had ample opportunity for carrying out their battle cry: Death to the Jews. For of the ten million Jews in Europe, eight million lived in the Russian and Austro-Hungarian empires.

Millions of Jews were rendered homeless. Committees were organized to raise funds for the ever-swelling ranks of Jewish refugees who fled from one town to the next, trying to keep out of the way of the armies. Golda worked with People's Relief and with an organization called Aid in Need, formed by Jewish workers in Milwaukee to help hungry and homeless European Jews.

Then a report came in from Pinsk. Over forty men had been lined up and shot by the wall of a church which Golda had often passed as a child. Their crime? Receiving funds from the American Jewish Joint Distribution Committee and distributing this money to desperate families in Pinsk. Had her uncles been among those murdered? Had *Zayde?*

She felt broken apart inside. For nights she could not sleep. What *good* did it do, running around, making speeches, collecting money for a new generation of suffering, displaced, wandering Jews? There had to be a better answer than this. There *had* to be one place in the

world where Jews could at last be free from persecution.
There *had* to be a Jewish homeland. And it must be
created as soon as possible. All her beliefs suddenly solid-
ified into one single purpose. As soon as she could she
would go to Palestine and devote her life to this goal.

She joined Poale Zion, the Labor Zionist Party—the
party which had as its slogan the saying of the Hebrew
sage, Hillel:

> *If I am not for myself, who will be for me?*
> *But if I am for myself only, What am I?*
> *And if not now, when?*

If not now, when?

She was seventeen. She had no training. She had no
money. The war was spreading to the Middle East. It was
not possible to leave for Palestine "now." But she would
work, start saving up passage money. And, when the
war was over, she would go to Palestine!

But what about Morris? How would he feel?

She soon found out.

In a letter dated August, 1915, Morris wrote: *I do not
know whether to say that I am glad or sorry that you have
joined the Zionist party, and that you seem to be so
enthusiastic a nationalist. I am altogether passive in the
matter, though I give you full credit for your activity, as
I do to all others engaged in doing something toward helping a distressed nation. . . . The idea of Palestine or any
other territory for the Jews is, to me, ridiculous. . . . The
other day I received a notice to attend one of the meetings . . . but since I do not care particularly as to whether
the Jews are going to suffer in Russia or the Holy Land,
I did not go.*

When she had finished reading the letter, Golda wept.
Now that she had determined the course her life would
take, it seemed inevitable. She *must* live in Palestine. Yet,
she loved Morris Myerson and wanted to be his wife.
Afraid of his reactions, she had written him only that she
had joined the Labor Zionist Party. Would he break with

her completely when he learned that she wanted to move to Palestine?

When she left Denver, Morris and she had agreed that although they were secretly engaged, this should not mean they would cut themselves off from seeing other people. Golda had, consequently, continued going to meetings, to concerts, to fund-raising events, and to dances with a number of attractive young men. And, as her friend Regina reported, "Four out of every five boys we met fell in love with her."

Some of these boys who fell in love with her were ardent Zionists. Perhaps life would be simpler if she and Morris did end their affair, if she married a man who was determined to spend his life in Palestine.

There was only one complication; it was Morris she loved.

Meanwhile, she set about making money for her passage to Palestine. She worked part time at the Sixteenth Street and North Avenue branch of the Milwaukee Public Library.

In the spring of 1916 she graduated. Next to her picture in the class yearbook was written:

> *Those about her*
> *From her shall read the perfect ways*
> *of honor.*

She entered Milwaukee Normal School for Teachers and took a part-time job at a Yiddish-speaking folk school which advocated Labor Zionism. But even this seemed too far removed from her goal: So she started speaking for the Labor Zionists' Poale Zion.

The organization soon discovered that the eighteen-year-old girl had a remarkable talent as a speaker, and they sent her on speaking engagements around the country. Her mission: to try to stir the complacent American Jewish youth, awaken them to the philosophies and the necessities of Labor Zionism.

One Friday night she was scheduled to speak in Milwaukee, not in a meeting room or an auditorium. She would speak on a street corner. Standing on a soap box.

Her father heard about the plan and was horrified. Women, he thundered at Golda, did not *do* such things! His daughter, to stand on a soap box exhorting people on the street! "If you dare to go ahead with that speech," he threatened, "I'll come down there and pull you off home by your braids!"

"I'm sorry, Papa," Golda said, firmly, "but the speech has already been announced."

She took the precaution of telling members of Poale Zion that her father might create a scandal that evening, and since she did not cherish the notion of being dragged off the soap box, she asked that they form a protective circle around her as she spoke.

This was done. But it was almost unnecessary, for the crowd which gathered on the street corner that night was so large that Moshe Mabovitch would have had a hard time shoving his way through. Most of the bystanders had stopped out of curiosity. It was not every day that one saw an attractive young girl standing on a soap box and talking about a faraway land called Palestine. They soon found themselves spellbound, caught up by Golda's impassioned oratory.

As she spoke, Golda noticed her father at the edge of the crowd; noticed thankfully that he did not, after all, seem bent on making a scene.

Afterward, Poale Zion members gathered around her with congratulations. It was a fine speech. One of the best she had ever made. They wanted her to come back to the office for a party. She went, but she left early.

When she got home, her mother was sitting at the kitchen table sewing.

"Where's Papa?"

"In bed."

Bluma looked up. She was smiling a little. "He came in. He sat down. He shrugged. He said, 'Where did she get this talent for speaking?' Then he stood up. He said, 'God knows what this girl may be able to do!' And he went to bed."

From that night onward the Mabovitches offered no more objections to anything Golda wanted to do. They seemed to realize that they had somehow bred a very special child. Their best contribution now would be not to interfere.

Morris, however, was a different matter.

His consumptive sister recovered and went back home to Philadelphia. And Morris came straight to Milwaukee.

Golda met him at the railroad station—and it was as though they had never been apart.

Until the matter of Palestine came up. Which it did, almost at once.

Some months ago Morris had written to her, *Have you ever stopped to think whether your Morris has the one attribute without which all other refinements are worthless, namely "the indomitable will"?*

Now, however, Morris displayed "indomitable will." He wanted to marry Goldie, yes. But he would not move to Palestine.

Golda wept, she implored. Morris' will remained indomitable.

Golda wrote to her sister Shana, who was now living in Chicago where Shamai worked for a Jewish newspaper. Shana had always been the most important influence in Golda's life. What would her older sister advise her to do now?

Shana wrote back giving her own views about the Zionist dream—views which seemed to have changed somewhat since the Pinsk and Denver days. *I don't want to shatter your dreams. I know what it means. But, Goldie, don't you think there is a middle field for idealism right here on the spot?*

Golda's dreams were not shattered by this letter. But *she* was shattered. Her dreams remained intact. Palestine had become a part of her. To live there on a kibbutz, to help rebuild the homeland with her own hands—this seemed the most beautiful and essential thing she could do with her life. If Shana did not understand, if Morris did not understand—well, she would have to go on alone.

Poale Zion asked Golda to go to Chicago; her mission: to try to awaken the complacent Jews of that city.

Before she left, Golda told Morris Myerson that if he did not agree to move to Palestine, she could not marry him.

Morris replied that although he loved her desperately, he could not agree to live in Palestine. He was not a Zionist; he was not, therefore, fortified to face the hardships, the struggles, the dangers which life in Palestine entailed. He tried to reason with her, to humor her, to plead with her.

To no avail. Golda broke the engagement and left for Chicago. She stayed in a rented room with a friend named Raizel Shapiro. She worked hard. Sometimes in the evening, she visited Shana and Shamai or her old friend Regina, who had moved to Chicago in 1916. Regina promised to accompany Golda to Palestine, and she too started a "Palestine bank account."

But Golda seemed to have changed. Her ebullience had vanished. She rarely smiled. "She was very moody and unhappy," Regina recalled later, "because of the break with Morris."

Golda's misery disappeared when she returned to Milwaukee. It was banished by two momentous statements.

The first was issued on November 2, 1917, by the British Foreign Secretary, Arthur James Balfour:

His Majesty's Government view with favour the establishment in Palestine of a national home for the Jewish people, and will use their best endeavors to facilitate the achievement of this object. . . .

It was incredible. When she left for Chicago it had been a matter of some 130,000 Zionists in the entire world. And a handful of Jewish settlements in Palestine. Now Great Britain, one of the world's most powerful nations, had promised to use her *best endeavors to facilitate the achievement of*—the Zionist dream! *A national home for the Jewish people!*

That simple declaration acted as a sudden charge of hope for persecuted Jews throughout the war-racked countries of Europe.

It also seemed to act as inspiration to the army of General Allenby. The British had been fighting a notably unsuccessful war against the Ottoman Turks, who—for four centuries—had dominated the Middle East, including the territory called Palestine. However, one month after the issuance of the Balfour Declaration General Allenby's army liberated Palestine. His troops entered Jerusalem on the joyous Jewish holy day of Chanukah, the Feast of Lights.

How had it all happened? What had brought about this historic Balfour Declaration?

The answer lay primarily in the activities of one man, a chemistry professor born in the tiny village of Motol, near Pinsk. His name was Chaim Weizmann. Shana had often attended secret Zionist meetings at the home of his married sister, Chaia Weizmann Lichtenstein.

Chaim left Russia to take up residence in England. A brilliant chemist, he was asked by the British government to find a way of producing synthetic cordite, an explosive which they said was essential to the British war effort. Weizmann discovered the process, turned it over to the British government. And, thereafter, found doors open to him which otherwise would undoubtedly have been closed.

Weizmann, like his sister Chaia, was a dedicated Zionist. And he made use of his British connections to make converts to his cause. One of these was Arthur James Balfour, who remarked one day to Weizmann, "You know, I believe that when the guns stop firing, you may get your Jerusalem."

From the time that single sentence was uttered, Dr. Weizmann worked without stopping. He won the backing of influential British leaders. And on November 2, 1917, the Balfour Declaration was issued by the British Foreign Office.

The second momentous statement to greet Golda upon her return to Milwaukee was issued by Morris Myerson.

He came to call on her. He declared that the breaking
of their engagement had made him realize one thing
clearly. He adored Goldie. He could not live without her.
He was therefore prepared to live with her anywhere in
the world. Even Palestine.

The wedding took place on December 24, 1917. Golda
insisted on a simple wedding—no long white dress, no
long guest list. This was, she said, in keeping with her
Labor Zionist philosophy. Papa agreed with enthusiasm,
since he could not, as Golda well knew, afford to give his
daughter a traditional "white wedding."

The wedding was held at home. Only the immediate
family and a few friends were invited.

There was, however, one element about the wedding
which was somewhat unusual. The service was performed,
at his own suggestion, by the Chief Rabbi of Milwaukee.
Rabbi Schoenfelt was a short, rotund, scholarly gentleman
with a long beard. He was not a man given to rosy words
or extravagant statements. At weddings or funerals he had
rarely been known to part from the traditional text in
order to offer his own personal comments. But when he
performed the service which joined Golda and Morris in
holy matrimony, Rabbi Schoenfelt astounded the small
assembled gathering. He went into a veritable eulogy about
the nineteen-year-old girl, her sense of purpose and
dedication, her tremendous inner dignity. He described
his first associations with her during a massive street
parade and demonstration which Golda had organized to
protest the pogroms in Europe. And he concluded by
saying that he was proud indeed to be performing the
service which united this remarkable young couple as
husband and wife.

Chapter 7

The war was over. The "Palestine bank accounts" had been emptied. Golda, Morris, Regina, and their friend Yossel Kopelov had bought boat tickets. And Golda had come to Chicago to bid her sister good-bye.

During the ritual of farewells, Shamai remarked in a joking way to his wife, "Maybe *you'd* like to go to Palestine too?"

And Shana replied, "Yes, if you'll give me money for expenses."

Shamai stared at his wife. She sounded quite serious. He gave her a sick-looking smile.

Even Golda looked at her sister, startled. Shana had two small children. Judith was eleven, but Hayim was only three. Did she mean to take them with her? And leave Shamai behind? Golda knew that her sister suffered when away from her husband for so much as a week.

Yet, it seemed that this was exactly what Shana had in mind. She had *talked* about Palestine long enough—during the secret meetings in Pinsk . . . during heated discussions in Denver . . . even here in their comfortable apartment in Chicago. It was time for talk to turn at last to reality. So it was decided that Shana and the two children should accompany Golda and Morris to Palestine, while Shamai remained in Chicago where he could continue to work and send them money. When Shana and the children were "set up" in the Holy Land, Shamai would join them.

They boarded the S.S. *Pocahontas* on May 23, 1921.

The ship was bound for Naples where, so the plan went, they would take another ship to the Palestinian port of Jaffa. The ocean voyage from New York to Naples ordinarily lasted two weeks. It took the *Pocahontas* forty-four days.

In midocean the crew went on strike. They flooded the engine room, and the ship listed dangerously. They opened two portholes in the supply room and water rushed in, ruining most of the food. They salted the remaining food so that it became inedible. Then, for good measure, they salted the sweet drinking water. Soon there was nothing to serve the passengers at mealtimes but rice and salty tea.

Fires broke out. The boiler pumps stopped. Members of the crew were clapped into irons. The captain's brother went mad and wept and screamed throughout the voyage. One of the passengers broke her leg; there was no doctor to set it. Another passenger was thrown overboard. A third died. When the ship finally reached Naples, the captain was faced with arrest for his lack of judgment in proceeding with so mutinous a crew. He thereupon committed suicide.

But at least the ill-fated ship had gotten Golda and *her* crew to Naples. They checked in at the Imperial Hotel, which, despite its regal name, was a drab place on the waterfront. Rooms were $1.50 a day. Since they could not afford restaurant meals, they smuggled in food under their coats and cooked secretly in the room, using a small primus stove.

They found, to their dismay, that they could not take a ship from Naples to Palestine as they had planned. On May 1, Arab riots had broken out in the Palestinian port town of Jaffa and had spread throughout the area. Forty-three Jews had been slaughtered, almost as many as in the Kishinev pogrom.

They knew, of course, about the riots before they sailed. Shamai, in fact, had tried to prevail upon Shana not to leave until things settled down. But she had replied airily that by the time they arrived the country would surely be calm again.

But now she had to write Shamai from Naples: *It seems*

*we can't go further. They don't sell tickets. We got a
funny answer from the shipping companies, really something to laugh at. Christians and Moslems can go to
Palestine, but they can't sell tickets to Jews. They do this
for our own sakes because the Arabs in Jaffa throw the
Jews into the sea. So here you have a sad joke—no Jew
can enter Eretz Israel.**

Finally, they managed to get visas to Egypt. They traveled by train to the Italian port of Brindisi and then took
a three-day ship voyage to the Egyptian port of Alexandria
—three days of sleeping on deck, without one hot meal.
Nonetheless, they were in high spirits, singing and practic-
ing their Hebrew. They were actually nearing the Holy
Land!

At the station in Alexandria they were met by their
first overwhelming onslaught of "the Middle East." Dry,
baking summer heat; hordes of flies. And beggars. Beggars
pulling at their clothes, whining, demanding, shrilling.
Blind or crippled mothers holding up rag-wrapped children.

When they finally boarded the train, the heat was so
unbearable that they very nearly got off again. The train
too was filled with barefoot, stinking beggars, who kept
crowding around the Americans, pleading for *baksheesh*,
a handout.

At Kantara, the Egyptian border town, there was no one
in the passport office. So they had to wait until an official
finally showed up—at midnight. Meanwhile, again, they
were prey to Arab beggars who surrounded them like
locusts. By the time the Americans finally boarded the
train to Palestine, most of their suitcases had been stolen.
(They had, fortunately—or so they then thought—left
their trunks in Naples to be shipped after them to Jaffa.)

They were ushered into the Promised Land by a raging
sandstorm. Though the train windows were closed, desert
winds swept the sand in through holes and cracks, and
the sweltering passengers were soon coughing, choking,
trying to rub the sand from their eyes.

---

* The Land of Israel.

At noon the next day—it was July 14, 1921—the exhausted Americans finally arrived in the new Jewish city of Tel Aviv. At home, in Zionist discussions, Tel Aviv had emerged romantically wrapped in dreams. Tel Aviv, the first all-Jewish city to be built in 2,000 years. Tel Aviv— Hebrew for Hill of Spring. It sounded splendid. Inspiring. A suitable first stop for Jews returning to the homeland they had never seen.

Tel Aviv. They stepped down from the train into ankle-deep sand. *City? Hill of Spring?* The place seemed little more than an arid flat stretch of sand baking under the scorching midday sun, surrounded by desolate sand dunes. In the distance were several clusters of squat houses. A camel caravan plodded slowly along the horizon.

Yossel Kopelov was the first to break the silence. "Well," he announced in a loud firm voice, "I'm going back home!"

Yossel was known as a humorist, so they chose to take his remark as a joke—although, in fact, it reflected the feelings of all, with the exception of Golda who pointed out the lone but beautiful tree by the railroad station and said something about its being a symbol of the Jewish people, managing to flourish despite adversity.

No one commented further on the matter.

A man was plodding toward them through the sand. When he reached them he stopped, smiled cheerfully, wiped the sweat from his face with a dirty rag, and announced that he was the proprietor of the only hotel in town.

So they picked up those suitcases which still remained and followed him. Eventually they arrived at a one-story building with a proud sign hanging out in front: MALON BARASH (Hotel Barash). With high enthusiasm, Mr. Barash booked a two-room "suite" for the five adults and two children.

Things began looking up. The rooms were large and comfortable. Furthermore, a note had been left for them by friends from the States, the Hadaris, who would drop in and see them that evening. Even Morris, who had retreated into a cocoon of glumness, began to brighten somewhat—especially after he'd had a wash and a shave.

However, the Hadaris came to inform the new arrivals that they were leaving for the States the next day. They "couldn't take it." Morris, who had trustingly left his precious American razor on the sill of the open window, came back to find that the razor had been stolen. And a sleepless night was spent by all, for the beds were alive with bugs.

When Yossel complained to the proprietor the next morning, Mr. Barash exclaimed indignantly, "Bedbugs? Not in *my* hotel! I'll give you a pound sterling for every bug you find!"

"Good!" said Yossel. "It's our chance to get rich quick."

They did not, however, get rich quick. Indeed, they had a hard time finding any paying job at all. Golda, who remained the group's sole optimist, wrote to her brother-in-law Shamai three weeks after their arrival. *I say that as long as those who created the little that is here are here, I cannot leave and you must come. I would not say this if I did not know that you are ready to work hard. True, even hard work is hard to find, but I have no doubt that you will find something . . .*

Golda was the first of the group to be offered a job—as English teacher at the Gymnasium Herzlia, the first Hebrew high school in Tel Aviv. It was on the main street, Herzl Street (a street made of wooden planks), and was the largest building in town, a handsome Oriental-style structure. It also housed Tel Aviv's "chief industry," for half the town seemed to make a living either teaching at the school or taking in students as boarders.

Golda, however, turned down the job. "I came to *Eretz Israel* to work," she said, "not to teach English."

By "work" she meant work on the land, in the true Zionist tradition. Immediately upon arrival she had applied for membership in the kibbutz Merhavia, a communal settlement in the malaria-ridden Valley of Jezreel. But to join a kibbutz one had to be voted upon and accepted by the entire community. There were thirty-two men and eight women in Merhavia. Most of the men were bachelors. They consequently preferred unmarried women as members of their isolated community. Furthermore, they had many doubts about Golda, all centering on the fact that she was an American girl, reared in the "soft life" of the United States. How would she stand up to the rigors of kibbutz life?

At the first two meetings held on the subject, the Morris Myersons were turned down as members.

Meanwhile, Golda earned a little money giving tutoring lessons in English. Regina earned a little more as a secretary with the Silocate Brick Factory. And Shana went every day to the post office to see whether a letter or money order had come yet from Shamai. And every day the answer was the same: "No, there's nothing."

Indeed, for weeks, there was not one letter for any member of their group. They surmised, correctly, that the mail had been lost en route.

Their trunks also had been lost. Their repeated inquiries at the Jaffa port were met only with shrugs.

Their savings ran out. They could no longer afford the hotel. So they looked for a flat, which, like everything else in Tel Aviv, proved hard to find. They finally located two empty rooms in Lillienblum Street behind the Cinema Eden, the only movie house in town. The kitchen was outside, as was the outhouse. The rent was five pounds sterling a month. And the landlord, Mr. Hezroni, insisted that they pay an entire year's rent in advance. This they could not afford to do. Golda pleaded with eloquence. And finally Mr. Hezroni relented. He would accept six months' rent in advance.

Finally, in September, their trunks came—with half their contents missing. Shana wrote to Shamai: *Instead of sending the baggage to Jaffa, it went to Damascus, Syria. The Syrian Government wanted us to pay duty for everything, new and old. Can you imagine? . . . So Golda and M. went to . . . the American Consul and the High Commissioner . . . and, finally, with God's help, the baggage came. . . . Out of so many trunks we made various things. A table . . . nicely draped with curtain goods. With another two trunks we made a sofa. With another two we made a dresser. . . . I tell you it's pleasant now; only you are lacking . . . Everything is dear and there isn't much choice, but we eat and have enough of everything. . . .*

She did not, however, mention the market—where food was displayed in open stalls or on dirty blankets spread on the ground. Everything bared to the baking sun and to the constant swarm of flies. The meat they bought was usually rancid, the milk often sour.

Golda and Shana frequently found themselves reminiscing about the days of plenty when they lived behind the grocery store. Bluma had always refused to sell, or to serve, food which was not fresh. "Remember," Golda recalled, "how Mama used leftover milk to wash the leaves of the two rubber plants?"

And Shana remarked rather grimly, "If I could only *get* some leftover milk as pure as that was—to give to my children."

A few days later her little son Hayim contracted glaucoma, a serious eye disease. They had no money to take him to a doctor. Nor could Hayim get free medical care through the Kupat Holim, which was only for workers. "I *want* to work," she pleaded with the Kupat Holim doctor. "Give me a job!" But there was no work.

For the first time Shana broke down and wept. "Is this the welcome we receive in the land of the Jews?"

Finally, in an attempt to get medical attention for her son, she volunteered to work as a nurse in the town's rather primitive hospital. After six months, working full time without pay, she was given a job—with salary—supervising the kitchen. And Hayim got free medical care and was cured.

Golda, meanwhile, had received good news. Shortly after Rosh Hashanah, the Jewish New Year, when kibbutz members made their final decision on new applicants, the Morris Myersons were informed that they had been accepted for a probationary period by the kibbutzniks of Merhavia.

Elated, Golda packed their belongings. She also took along—over Shana's protestations—the phonograph they had brought from the States. (*I still believe,* she later wrote, *that the scales were tipped in our favor by the phonograph! It was the first phonograph in the country without the horn—and many records came with it. It's still there in Merhavia!*)

Although the unmarried members of Merhavia lived in dormitories, the married Myersons were given a room to themselves. Morris made furniture for it—two cots and a table. His work assignment was to dig stones out of a rocky hillside, which the kibbutzniks planned to make a fertile field. Golda was assigned to pick almonds.

After he returned from the first day of work under the broiling sun, Morris said very little. And as the days went on, he spoke less and less. A born introvert, he was appalled by the lack of privacy in kibbutz life, where everyone washed together in a communal washroom, ate together in a communal dining room, met every evening for a conversational *cumsitz* (get together), a song fest, or a party, where they danced the *horah* dressed in the clean clothes they had taken from the communal clothing shelves. And he was appalled by the fact that every aspect of life was run by committees. Furthermore, he had come to Palestine for one reason only. His love for Golda. Zionism had never held any great attraction for him. And without the sustaining ideological beliefs which were basic to Zionism, slaving all day in the fields under the scorching sun could become depressing indeed!

Golda's sole sorrow was that Morris was unhappy. Otherwise, the kibbutz life fitted her ideology and her personality to perfection. She worked well and with enthusiasm at any job assigned her by the Work Committee. And her energy seemed endless. After a day in the fields she would dance the stamping *horah* longer than anyone else, or she would talk late into the night at a *cumsitz*.

When the trial period ended there well still a few— mostly women—who complained that Golda had too many "American refinements." For example, she sometimes wore silk stockings to dinner. And she would insist on ironing her dress if it were rumpled. But the men members of Merhavia had very few complaints. One of them declared her "charming and inspiring," which seemed to reflect the opinion of all.

Consequently, to Golda's elation and Morris' alarm, the Myersons were elected as permanent members of Merhavia.

Six months later the Work Committee sent Golda to take a special course in poultry breeding. Golda had hated chickens ever since the days in Pinsk when the rivers flooded and drowned poultry came floating down the wet streets. But the kibbutz, which had always bought its eggs from neighboring Arabs, decided to go into production for itself. So Golda went off to learn about breeding chickens. And within a year proceeds from the sale of eggs became an important factor in Merhavia's economy. ("The kibbutz made me an expert in growing chickens," Golda said later. "Before that I was afraid to be in the room with even one chicken.")

One day she wrote home to her parents reporting on the success of her hatcheries. She also mentioned with glee that the cow had finally given birth. Her father wrote back that he was delighted to hear the news. And when would *she* become as productive as the cow?

In Milwaukee Golda had insisted that she wanted her children to be born and raised in Palestine. But now, in Palestine, Morris was insisting that—although he very much wanted children—he refused to have them brought up in a communal Children's House by a housemother who was rotated every few months. He demanded that Golda leave the kibbutz so they could establish a normal family life and have children.

Golda refused. She had married him on the condition that he come with her to Palestine. And he knew that— to her—Palestine meant communal living on a kibbutz.

Then Morris contracted malaria and was taken off to the hospital in Tiberias. When he returned to Merhavia he was too weak to do much work. And he objected strenuously to continued exposure to a life in which malaria was such a constant threat that quinine tablets were served at every meal.

His letters to his mother became increasingly gloomy. Finally, his mother wrote demanding that Morris leave Golda and return home to Philadelphia. If he agreed, she would immediately forward him the passage money.

But there was one trouble; the same trouble which had existed all along. He loved his wife. He could not leave her.

Finally, Golda—torn with guilt, compassion, and love for her husband—agreed to a compromise. If Morris would remain in Palestine, she would leave Merhavia, move with him to Tel Aviv or Jerusalem, become the housewife he wanted her to be, and have his children.

Chapter 8

It was the spring of 1924. They moved to Jerusalem, the holy city in the Judean hills.

Next year in Jerusalem.

Since the age of five, when Shana had first told her about Zionism, this Passover prayer had taken on forceful meaning for Golda. Now she was here, living in the city which had been the spiritual capital of the Jews for twenty centuries.

Jerusalem. The city King David had enlarged and rebuilt from a squalid town; a town which King Malchitzedek had named Urusalim in the days of Abraham: Urusalim, which meant the City of Peace.

It held all the mystic beauty she had ever imagined. Especially at sunset. She and Morris would often walk together over one of the stony roads which stretched into the gaunt Judean hills, and they watched as the yellow limestone buildings reflected the glow of the sinking sun and the city shimmered with a golden aura. Sometimes they stayed till the moon rose and the valleys brimmed deep with shadows, and the Past seemed to overtake the Present.

In the daytime, however, the Present took over. They lived in a wretched two-room flat. The kitchen was a tin shack in the yard; the stove was a small oil primus. Unlike Tel Aviv, Jerusalem had no electricity, but many of the homes were lit by gaslight. Not theirs, however. They had only oil lamps—the same type they had used back in Pinsk.

Morris had found a job as bookkeeper with Solel Boneh, the building cooperative, which is why they had come to Jerusalem. He made, however, only eight pounds a month—less than forty dollars. Furthermore, this was paid not in cash but in credit slips—accepted by the local food stores but not by the landlord of their apartment. Consequently, to pay the rent, the Myersons let one of their two rooms to a boarder.

Soon after they'd settled in, Golda was visited by Regina, who had moved to Jerusalem in May, 1921, when she got a job with the Zionist Commission. Regina had Golda's address on Yegiah Kapaim Street. However, since the section in which the Myersons lived had no numbers on the houses and no names on the streets, Regina had made several forays in vain search for her old school friend. Finally, she came across a grocer who shook his head blankly when she gave the address. But when she mentioned Golda's name, he brightened. "Oh!" he exclaimed. "She lives next door to *Shaike der Farber* [Shaike the housepainter]." So Golda was finally reunited with the girl she had known since the second grade.

After tea and some "catching up" chatter, Golda mentioned the letter her father had written about the cow which had calves. "Well," she said then, "I couldn't let myself be outdone by a kibbutz cow!"

Menachem Myerson was born on November 23, 1924. Morris, waiting in agony outside the room, was certain his wife and child had died, for he heard not one scream, not even a moan. Then, finally, after endless hours, came the mewling cry of a newborn child. And the doctor came out to announce to Morris, "You have a beautiful baby boy. And your wife is fine. She's a very brave young lady."

Menachem was, indeed, a beautiful boy with soft brown curly hair, large brown eyes, and a ready smile. His parents adored him. And Morris was happy. The moroseness which had enveloped him at Merhavia fled completely. This was his world as he wanted it. He was the breadwinner. She was the housewife. She went shopping every day; she looked after the child. And Morris loved Jerusalem; his soul seemed to belong here in this ancient city of dreamers, poets, philosophers, and scholars. Though the city still lacked such refinements of civilization as running water and sewers, it did have numerous bookshops. And this, for Morris, *meant* civilization.

If Golda was less happy than he, she suppressed it—or tried her best to.

But one spring evening when Menachem was six months old, it somehow all broke loose. She wept. She pleaded. She loved Morris. She loved the baby. But she was a Labor Zionist. She had not come all the way to Palestine to be a Jerusalem housewife. She wanted to go back to Merhavia. She wanted to work with people who were helping to recreate the Jewish homeland.

Morris said very little. He merely shrugged. "So, go to Merhavia. I'll stay here. If you want to come back, I'll be waiting."

She took the baby and went to the kibbutz. This time they made her the *metapelet*—the housemother—in charge of the Infants' House. Instead of one remarkably good baby, Menachem, she now had five—who were not so remarkably good. As soon as one stopped crying, another seemed to start. Then they all got sick at the same time: an infectious illness.

Golda diligently sterilized the infants' bathtub—with crude alcohol, since there was no medical alcohol. Her fellow kibbutzniks were indignant at this extravagance.

Caustically they dubbed her small charges "Golda's brandy babies."

As before, she worked hard. But somehow the ebullient spirit seemed to have gone out of her. She missed her husband. She loved him. What was she doing here in Merhavia breaking up her marriage?

Six months later she went back to Morris; back to Jerusalem; back to the life he wanted her to live.

The following spring, in May, 1926, Sarah was born. She too was a beautiful baby, blond, blue-eyed. However, she cried a good deal more than any of the crying babies in the kibbutz. Golda worried, took the child to a doctor. The verdict? "Colic. She'll grow out of it," the doctor said.

But she did not grow out of it.

Finally they found a pediatrician who was able to diagnose the malady. "It's her kidneys," he said somberly. "We'll have to put her on a special diet. And watch her very carefully."

The two children had been sleeping with their parents in one room. But it was obvious that the cramped, hot quarters were not conducive to the rest and quiet that the baby needed, so the boarder was asked to leave. And Menachem and Sarah shared the extra room.

But with the boarder gone, the Myersons did not have sufficient money to pay the rent and to pay Menachem's tuition at nursery school. Golda could have gone out to work and hired someone to look after the children. But she was determined now to be the kind of wife that Morris wanted. So, in order to be with her children and still make a little money, she took in washing. The flat, fortunately, had a large bathtub. And the British fortunately had recently laid water pipes. Golda at least did not need to draw water, pail by pail, from the well, as she'd done when they first arrived.

However, clothes could not come clean in cold water, which meant that pot after pot of water had to be heated on the primus stove. It was a laborious job, and she spent many hours each day kneeling by the bathtub sloshing heavy wet clothes up and down on a rough washboard.

Shana, in Tel Aviv, was faring little better.

The letters between the two sisters held few references now to the ideals of Zionism. They dwelt on such mundane subjects as unpaid bills and children's illnesses. Shana's greatest hardship was the separation from Shamai, who was still in Chicago working to make money to send to his wife and children.

Golda's greatest hardship was the degrading embarrassment of avoiding the butcher because of unpaid bills, pleading with the milkman for credit, begging the landlord to wait just a little longer for the rent.

One day she was returning from shopping at the food stalls of the old walled quarter, the Mea Shearim. She met an official of the Histadrut, the trade union for Jewish workers in Palestine. She knew the man, for at Merhavia she had been sent as delegate from the kibbutz to various Histadrut conferences.

When he heard that she had "retired" he was both surprised and indignant. The Yishuv—the Jews of Palestine —could not afford such a luxury. She had special talents which were badly needed.

Shortly afterward Golda was called into the Histadrut office and offered the job of secretary of the Moatzot Poalot, the Women's Labor Council. As she listened to what the job would entail, she felt charged with joy and determination.

She *had* tried to be the wife Morris wanted her to be. She had, with real determination, cut herself off from all outside contacts. She had been a wife and a mother and nothing more for four years. She loved her husband, her children. But why could she not continue to be a good wife, a good mother—and at the same time work for the cause she believed in more deeply than anything else in the world?

That evening Menachem came in clutching a scrawny kitten he had found in an alley. He wanted to keep it.

Golda looked at the animal dubiously. Once, in Pinsk, as a child of five she had tried to separate two fighting cats. They turned on her, gashed her legs deeply. Ever since she had hated cats.

"Please, Mama!" Menachem said, looking up at her.

"It probably has fleas!" said Golda.

Suddenly she remembered a similar scene, a long time ago. Little Tzipka had found a mangy stray dog and had begged to keep it. "It probably has fleas!" Bluma had said. But when Tzipka cried, Bluma relented. "All right. Keep it. But just for *one* night! In the basement."

The dog stayed till it died, five years later.

"Please, Mama!" four-year-old Menachem said again.

Golda knelt down, embraced the little boy and the kitten. "All right," she said. "I may have to go away sometimes. On trips. For a new job I'm taking. We'll wash the kitten. Then he can sleep in your bed so you'll never be lonesome."

A smile spread over Menachem's face. "Thank you, Mama," he said.

Once Golda had determined to take the job, nothing would deter her. She tried her best to explain it to Morris. They were two completely different types of people: extrovert and introvert. They had made the mistake of falling in love. But it could work, if he gave her some freedom to do what she felt she must do. It could work, if only he would understand.

Morris looked at her. His lips were tight. "I'll try," he said.

He did try. But Golda was away from home far more frequently than anyone—even she—had imagined she would be. The executives at the Moatzot Poalot soon discovered that the attractive young woman they had hired as secretary of the organization was a forceful and eloquent speaker. The fact that she had been brought up in America and spoke perfect English was also vitally important when it came to winning understanding and sympathy for the Zionist cause in England. And this became an ever more essential undertaking.

In 1920, Great Britain, "mother of the Balfour Declaration," had been given a mandate to govern Palestine. The following year Britain had taken her first step in turning her back on the Balfour Declaration—which declared that His Majesty's government viewed *with favor the establishment in Palestine of a national home for the Jewish people.*

But in 1922, the British—without consulting anyone— had chopped off more than three-quarters of Palestine, which they handed over to King Abdullah for an Arab kingdom. (He promptly renamed his new domain Trans-Jordan.)

Despite the fact that Great Britain had arbitrarily given away most of the Jews' twice-Promised Land, in 1922 the League of Nations ratified the mandate which Britain held over Palestine.

In 1929 the Jewish Agency was created to represent the Jews of Palestine in their relationship with the Mandatory Government. And after that year, 1929, Golda found herself traveling more and more often to Great Britain. Her mission? Golda put it simply in a letter she wrote to Shana: *I think that we must miss no opportunity to explain what we want and what we are to influential people.*

She said something more in that letter. She pleaded with Shana, her adored older sister, for understanding.

I ask only one thing, that I be understood and believed. My social activities are not an accidental thing: they are an absolute necessity for me. I am hurt when Morris and others say that this is all superficial, that I am trying to be modern. It is silly. Do I have to justify myself?

Before I left, the doctor assured me that Sarele's health permits of my going, and I have made adequate arrangements for Menachem. And yet you can understand how hard it is for me to leave. But in our present situation I could not refuse to do what was asked of me.

"In our present situation I could not refuse to do what was asked of me."

She was thirty-one when she wrote that sentence. It was a sentence which she was to repeat in other words and in other ways for the next four decades. It was a sentence which became the most important guideline of her life.

Chapter 9

Golda was at a conference, making a speech. As she stepped from the rostrum a cable was handed to her. An ordinary occurrence now. The year was 1932. She had become a fairly important personage. She received numerous cables. But not like this one. It was from Morris.

SARELE DESPERATELY ILL.
COME HOME AT ONCE.

When Golda walked in, her little girl was lying on the cot, so pale that her skin looked almost transparent. "Mama," she whispered, and smiled. Eight-year-old Menachem was sitting by his sister's bedside. He looked at his mother with large accusing eyes and said nothing at all.

She embraced the children, then followed Morris into the next room.

"The doctor says there's very little hope." His voice was flat with anguish.

"We'll—find another doctor."

Morris turned away, walked to the open window, and stood, staring out.

During the past two years they had been to many doctors; some of them had come recently from Europe and were graduates of the great medical schools of Germany and Austria. All of them agreed on the cause of the child's illness: the kidney disease she'd had since infancy.

All had agreed on the treatment. A special diet. Sarele was allowed to eat only carbohydrates.

And now it seemed that the doctors agreed again. There was little hope that the child would live.

Presently Golda left the house. She went to the Histadrut office. For the first time she made a specific request. Would they send her, please, to the United States? She would do anything, serve in any capacity. But she must be sent at once to the United States.

She had recently read that doctors in New York City were doing new work on kidney disease.

She was given an assignment. There was an organization in New York City called Pioneer Women. Its purpose was to sponsor activities which encouraged women to play a greater part in the reclamation of the homeland. Pioneer Women had been organized eight years ago. It had accomplished a certain amount, but its membership was still small. Furthermore, it consisted almost entirely of Yiddish-speaking, Zionist-oriented immigrant women. Golda's assignment: to spread the message of Pioneer Women to "Americanized" Jewish women throughout the country; to arouse their interest; to enlist their aid and their financial backing.

When Golda informed their present pediatrician that she planned to take Sarah to the States, the doctor looked at her as though she had gone mad. "Well," he said flatly, "you'll kill her, that's all. She's in no shape for a trip like that."

Wracked with doubt, with despair Golda turned to Morris for help in making the crucial decision. Finally, after tortured hours, the parents agreed. She would leave for the States as soon as possible, with both children. Morris had been offered a position with a large import firm in Haifa; it would be the most promising job he had ever held. So it was decided that he should remain in Palestine.

The next morning Morris went to the travel office to make reservations. He returned home more despondent than ever. The only ship they could get passage on was the *Bremen,* which left from Le Havre. They would have to travel by train from Tel Aviv to Egypt, then by ship from Port Said to Marseilles. Another train to Paris. Still another to Le Havre. As for the long ocean voyage itself —they could only hope. They had grim memories indeed of the last transatlantic crossing.

Many times Golda or Morris, or both together, decided definitely to cancel the reservations. As Sarele lay in bed weak and wan, it seemed impossible that the child could even survive the train trip to Port Said.

Yet, somehow Golda felt that hope lay only on the other side of the ocean.

One day the doctor came. As usual, he put Sarah on the kitchen table, and drew blood from her vein. Always before Golda had managed to smile, to be strong in front of the child. But this time, torn by the impossible decision, she broke down suddenly. She wept.

Sarah looked up and said to her, "Mama, don't cry."

It was the quiet courage of the six-year-old child which made Golda decide finally that they must take the chance.

The trip was as arduous as they had anticipated. But Sarah survived it. Indeed, on the *Bremen* she seemed to rally somewhat. They had a small cabin in tourist class, but on the first day at sea a steward took Menachem up to the first-class section of the ship and into the children's playroom, which was empty. The little boy found himself in a brightly painted world of hobby horses, seesaws, dolls, small furniture, stuffed animals, and games. When he described it to Sarah, she insisted on coming along the next day.

Like Menachem, she had never even dreamed there could be a place as splendid as this first-class playroom, where everything was made to order for children. She spent many hours every day dressing and feeding and rocking her new-found family of dolls.

Twelve days later, at dawn, the ship sailed past the Statue of Liberty. Golda, standing on the deck with Menachem beside her, found herself deeply moved.

Give me your tired, your poor, your huddled masses yearning to breathe free . . .

Perhaps someday *Eretz Israel* would be able to offer the same message of sanctuary and hope to the persecuted Jews of the world.

Mrs. Fanny Goodman, an old friend from the Poale Zion days, had insisted that Golda and the children stay with her. So they took a taxi to Fanny's apartment in Flatbush, Brooklyn.

A short, plump, motherly woman, Fanny bustled about, trying to make them feel at home. Golda put Sarah straight to bed, then went off to telephone a doctor whose name she had been given.

Within a short time the child had been admitted to Beth Israel Hospital, a tall, splendid, newly built brick building on Stuyvesant Square East. Sarah had a bed by the window. From the third-floor pediatrics ward she could look out and see the tops of trees in the small park across the street.

But the little girl turned away from the window, buried her face in the pillow, and cried when it came time for Golda to leave. She clung frantically to her mother's hand, to her dress. "Stay with me, Mama! Don't leave me all alone!"

Golda, near tears herself, tried to explain that visiting hours were over, that she would return first thing the next morning. Finally, with the nurse's help, she disengaged herself from her daughter's clutching hands. She well understood the child's terror. Aside from being left alone in a strange place, Sarah knew no English—which made her isolation absolute.

At home in Fanny Goodman's Flatbush apartment, Menachem was equally miserable. Since he spoke no English, he refused to go out in the street to play with other children. He would sit on his cot reading over and over the few books he had brought with him. If he spoke at all it was of his Papa or his cat. Golda and Fanny tried to encourage him to learn a little English. After all, school would start in a few weeks. He would be lost if he didn't at least know the rudiments of the language.

But Menachem did not want to go to school in Flatbush,

Brooklyn. He did not want to learn English. He wanted only one thing—to go home to Papa and Palestine.

Golda could not take him along when she visited Sarah, for the hospital allowed no children as visitors. And she could not, of course, take Menachem when she went to work. She tried as best she could to be mother and father to the lonely little boy. But there was never enough time. His misery settled inside her, like a dead weight, ever present. She felt torn to pieces by the need to be with him, the need to be with Sarah, and the ever-mounting pressures imposed upon her by her new job.

She often found herself irritated at the foolish questions asked by the well-to-do ladies who came out of curiosity to hear her speak at meetings of the Pioneer Women.

"Mrs. Myerson, when was the first kibbutz started? And why?"

"First of all," Golda would answer tartly, "it's not pronounced like a kibbitzer at a bridge party. The accent is on the second syllable. Ki-BBUTZ!"

Then seeing the look of chagrin on her questioner's face, she would soften her tone. After all, she had not been sent here to answer questions with irritation. Her mission was to inform, to inspire, and perhaps win financial backing from wealthy American Jewish women who knew nothing of Zionism or Palestine.

"You ask when the first kibbutz was started. In 1909. You ask, why. Well, that's not such a simple story."

She would then launch into the story which was not so simple. She would tell them of the first wave of Jewish settlers—the First Aliyah, some 10,000 young scholars and shopkeepers who came to Palestine in the 1880's and 1890's. They came fleeing the violent new waves of pogroms which were sweeping Russia. Almost all were poor. Some were penniless, with no money even for railroad fare. So they walked all the way. It often took them two years. They trudged over the rearing, rugged mountains of the Caucasus where the snows were waist-high in the winter . . . down through Turkey . . . the province of Syria . . . Lebanon—strangers always in a hostile land. Except for the small Jewish communities who would house them, feed them, and give them a little money to go on. On to Palestine, the Promised Land.

But no longer a land of milk and honey. It had declined under centuries of conquerors to a land of festering malarial swamps, sun-seared desert, and eroded, rocky hillsides. A barren, dying, almost empty land.

The new Jewish pioneers came with high ambitions about reclaiming the land, making it fertile once more. But they lacked experience. Lacked funds. And their settlements foundered. In desperation, as one of the colonies was about to dissolve in a mire of despair, an early settler, Reb Feinberg, made a trip to Paris to see Baron Edmond de Rothschild, whose interest in Jewish causes was well known.

Feinberg met the Baron. Pleaded for a loan. And, as collateral, held out his own work-callused hands. The Baron agreed to give the pioneers 30,000 francs.

The results were so impressive that Rothschild gave more and more money to the Jewish settlements, then started establishing small agricultural colonies himself on some 125,000 acres of swamps or rocky hillsides which he bought from Turkish or Arab landowners.

At the turn of the century came the second wave of immigration—the Second Aliyah—inspired by the fiery founder of political Zionism, Theodor Herzl.

They too came chiefly from Russia, some forty thousand of them. But they scorned the type of settlements sponsored by Rothschild and a few other Jewish philanthropists who had entered the Palestine picture. The homeland, they felt, must be re-created by the labor and sweat of Jewish pioneers, working on land purchased by—and therefore belonging to—the Jewish people.

So the Keren Kayemet was formed, the Jewish National Fund. In the Jewish sections of cities, towns, and villages throughout Eastern and Western Europe and North and South America small blue and white boxes were nailed up in kitchens and shops. Collection boxes for the Jewish National Fund.

Jewish children were taught to drop their savings into

the box every Friday night. Housewives dropped bits of change into the box when they left a shop. Old men came around once a week to collect the money, which they brought then to the local office of the Jewish National Fund.

Pennies, dollars, kopeks, lire, francs, pounds, piasters began coming in from Jews of the world. And with this money more tracts of swamplands or barren rocky soil were bought from the Arab and Turkish landowners, a few dozen of whom owned most of the land in Palestine. The prices they charged were outrageously high. But the prices were met, for this, the Jews felt, was hallowed land. The historic homeland of the Jewish nation.

The pioneers of the Second Aliyah were even more idealistic than their predecessors. They refused to hire Jewish or Arab labor as the farmers of the First Aliyah had done. But working the impossible land as individuals soon proved an impossible task. So the ten young pioneers decided to try a new experiment in *communal* farming.

They took over 750 acres of swampland by the River Jordan, which they determined to reclaim without hired labor. And without pay. All their earnings would go into a common fund, from which supplies would be bought— and distributed to each member according to his needs. No member need worry about such matters as doctors' bills, food bills, insurance, rent, education for his children, care for his elderly parents. The kibbutz, as they called their collective settlement, would take over the personal responsibilities of each member.

The land they reclaimed would never belong to them. It would always remain the property of the Jewish National Fund and the Jewish people. And should one of the communal farmers leave Degania, as they called their community of wooden shacks, he could take nothing with him but the clothes on his back.

For months the ten kibbutzniks hacked away at tangles of undergrowth, dug ditches for drainage, planted Australian eucalyptus trees to soak up the stagnant swamp water, pulled up rocks and boulders by hand. A third of their members were always bedridden with malaria. Yet, after two years, they managed to clear and to cultivate several hundred acres. And they had set a unique successful pattern for communal living, one which was to be a cornerstone of the coming state.

"A few months ago," Golda told her now-fascinated audience, "I had a meeting with one of the founders of Degania, Joseph Baratz. We discussed those early days. He told me how one of the first ten members had been killed by Arabs. How two more died of malaria. But even so, their community increased. Baratz put it this way: 'One of our men had such a noble plan: no marriages for five years. Only work! So what happened? Came two girls from Russia. And five months later he was married—the fellow who proposed the plan. But he was not the first,' said Baratz. 'I was the first!' "

The ladies in the audience laughed at the story of Joseph Baratz; laughed because they were moved, almost to tears. It had been brought very close, for the first time: the struggle, the strength, the courage of Jews—Jews like themselves—who were working to reclaim the homeland.

And the ladies slipped checks for substantial amounts into the little blue and white box of the Jewish National Fund when it was passed around at the meeting.

Golda spent two years in America. Her success became almost legendary as she traveled about the States bringing the message of pioneering Palestine to American-Jewish women who "couldn't care less"—until they heard her. Then her down-to-earth simplicity, her rock-bottom sincerity, tempered by her warmth and her wit, somehow transformed "speeches" into memorable experiences for her audiences. And transformed thousands of apathetic American women into ardent—and contributing—Zionists.

The American trip was successful in another way as well.

Sarah was cured. The kidney trouble might recur, the doctors at Beth Israel Hospital said, but it could be handled now by special treatment and diet. For the first time the little girl could lead a completely normal life.

Chapter 10

"There's *Papa!*" Menachem screamed it out.

They had just come through customs. He ran to his father, who lifted him high in the air, then hugged him hard. "Hey, you're heavy!" Morris exclaimed. "I sent you off a little boy, now you're almost as tall as I am."

"Papa!" Sarah came racing to him. "Papa, we're *home!*"

Morris lifted his daughter in his arms, and when he set her down there were tears in his eyes.

Golda came toward him. She was carrying a large black cello case. *"Shalom,* Morris," she said softly.

"So," he said, "you're all home, thank God, safe and sound and—healthy."

When they climbed into a taxi, Morris patted the cello case which was sandwiched upright on the seat between him and Menachem. "And this, I understand, is the new member of the family!"

Menachem had written him long letters about the cello. How Golda had taken him and Sarah on one of her long trips. How they spent Passover in Detroit at the home of a friend. How after dinner the friend's eighteen-year-old son played the cello for them. *All of a sudden I knew, Papa,* Menachem had written, *that's what I want to be. A cellist!* So Golda had bought him a cello, and he'd started taking lessons.

"Papa, I really am getting good!" Menachem exclaimed. "No kidding!"

"I don't know which I'm more impressed by," Morris replied. "Your cello. Or your American slang."

"I'm going to study the violin, Papa," Sarah chimed in. "Then you won't have to go out to concerts any more. You can stay home and listen to *us!*"

Morris laughed softly. "You know," he said, "it's very very good to have you back again." Then he added, "No kidding!"

Since their father had to return to Haifa that evening, the children tried their best to fill him in on all the happenings of the past two years. They talked quickly, in their newly acquired perfect English, each interrupting the other with enthusiasm to recount still another exciting exploit or adventure. But they carefully omitted mention of the loneliness, or the tears.

It was the loneliness, however, which remained as the dominant memory. Years later, during an interview, Sarah recalled the period in these words: "Mother traveled all over the United States. Sometimes weeks would pass and we didn't see each other. My brother suffered a great deal from this and he often gave vent to his protests. He quarreled with Mother and tried to stop her from leaving the house to go to meetings. I was more tolerant, but I also felt lonely without her. We were always lonesome for Mother because we saw very little of her."

These separations—and all those which followed—were equally difficult for Golda. Some of the anguish she underwent can be seen in an article she wrote, anonymously:

> Taken as a whole, the inner struggles and the despairs of the mother who goes to work are without parallel in human experience. . . . There are some mothers who work only when they are forced to, when the husband is sick or unemployed. In such cases the mother feels her course of action justified. . . . But there is a type of woman who cannot remain at home for other reasons. . . . She cannot divorce herself from the larger social life. . . . And for such a woman, there is no rest.

Theoretically it looks straightforward enough. The woman who replaces her with the children is devoted, loves the children, is reliable and suited to the work; the children are fully looked after. . . . She, of course, has the great advantage of being able to develop . . . therefore she can bring more to her children than if she were to remain at home. Everything looks all right. But one look of reproach from the little one when the mother goes away and leaves it with the stranger is enough to throw down the whole structure of vindication. That look, that plea to the mother to stay, can be withstood only by an almost superhuman effort of the will. . . .

This eternal inner division, this double pull, this alternating feeling of unfulfilled duty—today toward her family, the next day toward her work—this is the burden of the working mother.

The children had hoped they would all move to Haifa so the family could be united again.

Golda merely told them that this was not possible, since she had been offered an excellent job in Tel Aviv. But they would all be together on the Sabbath.

That was, of course, only part of the story.

After the two-year separation the parents realized that they were happier living apart. Opposites, they say, attract. But when husband and wife are as diametrically opposite as Golda and Morris, perhaps the original attractions turn to frictions. Introvert and extrovert, each wanted, each needed a totally different type of life. Each had tried living according to the other's wishes: Morris in Merhavia, Golda in Jerusalem. Yet, during these periods each had despaired because the other was obviously unhappy.

Out of the deep respect and affection they felt for each other, they decided to try an unofficial separation.

Golda found a flat on the newly built Israel Street. They had two rooms, a kitchen, and a terrace in one of the white, three-story, cement-block houses. The children shared the bedroom. Golda slept on the couch in the living room. And every Friday afternoon Morris commuted from Haifa.

A ritual soon developed. The children would wait for him at the bus stop. When he arrived, the three would go around to the bookstores where Morris purchased the Manchester *Guardian,* the London *Times,* and placed orders for several new books he had heard or read about. Menachem and Sarah were permitted to buy a book each.

Then they would all troop home. Golda, an admirable cook, prepared dinner. Friends dropped in. The family spent the Sabbath together. And on Saturday evening, after sunset, Morris would take the bus back to the city of Haifa.

Golda's new job was the most exciting, the most fulfilling she had ever held.

Because of the acclaim she had won during her two-year stint in the United States, she was made a member of the executive committee of the Histadrut, the General Federation of Jewish Labor in Palestine.

The Histadrut was certainly the world's unique labor union. It had been founded in 1920, when there were few jobs in Palestine. So the new labor union had proceeded to make some jobs. With the dues of its first 5,000 members it set up small Histadrut-owned factories, which created jobs for another 5,000. And so the snowball rolled.

By 1934, when Golda went to work in the Histadrut headquarters, its membership numbered over forty percent of the Jewish workers in Palestine. This included, as might be expected, such categories as bus drivers, printers, plumbers, construction workers. It also included, as might not be expected, such categories as farmers, secretaries, doctors, even artists.

The Histadrut was often called the world's only capitalistic union. It set up its own chain of kibbutzim and a huge marketing cooperative to sell farm products in the cities and villages. It set up and owned many factories. It started its own publishing house to translate the classics into Hebrew. It started its own daily newspaper, *Davar (the World),* which soon had the highest newspaper circulation in the land. It had its own theater. And before any other country had general medical programs, Histadrut was giving its members full "womb to tomb" coverage through the low-cost health insurance of its Kupat Holim (the Workers' Sick Fund).

The Histadrut also had its schools. Menachem and Sarah went to one of them: Beithachinuch (School for the Children of Working Parents). Among its many educational goals was that of teaching the satisfactions and the skills of physical work. The children, consequently, had classes in kitchen, gardening, and workshops.

At first Menachem and Sarah came in for much teasing. They were called the Americans. They had forgotten most of their Hebrew, and as they relearned the language the words came out thick with American accent.

But within a few months they had adjusted well to their new school, new neighborhood, and new life.

Since the Histadrut school was set up primarily for the children of mothers who worked, school days were long, from eight in the morning till three or four in the afternoon, six days a week—which corresponded to adult working hours.

Golda could, therefore, go off to the office without worry—at least during those periods in which she remained in Tel Aviv. When she was away she had to depend on friends or hired sitters to stay with Menachem and Sarah.

The children, quite naturally, never got used to these separations—which meant continual anguish for their mother. But at least now Golda had given up worrying as to whether the course she was pursuing was the right one. In the Histadrut the Jews of Palestine were creating many of their own advanced forms of self-government. And to be a member of the Histadrut Executive Committee was to be one of the leaders of this government.

Within a year Golda was elected to the secretariat of the Executive Committee. Now, at age thirty-seven, she was truly one of the inner circle.

The following year she was made Chairman of the

Board of Directors of the Kupat Holim (the Workers' Sick Fund).

Despite these exalted positions, there was still very little money in the Myerson household. The reason lay deep in Histadrut philosophy. A worker was not paid according to the type of work he performed, but according to the number of years he had put into the job and according to the number of his dependents. Consequently, the cleaning woman who scrubbed the floor of Golda's office in the evenings could well have been making more money than Chairman of the Board of Directors Myerson.

Sarah later recalled this period in these words: "Our economic condition was never good. I remember that for a long time my mother had only two dresses. She washed one and wore the other. Buying a dress or a blouse constituted a problem which could not easily be solved. Often my mother was worried about financial conditions and the question of debts, although our demands were very modest."

One of these demands was Menachem's cello lessons. As soon as they returned from the States, Golda arranged that he should have private lessons. Since the cello was awkward and heavy for a small boy to manage on a crowded bus, Golda would often accompany him to his lesson to tote the cello—before she returned to the office to work through the long evenings and often into the late night hours.

Sarah had also been promised music lessons, so she started studying violin at the age of nine. But when it became apparent that she lacked her brother's brilliance as a musician, the lessons came to a halt, it being too difficult to pay two different sets of tuition fees. Sarah was not notably heartbroken.

She and Menachem did, however, give themselves lessons of a different sort. Their mother had refused to buy them bicycles. Tel Aviv traffic, Golda felt, was far too hazardous for children to try to make their way through the streets on bicycles. Within a decade a full-fledged city had sprung up almost miraculously out of the sand dunes —a city with a restless, on-the-go, round-the-clock mentality. All of which was reflected in Tel Avivians' driving techniques.

Golda perhaps set down stricter health and safety rules for her children than other parents did, precisely because she was away from home so often. In any case, Menachem and Sarah felt that this particular rule—no bike riding—was quite unjust. Why should *they* be the only ones who could not ride a bicycle? So they borrowed bikes from their classmates and became champion cyclists—an accomplishment which, however, they kept well hidden from their mother.

While Menachem and Sarah were going to school, taking music lessons, learning to ride bikes on the sly—and growing up quite unaware of the meaning of anti-Semitism —there were other Jewish children growing up under the constant shadow of fear and degradation.

Jewish children in Nazi Germany had been forced into segregated "Jew Schools." They were forbidden to enter public parks—unless the park had a special bench with a sign on it: JEW BENCH. (Or, in some cases, BENCH RESERVED FOR PIG JEWS.) In which case the Jewish child was permitted to sit on the bench and watch other children play.

The signs were everywhere. At the entrance to towns: NO DOGS OR JEWS ALLOWED. At the change booth of movie houses, swimming baths, concert halls: NO JEWS ALLOWED. And in shop windows throughout the land: WE DO NOT SELL TO JEWS. There were towns in which a Jew could not buy milk for his children. Or medicine. In some of the smaller towns it was almost impossible for a Jew to buy food because of the signs at the doorways of the dairies, the groceries, the butcher shops.

On September 15, 1935, a series of laws were passed: the Nuremberg Laws. Making every Jew in Germany legally and officially an outcast. With no rights at all.

Consequently, there was no punishment at all for those who broke into Jewish shops and homes to destroy and to steal. There was no punishment for the gangs who waylaid a Jewish child on his way home from school or an old rabbi leaving the synagogue—and beat them into insensibility.

Murder was, at first, a slightly different matter. Some of those who murdered Jews were actually brought to trial. But in ninety percent of the cases, the murderer was judged "Not Guilty" and walked from the courthouse a free man.

Jews, on the other hand, were arrested by the hundreds, then by the thousands. The only crime they had committed: being born a Jew. Who was a Jew? There had been, after all, much intermarriage between Jews and Gentiles in Germany. The Nuremberg Laws set it all down clearly. Any person with one Jewish grandparent was defined as being a Jew.

So many Jews were arrested that the prisons could not hold them. Criminals were set free so their cells could be used for Jews. Still the prisons overflowed, so special concentration camps were built; eighty-five percent of their inmates were Jews.

By 1936 over half the Jews in Germany had been fired from their jobs. And since few of them could find new work, their families started to starve.

Naturally they tried to get out of the country.

In the early years of Hitler's reign this had not been too difficult. But as the months went by a strange contradiction occurred. Though the Nazis proclaimed more stridently than ever that their goal was to make Germany *judenrein*—cleansed of Jews—they made it, at the same time, almost impossible for Jews to leave.

A cruel game was begun. A Jew wanting to emigrate had to get, through bribery in most cases, so many official documents and papers that he was forced to spend his days running from one government office to the next. Often, by the time the last paper had been acquired, the first one would have expired. And the nightmare process would have to begin all over again. The process included signing over everything one owned, to the German government. A Jew could leave Germany with no more than ten Reichsmarks, the equivalent of a few dollars.

Frequently, false exit visas were sold—at exorbitant

rates. Jews who, unknowingly, bought these were, of course, turned back at the border. But even those who did finally manage to acquire perfectly valid exit visas were frequently arrested at the frontier, brought back, and locked up in a concentration camp. As with the other Jewish inmates, that was usually the last anyone ever heard of them. (Although, on occasion, a postcard was received by a member of the family with the information that ashes of the deceased would be forwarded upon receipt of prepaid postage.)

In March, 1938, Adolf Hitler's armies goose-stepped into Austria, to be greeted with huge enthusiasm. As further proof of their loyalty to their new leader, Austrians immediately turned upon *their* 400,000 Jews with even more ferocity than the Germans had shown. Orders went out to arrest every male Jew between the ages of eighteen and forty-five.

Jewish children, women, and old people were set upon by laughing, jeering gangs. They were often hauled off to clean out the public latrines or forced down on their hands and knees to scrub the gutters. Sometimes, as an added joke, acid was put in the scrub water.

Quite naturally news of these extraordinary happenings reached the rest of the world. And the reaction of the rest of the world was quite extraordinary. The reports were met with disbelief, put down as "warmongering" or "propaganda." Or they were met with apathy and indifference.

Most world leaders seemed to regard Adolf Hitler as something of an unbelievable upstart. An ex-housepainter —who had failed even in that undemanding career. The illegitimate son of a peasant serving girl and a vagrant named, of all things, Shicklgruber! Statesmen who met Adolf Hitler were startled by his vulgarity and by his ignorance. This ranting little man with his black forelock and comic mustache would, they felt, somehow disappear as abruptly as he had arisen.

But the leaders of the Yishuv—the Jews of Palestine— did not have so optimistic a view. A few of them even foresaw that Hitler's real intention was to make the Greater German Reich *judenrein*—not by forcing the Jews out—but by keeping them in. And secretly, systematically murdering them all.

And there were Jewish leaders who predicted that Hitler would one day dominate most of the countries of Europe—which meant that far more than the half million Jews of Germany and Austria were in dire danger of extermination.

As early as November 25, 1936, Dr. Chaim Weizmann stood before the Palestine Royal Commission in Jerusalem and warned, "There are six million people doomed to be pent up where they are not wanted and for whom the world is divided into places where they cannot live, and places which they may not enter. Six million!"

What would happen to those six million people, those six million Jews?

Even in Palestine there were few who could envision the most monstrous nightmare in all the history of mankind: that six million Jews would be systematically murdered, most of them in the gas chambers of specially designed death camps where bodies could be conveniently reduced to ashes in huge furnaces made to order for human corpses. (Before being shunted into the oven, however, each corpse was gone over by trained technicians. One pried open the jaw, knocked out gold-filled teeth. In a single camp, Auschwitz, seventeen tons of gold were collected in this manner. Another technician shaved the heads of women. The hair was used in the manufacture of mattresses and textiles. An apprentice member of the team removed such items as watches, rings, and false limbs. Jewish fat was used to make inexpensive soap. Bones which did not burn in the ovens were used for the manufacture of phosphate. And the final ashes were made into fertilizer for German fields and flower gardens.)

It was not necessary, however, to envision such unimaginable horrors in order to work—almost with despera-

tion—for the immediate creation of a Jewish national
home in Palestine.

By the year 1938 the horrors which were happening
every day in Hitler's Reich were reason enough to turn
the words of Article 2 of the British Mandate into immediate reality.

> *The Mandatory shall be responsible for placing the
> country under such political, administrative and economic
> conditions as will secure the establishment of the Jewish
> national home. . . .*

Sixteen years had passed since that agreement was
signed. The Yishuv had developed all the institutions any
country needed to govern itself successfully. The time for
the establishment of the Jewish national home was due,
and overdue. There had to be some place in the world to
which the Jews of Hitler's Reich could flee. And certainly
no other nation was opening its arms to welcome the
desperate refugees. Quite the contrary. All other nations
in the world were busy raising official barriers aimed at
keeping the Jews out.

And at the head of the line of the barrier-raisers stood
the British Mandatory Power of Palestine.

Indeed, the British Foreign Office seemed to have completely forgotten the role of a Mandatory Power. Britain
had come to regard Palestine as a colonial possession, a
strategic possession which she wanted to keep—for
through Palestine she could hold a vital key to power in
the Middle East.

There was also the matter of Arab oil which, if war
broke out, could become essential to the survival of the
British Empire.

Consequently, the British Mandatory Power turned
deaf ears to the desperate pleas of the Yishuv leaders, and
listened with utmost consideration to those Arab leaders
who insisted that Palestine must not become a haven for
hordes of fleeing Jews.

Obligingly, in the year 1935 the British set down a

strict immigration quota. Only 60,000 Jews a year would be admitted to the Holy Land. The following year they cut that figure in half.

The words of the Balfour Declaration had become almost a mockery.

And the League of Nations, which had promised Palestine to the Jews as their homeland, was now almost a defunct world body.

What single nation—or group of nations—would take the responsibility of insisting that Britain release her hold on Palestine and turn the ancient homeland back to the Jews in this, the most desperate period in all Jewish history?

The answer was resoundingly clear.

The leaders of the Yishuv were fighting alone. Fighting against time. Fighting against the world.

Then, in May, 1938, came incredible news.

Franklin D. Roosevelt, President of the United States, was organizing an International Conference on Refugees. The nations of the world were being invited to send delegates to Évian-les-Bains, France. The delegates would determine ways and means of getting Jews out of the Greater German Reich and of helping these fleeing Jews reestablish their lives elsewhere.

The United States had not, after all, forgotten its historic heritage. The nations of the world had not, after all, turned their backs upon the Jews.

A few days later Golda came home and told her children that they would be staying with their Aunt Shana for several weeks during the summer.

"Why?" said Menachem. "Are you going away *again?*"

Golda nodded.

Menachem moaned. Sarah scowled. *"Another* conference, Mother?" Sarah asked.

"This," said Golda, "will not be just—another conference. It may turn out to be one of the most important conferences in all of Jewish history."

Chapter 11

The Évian Conference was held in the Hotel Royal, a luxurious hostelry with semicircular balconies overlooking the French resort spa and Lake Geneva where white triangles of sailboats slid along waters of picture-postcard blue.

The conference opened in the splendid, high-ceilinged Grand Salon at four o'clock on Wednesday afternoon, July 6, 1938. The chief delegates of the thirty-two nations were seated around a horseshoe-shaped conference table, eminent-looking gentlemen all. Their numbers, Golda had learned, consisted of three ambassadors, three ministers, thirteen envoys, and thirteen other diplomats of high status. Behind them were two semicircular rows of assistants. Three further rows of chairs had been set in the salon for the audience. Golda was a member of the audience.

It was, indeed, an impressive array of statesmen, representing the heart of the world. Late—but, thank God not too late—these thirty-two nations had heeded their collective conscience; had gathered—as nations had never gathered before—to help a persecuted people find new homelands. A heavy hum of conversation pervaded the Grand Salon. But Golda simply sat; isolated by the depths of her emotion.

The French Ambassador rose, and silence fell. As representative of the host country, he opened the conference. His speech was short, and worthy. He introduced Ambassador on Special Mission Myron C. Taylor, head of the American Delegation and Special Envoy of the American President, Franklin Delano Roosevelt.

Golda leaned forward in her seat, not wanting to miss a single sentence. And the words were everything she could have hoped for. "I need not emphasize," said the American Ambassador, "that the discrimination against minorities, the pressure that is being brought to bear upon them, and the disregard of elementary human rights contradict those principles which we have come to regard as the standards of our civilization." He continued on in this manner. And at the conclusion of his inspiring speech, Myron C. Taylor announced that the United States had raised the quota for German and Austrian immigrants to 27,370 persons per year.

He sat down, to polite applause. Golda frowned. She well knew that the American quota had already been filled for 1938 and 1939. People were being put on waiting lists for years ahead. People who could not afford to wait. It was *now* they needed a place to escape to. Furthermore, she felt that the figure 27,370 should be hidden in shame. Not used as a climax to all the high-flown words. In the single city of Vienna alone there were 176,000 Jews desperate to get out. The United States had called this conference of thirty-two nations. Was this the inspiration they offered to other countries—this paltry inching up of the immigration quota? A quota which included, of course, all Germans and Austrians, not only Jews.

As it turned out, however, the speech of the American Ambassador, Myron C. Taylor, was far and away the most inspiring offered at the conference. And the infinitesimal quota-raising which he announced was virtually the only positive step taken by any of the thirty-two "Évian nations."

Stunned first by incredulous disbelief, then by despair, Golda listened as, day after day, meeting after meeting, delegates from the various nations rose each to explain that his country understood of course the gravity of the situation and wanted to help. But was, unfortunately, unable to do so.

They presented a varied parade of reasons.

England pointed out that she was a densely populated country "at present engaged in a difficult fight against unemployment." To allow in masses of Jews at this point would only make for anti-Semitism. "No country," announced the British delegate, "can be expected to take people who have been robbed of their means of existence before even embarking on their emigration."

This, it turned out, was a clarion cry uttered by almost all the speakers. Their chief criticism of the Nazis seemed to be that they would not allow Jews to bring their wealth with them.

France announced that she had already taken in 200,000 refugees and could not take more—though doubtless the newer, underpopulated countries of the world would welcome an influx of refugees.

Switzerland, long the haven of freedom and democracy, pointed out that unfortunately she had several thousand Swiss citizens stranded in Spain because of the Spanish Civil War. She had to look after her own citizens first.

There were many other nations with the same problem. Peru, for example, had to help the Peruvian Indians. Integrate them into the Spanish Catholic life of the state.

Numerous countries had, unfortunately, legal restrictions which left them unable to help. Brazil, for example, had a new law. Every visa application must be accompanied by a certificate of baptism. Ecuador could accept only agricultural workers. (Since Jews of the Greater German Reich were forbidden by law to work in agriculture, that let Ecuador off the hook.) The immigration laws of Nicaragua, Costa Rica, Honduras, and Panama all classified intellectuals and merchants as undesirables. (Unfortunately, half the Jews of Germany and Austria fell into the "intellectual" category—doctors, lawyers, professors, and other such. Most of the rest were businessmen: "merchants.") Bolivia put the matter squarely and simply. Its laws forbade the immigration of Jews.

Australia? "Up to now," said the honorable delegate, "we have had no racial problem. And we do not wish to create one."

Other underpopulated nations put forth the same policy
in different and more flowery words.

Was there no country in the world which would set the
example? Act as a haven?

Between the meetings Golda spent her time trying to
talk to attachés, advisers, experts, and officials representing the thirty-two nations. She went up to them as they
strolled on the hotel lawns. Sat down by them in the hotel
lounges. Talked to them by telephone. Arranged meetings
in the delegates' suites. She was received in most cases
politely. In some cases sorrowfully. In all cases she was
told there was nothing the delegates could do. They had
received their instructions from their own governments
before they left home.

The press—perhaps *they* would arouse the conscience
of the world!

Many members of the press were present. But, incredibly, by the time the stories appeared in print, they had
been whittled down to splinter size. Not a single Évian
story appeared on a single front page. On the opening
day of the Conference, for example, the New York *Times*
covered Évian in a half column on page thirteen. (A full
column was devoted that day to the news that Adolf Hitler
had opened an art exhibition in Munich.) Subsequent
half-column stories on Évian appeared in the *Times* on
pages twelve, fourteen and, on the final day, page twenty.

News was certainly made that final day, for a special
resolution was passed. *The delegates of the countries of
asylum are not willing to undertake any obligations toward
financing involuntary emigration.* Since it was well known
that the German government allowed no Jew to leave the
country with more than ten Reichsmarks, the equivalent
of one pound or something less than five dollars, that
single resolution made every Jew from Germany or Austria
officially and automatically unacceptable to "the countries
of asylum."

Prior to adjourning the Conference on July 15th, the
Évian delegates appointed an Intergovernmental Committee on Refugees to study the matter further and make
recommendations.

Before she left Évian, Mrs. Golda Myerson, "the Jewish observer from Palestine," held a press conference. The questions asked by the journalists sounded more like condolences.

Golda was not a tall woman. She was only five feet four. But she seemed tall as she stood there before newsmen from various countries of the world. She seemed somehow a stalwart rock, in a sea of compassion.

"There is one ideal I have in my mind," she said. "There is one thing I want to see before I die, and that is that my people should not need expressions of sympathy any more."

When she reached home, Golda was once again interviewed by reporters. Did she see any hope at all, she was asked, in the Intergovernmental Committee on Refugees —or was this merely the conference's method of buckpassing?

Golda replied that she had met George Rublee, director of the new committee and that he was a decent and dedicated man. Yes, perhaps hope *did* lie here—in the person of Rublee and his Intergovernmental Committee on Refugees.

George Rublee and his Intergovernmental Committee were assigned offices in London. They worked hard. They presented a number of plans to the thirty-two nations which had attended the conference at Évian-les-Bains. Each plan they proposed was rejected.

Then, four months after the distinguished delegates at Évian had packed their valises and returned home, there erupted throughout the Reich the most disastrous night of horrors the century had yet seen.

It was set off by one bullet. A Jewish boy entered the German Embassy in Paris and shot and killed a German Third Secretary.

In retribution, 20,000 Jewish men over the age of seventeen were arrested and shipped to concentration camps; 171 Jewish apartment houses were completely destroyed; 815 Jewish stores were demolished; 191 synagogues were set on fire. In towns and villages throughout the land an unrecorded number of Jewish homes and shops went up in flames. Competitions were held to see which village would be "purified" of Jews first. Men, women, and children were dragged from their homes. Some were tethered by their feet to horsecarts, so their heads would bounce and crack on the cobblestones. Some were tied up, thrown into rivers, and left to drown. Some were hung.

In the cities, Jews were thrown out of apartment house windows and out the windows of speeding trains. Many Jews were shot while trying to escape.

Those who had murdered Jews were not punished in any way. The total number of Jews murdered was not announced.

What was announced—by German insurance companies—was the fact that some twenty-five million marks' worth of damage had been done. The matter of broken window glass alone came to a figure of five million marks. (This horrendous Night of November Tenth was henceforth also referred to as the *Kristallnacht:* the Night of the Broken Glass.)

Unfortunately, most of the "Jew stores" were merely rented by Jews—in buildings which belonged to German Gentiles, therefore their demands for repayment or replacement could not be ignored. Yet the insurance companies insisted they would go bankrupt if they were forced to make good on the policies.

The German government decided the matter in a simple manner. The Jewish subjects of the Reich would pay for the damage. Collectively, they were subjugated to a fine of one billion marks, as penalty for *"their abominable crimes, etc."* This amounted to one-tenth of the total estimated fortune of the Jews of Germany and Austria.

The governments of the world reacted with appropriate horror to the news of the *Kristallnacht.* Since, at last, their shock and concern seemed genuine, George Rublee put forth his most comprehensive plan. The details were carefully worked out during long, laborious sessions of the

Intergovernmental Committee on Refugees. The plan in essence was this: each of the thirty-two Évian nations should agree to take in 25,000 Jewish refugees.

Each of the thirty-two Évian nations diplomatically declined.

George Rublee continued to put forth plans—which the nations of the world continued to reject. Finally, in disgust and despair, Rublee resigned. First, however, he issued an official report. The situation, he said, was hopeless. All doors were locked against the Jewish refugees. Yet, despite this fact, more official restrictions were being issued all the time by countries all over the globe.

There was, it seemed, only one small group of people in the world urgently wanting to, waiting to receive the Jews of Europe. The Yishuv: the Jews of Palestine.

By 1939 over 60,000 German and Austrian Jews had made their way to Palestine. This was the so-called Fifth Aliyah, or wave of immigration. And it was different from the Aliyahs which had come before. The first four "waves" were made up, in the main, of Jews from Poland and Russia; students, scholars, small shopkeepers. Ardent Zionists all of them, convinced that the way to reclaim the homeland was to work on and revive the land with their own labor, their own sweat.

The Jews of the Fifth Aliyah were, in the main, not Zionists. Indeed, most of them had regarded themselves as assimilated Germans or Austrians. Now they were fleeing for their lives. The vast majority were city-born, with university degrees. They were doctors, scientists, chemists, engineers, professors, financial experts, government career men.

There were also the children. Thousands of children. Jewish parents unable to escape themselves performed that almost inhumanly heartrending act. They had sent their children off with strangers into unknown worlds.

On May 3, 1939, an article by Golda Myerson was published in *D'var HaPoelet,* a periodical of the Histadrut. It started off by speaking of the children.

*Every day brings forth new edicts which engulf more
hundreds of thousands of people; and we know that Jewish mothers are asking for only one thing: take our children away, take them to any place you choose, only save
them from this hell! . . . The whole Jewish community in
this country knows full well that there is only one way
we can assure Jewish mothers of their children's future:
if we bring them here, to this country. . . . Here they'll be
safe: safe for their mothers and safe for the Jewish people.*

On the seventeenth day of May, 1939, a paper was
issued by the British government—a so-called White
Paper. With one cold sentence it wiped out all the promises of the Balfour Declaration and all the proclamations
made by the League of Nations guaranteeing the Jews a
national homeland in Palestine:

*His Majesty's Government therefore now declare un-
equivocally that it is not part of their policy that Palestine
should become a Jewish State.*

To put teeth into this new decision two specific restrictions were set down.

Always before Jews had been free to buy whatever
land the Arab *effendis* cared to sell them. Henceforth,
Jews would be allowed to buy land only in five percent of
the country. Where then would the new Jewish immigrants
settle?

The second restriction took care of that question. During the next five years a maximum of 75,000 Jews would
be admitted. And after five years? *No further Jewish immigration will be permitted, unless the Arabs of Palestine
are prepared to acquiesce in it.*

Since it did not seem likely that the Arabs of Palestine
would be prepared to increase this quota, the White
Paper of 1939 meant that in five years time the historic
Jewish homeland would be closed to Jews.

Why? What was the justification for the White Paper of 1939?

Was it, perhaps, that the Arabs did not have sufficient territory and needed more?

They had four million square miles in the Middle East.

What of that more limited area of which Palestine was a part—the land freed from Turkish rule after World War I? Would the Jewish national home take up an undue proportion of *that* territory?

Five large—and largely underpopulated—Arab countries had been created from that land: Saudi Arabia, Iraq, Syria, Lebanon, and Trans-Jordan. They spread over 1,200,000 square miles. The section of Palestine which had been designated as the future Jewish homeland was a mere 10,000 square miles. Less than one percent of the total area.

Perhaps, however, the chief centers of Arab culture and religion lay in Palestine?

But they did not. Mecca and Medina, the holy cities of Arabia, the sources of the Moslem faith, all lay deep and undisturbed in Arab lands. Cairo, Damascus, Baghdad, and every other important city and center connected with Moslem and Arab history were also in Arab lands. Indeed, even those Arabs who lived in Palestine had for centuries thought of it only as the southern section of the province of Syria. At no time in all of Palestine's centuries-old history had there ever been an independent Arab state in Palestine.

Whereas the land now called Palestine had been universally known for well over a thousand years as "the land of the Jews." And since the fall of the Jewish state? The official British report of the Palestine Royal Commission (July, 1937) put it this way:

> *While the Jews had thus been dispersed over the world, they had never forgotten Palestine. If Christians have become familiar through the Bible with the country and its place-names . . . the link which binds the Jews to Palestine and its past history is to them far closer and more intimate. Judaism and its ritual are rooted in those*

*memories. Among countless illustrations it is enough to
cite the fact that Jews, wherever they may be, still pray
for rain at the season it is needed in Palestine. . . . This
belief in the divine promise of eventual return to Palestine
largely accounts for the steadfastness with which the Jews
of the diaspora clung to their faith and endured persecution.*

It was obvious that in a matter of months Europe
would erupt into a massive war. When that happened there
would be no more escape routes at all for Jews in the
Hitler-dominated countries of Europe. Now was therefore
the last chance to get as many Jews as possible into the
promised homeland.

Yet the British government had chosen *this* drastic moment to issue its White Paper.

Golda Myerson was one of the Jewish leaders who met,
in outrage and despair, to frame the official Zionist answer to the White Paper. One sentence of the statement
read: *It is in the darkest hour of Jewish history that the
British Government proposes to deprive the Jews of their
last hope and to close the road back to their Homeland.*

The full statement was duly published in leading newspapers of numerous countries.

The question which now echoed around the world was:
Why?

Chapter 12

The answer to that question started forming in the days when Golda and Morris first moved to Merhavia—when they, and the century, were in the early twenties.

Relations between Arabs and Jews were then, in the main, friendly.

At the Versailles Peace Treaty where the lands freed from Turkish dominance were newly divided, an agreement was signed between *His Royal Highness the Emir Feisal, representing and acting on behalf of the Arab Kingdom, and Dr. Chaim Weizmann, representing and acting on behalf of the Zionist Organization, mindful of the racial kinship and ancient bonds existing between the Arabs and the Jewish people, and realizing that the surest means of working out the closest possible collaboration in the development of the Arab State and Palestine.*

One of the clauses in the agreement stated: *All necessary measures shall be taken to encourage and stimulate immigration of Jews into Palestine on a large scale. . . . In taking such measures the Arab peasant and tenant farmers shall be protected in their rights, and shall be assisted in forwarding their economic development.*

And it happened as the forward-looking King Feisal had predicted. The Jews taught the Arabs new methods of crop rotation, fertilization, irrigation. They brought in many new types of crops, including fish which they farmed in fishponds which they dug, inland.

Furthermore, the Jewish contribution to the well-being

of the Arab farmer spread far beyond economic lines. For example, Jewish doctors in the farm settlements also tended neighboring Arabs. And free Jewish medical clinics were open to Arabs—who came in droves.

The Arab population in Palestine doubled from 1920 to 1939. This was due, in part, to natural increase. Before the Jews came, the average life expectancy of the Arab in Palestine was a mere thirty-five years. With the medical care brought to them by Jewish settlers, far fewer Arabs died.

Also, there were huge waves of Arab immigration from neighboring Arab countries to Mandated Palestine. The newcomers were drawn by the new jobs opening up in the developing cities, towns, and countryside. And they were drawn by the ever-rising standard of living among the Arabs of Palestine.

During the same two decades in neighboring Trans-Jordan—which was closed to Jewish immigration—there had been no rise in Arab population at all.

In one of his many later letters to prominent Jewish leaders, King Feisal wrote: *We Arabs . . . look with the deepest sympathy on the Zionist movement. We . . . wish the Jews a most hearty welcome home. We are working together for a reformed and revived Near East, and our two movements complete one another.*

If the Arab leaders and the Arab peasants welcomed the arrival of the Jews, what then went wrong?

Most of the land in Palestine was owned by a few dozen families of Arab *effendis*. Several of these families were as far-seeing as King Feisal. Most, however, were not.

Or, at least, they "saw" in quite a different direction.

They saw that the Arab peasant who worked on a Jewish farm earned far more money and lived in far better conditions than did the peasant who worked for an Arab *effendi*. What if Arab peasants, inspired by the example and the aid given them by the Jews, started to rebel against the *effendi*-dominated feudal system under which they were kept in dire poverty and ignorance? What, indeed, if this rebellion spread to other Arab lands?

Some of the worried *effendis* did not even live in Palestine. They had splendid villas and chateaus in Paris, Cairo, Damascus. But their massive wealth came from their lands in Palestine—lands which were worked by *felaheen*, the Arab peasants whose lives were no better than that of twelfth-century serfs of Europe.

This small but powerful group of Arab landowners had one ambition: to keep things exactly as they had been before the Jews started coming back to the Holy Land. Their program was twofold: allow no more Jews in, and get rid of the Jews already there.

How to achieve this?

The Arab peasants were easily led, excitable, and almost fanatically religious. So emissaries of the *effendis* went into the mosques, the Arab cafés, and coffee houses, bringing the Message: The Jews were invaders, stealing the peasants' land. (Conveniently overlooked was the fact that Arab peasants did not own the land they worked. The land was owned by the *effendis,* who—at the same time— kept selling the worst of it off to the Jewish National Fund for large amounts of "Hebrew gold." The *effendis* saw no risk in this, for what use could be made of waist-high swamps, alive with malarial mosquitoes, rats, and all manner of poisonous snakes? What use could be made of tracts of desert near the Dead Sea which never in recorded history had produced so much as a single weed?)

In passionate speeches the peasants were informed that they would be driven from their homes; that the Jews would destroy their holy mosques.

Despite all this, throughout the countryside relations between Arabs and Jews remained generally friendly. In the cities too, Arabs and Jews continued to live side by side in their own separate quarters, to work together, to respect each other's religions and differing ways of life.

But it does not take many to start a riot.

It usually, however, requires a leader—and that the Arab *effendis* had. He was a member of the Husseini family, one of the wealthiest and most powerful clans in Palestine. His name was Amin. Because he had taken the pilgrimage to Mecca, he was also entitled to the status symbol "Haj."

After World War I, Haj Amin got himself a strategic job in the office of the British Military Governor of Jerusalem. He also worked as a journalist in the Arab press. His astounding "news stories"—holding no truth whatever—were read out to illiterate Arabs, who quite naturally regarded the stories as fact since they were printed in the newspapers. They were told, for example: *Twenty million Jews are flooding the country to uproot you!* (This at a time when the Jewish population of Palestine numbered some sixty thousand.)

In 1921 Amin added to his title of Haj. The position of Mufti Haj Amin was also appointed head of the Supreme threatening the other candidates, Haj Amin "won" the post. But even this title was not grand enough. He promptly bestowed upon himself the title of Grand Mufti, which of course gave the impression that the Mufti of Jerusalem was the most powerful Mufti of all.

The proud Husseinis then saw to it that the Grand Mufti Hai Amin was also appointed head of the Supreme Moslem Council for Palestine. This meant that he had tremendous supplies of money at his disposal.

The money was spent for propaganda and to hire terrorist gangs.

Haj Amin organized his first pogrom in the walled Old City of Jerusalem, inhabited chiefly by elderly Jewish rabbis and scholars. The date was Passover, 1920. Four Jews were killed.

His next pogrom was somewhat more successful. It occurred in Tel Aviv and Jaffa. Forty-three Jews were killed. It started on May 1, 1921, and lasted two days. But its effects went on far longer. It was, for example, because of this pogrom that Golda and her small crew who had just crossed on the *Pocahontas* could not enter the Holy Land through the port of Jaffa—where, weeks after the riot, inflamed Arabs were still throwing Jewish immigrants into the sea.

In 1929 the Grand Mufti Haj Amin el Husseini organized his third campaign—by distributing falsified photographs showing that "world Jewish conspirators" had exploded bombs in the Mosque of Omar. This time 140 pious old Jews were slaughtered in the religious quarters of Safed, Hebron, and Jerusalem.

The Myerson were living in Jerusalem at the time. Golda was at home with the two small children. But they heard the screams, for their house was near the Mea Shearim, a quarter inhabited by highly orthodox Jews.

Morris, too, heard screams and ran into the street to see a few old men fleeing in terror before a mob of Arabs in long, flowing robes, brandishing sticks, rakes, hoes, and firearms. A rock hit one of the fugitives in the head. He fell to the ground. His shrieks rang out as the Arabs fell upon him, beating him with heavy sticks. When the mob rushed on, the old man lay dead.

But the ambitions of Haj Amin extended beyond the massacre of some pious old men. He wanted to dominate the entire Arab world. And he soon had a fine ally: Adolf Hitler.

In top-secret documents—published later—Hitler promised the Haj that as soon as the German armies had conquered Europe, had *totally destroyed the Judeo-Communist empire, the German armies would reach the southern exit from Caucasia. As soon as this happened, the Führer would give the Arab world the assurance that its hour of liberation had arrived. . . . In that hour the Mufti would be the most authoritative spokesman for the Arab world. It would then be his task to set off the Arab operations which he had secretly prepared.*

The organization of such preparations could not, obviously, wait for the arrival of Hitler's armies on the doorstep of the Middle East.

Furthermore, if the Grand Mufti were to be the spokesman for the Arab world, that Arab world would have to be united.

The Grand Mufti called together some Moslem leaders and formed a Pan-Arabic Federation. They would unite on a holy mission: the total destruction of the Jewish

homeland. The Grand Mufti, of course, was the head of
this new federation.

The "holy war" started in 1936. The Grand Mufti
ordered a campaign of terror throughout the country. But
the Arabs of Palestine proved remarkably uncooperative.
Why should they fight the Jews, when, primarily because
of the Jews, they were living better than any other Arabs
in the Middle East?

So the Mufti hired terrorist gangs from Syria, headed
by the notorious and highly paid Fawzi el Kawkji. In
order to encourage the Palestinian Arabs to cooperate, the
Syrian gangs first concentrated chiefly on them. One hundred and thirty-six of the most highly respected Palestin-
ian-Arab leaders were assassinated by the Mufti's gunmen.
Among them were the ex-Mayor of Jerusalem and the
Mayor of Hebron. In addition, an unrecorded but ad-
mittedly high number of Arab workers in the cities and
Arab *felaheen* in the countryside were slaughtered—those
who had "cooperated" with the Jews and those who had
refused to house and hide the Syrian henchmen. Often
mutilated bodies were strung up in Arab villages—as
warning.

This form of persuasion proved effective. The Palestinian Arabs were now afraid *not* to comply with the Mufti's
orders. The simplest—and most face-saving—way out was
to believe the propaganda barrage which had been aimed
at them for over a decade.

For the next three years a countrywide campaign of
terror raged through the land. Arab bands by the hundreds attacked Jewish settlements at night, slaughtering
men, women, and children.

The British, who were supposed to be keeping peace in
Palestine, reacted to all this as they had done since the
first Arab riots in 1920. They called commissions of inquiry. And each commission decided that the best course
was to pacify the Arabs by limiting Jewish immigration
more, and still more.

The Jews reacted by organizing an underground army
called the Haganah. *Haganah* is the Hebrew word for
defense. Realizing that their Arab neighbors were led by

Syrians from across the border, realizing too that Arabs who refused to "cooperate" were still being murdered by the Mufti's men, the Jews never attacked Arab villages.

Nevertheless, they defended their settlements well. Every farm settlement soon had its own Haganah set up. Men and women who worked in the fields during the day, patrolled at night, and, when necessary, resisted attack—with weapons which ranged from Molotov cocktails to pistols of historic ancestry. All weapons had to be smuggled in, for if British soldiers (who were constantly checking) found a Haganah arms cache, everything would be confiscated.

Because of the Haganah, the Arab terrorists preferred to ambush undefended buses and trucks, even donkey carts on the roads. To travel down a country road was to court death. Many Jews were not only murdered but mutilated: arms, breasts, heads cut off, stomachs slit open.

Golda was often reminded with horror of the report on the Kishinev pogrom which she had overheard at the age of five. Now these brutalities were happening here, every day, in the homeland.

The terrorists did not neglect the cities.

Like other Tel Avivians of that time, Golda and the children used to move every year from one rented apartment to another. And in each apartment Menachem, like other boys in the cities, would store up an arsenal of rocks with which to protect his family should Arab terrorists break in.

As the threatening thunder of war came closer in Europe, the British decided that the best way to keep their hold on Egypt and the Suez Canal—the strategic link to their entire empire—was to promote Arab nationalism. They reasoned that if the Arab countries united into one great power, the Arabs could then more easily be brought into the coming war on the side of the British. Whereas, if they remained separate nations torn, as they were, by internal strife and external jealousies, they would be easy bait for the German Reich to swallow up, one by one.

So, the British did all they could to foster the feeling of

Arab unity: Arabia for the Arabs. They did not, perhaps, realize that in doing this they were playing right along with the plans and ambitions of the Grand Mufti and his friend Adolf Hitler.

They did realize that there was only one rallying cry around which all the Arab leaders seemed to unite: the holy war against the Jews of Palestine.

This might be unfortunate for the Jews, who had, after all, worked so hard and accomplished so much in the Holy Land. But war was coming, and there was that vital factor of Arab oil. Whereas what did the Jews have to offer—except their desperate need?

Or could they too be considered a vital commodity of war? As she begged and pleaded with numerous British government officials, Golda Myerson put the equation simply: "Let our people into Palestine. If you don't, the Nazis are bound to turn them into a factor in the war effort of the Nazis. Let us bring them in, and they will be a very important help in the war effort for the Allies."

But the British decided to pay no attention to such arguments.

As a final grand prewar gesture to appease the Grand Mufti once more and to win favor with all the Arab nations, Great Britain issued the White Paper of 1939.

Shortly thereafter, the Grand Mufti left for Germany, where he remained as the guest of Adolf Hitler.

With the Mufti gone, the terrorist attacks on the Jews of Palestine subsided.

But three and a half months after the White Paper was issued, World War II broke out. Millions of Jews were now trapped in Europe. And it soon became clear that *their* terrors had only begun.

Chapter 13

At the start of the war the squat, bushy-haired Yishuv leader named David Ben-Gurion made two pronouncements:

"We do not regard the Mandate as our Bible, but the Bible as our Mandate."

"We shall fight the War as if there were no White Paper, and the White Paper as if there were no War."

The Jews of Palestine lived by those two statements for six long years, the most ghastly years in the four-thousand-year-old history of their people.

God had promised this land to the Jews *for an everlasting possession.* This was not the time to fight for world recognition of the Biblical promise. The promise, however, was helpful to keep in mind for the law-abiding members of the Yishuv who now became involved in what the British termed "illegal immigration."

Golda's activities during the war illustrated the conflicts and contradictions faced by thousands of Palestinian Jews as they carried out the second of Ben-Gurion's pronouncements.

In the daytime all her drive and dedication was spent working *for* the British and the Allied war effort. But sometimes, in the nights, she worked secretly, and at risk of imprisonment, against the British—at least against the British-imposed immigration quotas. She helped to smuggle Jews into the homeland.

A handful of Palestinian Jews—they numbered no

more than ten—were in Europe working with a network of some fifty local Jews. Their mission? To try to smuggle Jews across the borders, onto ships, over the Mediterranean, and into Palestine. All in secret. For, busy as they were with the war effort, the British nonetheless devoted planes and patrol boats to police the coastlines of Palestine in order to make sure that no ancient ship jammed with Jews should succeed in landing on the night beaches.

The entire operation of the so-called Mossad le Aliah Bet—the Committee of the Illegal Immigration—had to be carried out in secret along every step of the route, for if the British found out about a "shipment," the illegals would be kept under surveillance by British planes as they crossed the Mediterranean Sea. And when they entered the three-mile limit, they would be captured by British patrol boats. This was not a difficult feat, since the only vessels the Mossad could muster were old cargo ships or river boats barely able to make the Mediterranean crossing.

When captured, the illegals were sent back to Europe—and almost certain death. Or they were sent out to sea with no additional supplies—in which case they were rarely heard from again. Or they were allowed to enter Palestine, *but* their numbers were subtracted from the next allotment of legal quotas. The illegals, therefore, unwittingly condemned other Jews who would otherwise have received a precious legal certificate of entry to Palestine.

Nevertheless, almost miraculously, some Mossad ships did get through. Thousands of illegals did land in secret on the night beaches, to be met by waiting cars, horse-carts, buses and spirited off to some outlying kibbutz, where they promptly became new citizens of Palestine—citizens with false papers.

One strategic aspect of these operations were the secret ship-to-shore landing procedures. Golda at this time had an apartment overlooking the sea and the beach. Because it was hoped that the British would not dare to break in on the nighttime privacy of this highly respected Yishuv official, Golda's apartment became one of the centers for directing illegal immigration.

Sarah and Menachem were also involved. But, as with all other Yishuv families, parent and child usually did not know of each other's activities. One evening, for instance, Golda closed the door of the bedroom in order to compose, in privacy, a leaflet about the illegal ship, the *Struma*. This leaflet, in English, was aimed at British soldiers in Palestine. The hope was that it would make them "less vigilant" about capturing illegals and sending them back. Golda told the story of *Struma* in simple words. How this fifty-foot Danube river boat, jammed with illegals, had sat for two months in the port of Istanbul while desperate appeals were made for permits so the Jews could enter Palestine. The British refused the permits. And the Turks refused to let the ship remain in their harbor. The vessel was finally towed off into the Black Sea where, within several hours, it sank. Of the 769 Jews aboard, there was only one survivor.

Golda finished writing the *Struma* leaflet late that night. It was picked up by a Haganah courier the next morning and taken to a printer. The following dawn Golda's fifteen-year-old daughter left the house. Sarah, a member of the Haganah youth group, had been given the assignment of pasting on walls and billboards the leaflets on the *Struma*. She did not know that her mother had written the leaflet. Nor did Golda know that Sarah had put it up, risking imprisonment by doing so.

The *Struma* sank in February, 1942. It was one of the last illegal ships to leave Europe, for as the Nazi war machine steamrollered over Europe it became virtually impossible for any Jews to escape. There were even months when it was impossible to get out the 1,500 Jews whom the British permitted to enter Palestine legally under the regulations of the White Paper.

In that same year, 1942, the Nazis moved into a new phase of what they called "the Final Solution of the Jewish Question." They would get rid of Europe's Jews—those who had not already perished in the slave labor camps or elsewhere—by systematically murdering them all.

They did not quite succeed.

When the war was over some 106,000 Jewish survivors still remained alive in the concentration camps; skin-covered skeletons who were stared at in unbelieving horror by the Allied soldiers who liberated the concentration camps.

In a later speech Golda summed up the human statistics in these words:

"Hitler did not solve the Jewish Question according to his plans. But he did annihilate six million Jews—Jews of Germany, France, Belgium, Holland, Luxembourg, Poland, the USSR, Hungary, Yugoslavia, Greece, Italy, Czechoslovakia, Austria, Rumania. With these Jews there were destroyed over thirty thousand Jewish communities which for centuries had been the center of the Jewish faith, learning, and scholarship. From this Jewry stemmed some of the giants in the fields of arts, literature, and science. Was it only this generation of Jews that was gassed? *One million children*—the future generation—were annihilated. Who can encompass this picture in all its horror and its consequences for the Jewish people for many generations to come?

"And what about those who remained alive? Who are they? Each individual is a splinter of a family destroyed—each one lives in the nightmare recollection of his dearest and closest led to the crematorium. Mothers who have seen their babies thrown into the air and used as targets for Nazi bullets. Thousands upon thousands of Jewish women who will never be mothers because of the Nazi 'scientific experiments' performed on them. . . . All victims of the attempt to solve the Jewish Question."

During the war years the Jews of Palestine had endured a different type of torture. They knew about the death camps, the gas chambers. But there was nothing they could do to save the European Jews who were being systematically murdered.

After the war ended, Golda Myerson stood before an Anglo-American Committee of Inquiry and she tried her best to put into words that which was, in fact, inexpressible.

"Maybe you will realize," she said to the august tribunal, "what it meant to us during those years of war to watch from here millions of Jews being slaughtered—what it meant to us to see that going on, and again to have the curse of helplessness brought down upon us. We couldn't save them. We were prepared to do it. There wasn't a thing that we weren't prepared to share with them. . . . But the White Paper forced us to sit here helpless at a time when we are convinced that we could have saved, not millions, but probably hundreds of thousands, and if only tens of thousands, and if only a few. . . .

"Gentlemen, I am authorized on behalf of the sixteen hundred members of our Labor Federation to say here in the clearest terms that there is nothing Jewish labor is not prepared to do in this country in order to meet and accept large masses of Jewish immigration with no limitation and with no condition whatsoever. This is the purpose for which we have come to Palestine. Otherwise, our life here, too, becomes senseless."

Golda had spoken by now before virtually every important committee of inquiry which had appeared on the Palestine scene during the past decade. But this time—for the first time—she spoke with the faint warmth of hope. For this time—for the first time—the committee of inquiry was composed not only of British delegates. This time there were Americans on the tribunal as well.

The hope was that *this* committee would decide that now—at last, and almost too late—the remnants of Europe's Jewry would be permitted to enter the homeland. There still was no other country in the world willing to take them. Sick, maimed, and desperate, they still sat in camps, many of them in the same camps from which they had been liberated. Now, however, they were not called death camps or concentration camps. They were called DP camps. Displaced persons camps.

The British claimed that they had imposed the White Paper in order to assure Arab cooperation in the Allied war effort. But it was now pointed out to the Anglo-American Committee of Inquiry that this White Paper policy had not proved notably successful as far as winning over the Arabs was concerned. During the war the Arab nations had either been openly pro-Nazi or, at best, uncooperatively neutral.

It was further pointed out to the Anglo-American committee that the Jews of Palestine had made valiant contributions to the Allied war effort. During the first week of the war most of the young men and women of the Yishuv had volunteered to fight with the British Army. But they were turned down. Why, said the British, should they train and arm Palestinian Jews who might, at a later date, make trouble for them in Palestine? They did, however, allow individual Jews into service units. And they permitted Yishuv volunteers to attempt virtual suicide missions. Palestinian Jews parachuted behind enemy lines in Europe. They blew up enemy installations on the Mediterranean. They captured strategic points in Syria, which had gone over to the Nazis. Most of the volunteers were killed. (One narrowly escaped death in Syria. But he lost an eye. His name was Moshe Dayan.)

The German war plan had been to sweep up from North Africa, drive the British out of Egypt, take Palestine, then Iraq, Iran, and on to India while other German armies were conquering Europe and Russia. At which point the Nazis, with their Japanese allies, would be masters of the world.

When it looked as though the Germans would, indeed, take Egypt, the British had hastily started training a Jewish resistance force—to go into action if Palestine fell to the Nazis. During the first year of the war, the British had also permitted some 30,000 Palestinian Jews to join their Army, where they took part in the desperate battles in North Africa, Greece, Crete, the landings in Italy, up through France and, finally, Germany.

After the landings in Italy, the British finally permitted the Jews of Palestine to fight in their own Jewish Brigade.

And the Star of David shoulder patch soon became a symbol of fearlessness throughout Europe.

The Balfour Declaration had been issued, in large measure, as a reward to one Jew, Chaim Weizmann, for his contribution to the British war effort during the First World War.

Could the Balfour Declaration not, finally, be *implemented* as a reward to the Yishuv—a nation of Jews—for their contribution to the war effort during World War Two?

Could there be any further excuse at all for the British White Paper which kept the Jewish survivors of Hitler's holocaust locked out of Palestine?

The Anglo-American Committee of Inquiry answered these questions in a report backed by every member. They advocated that the British White Paper be abolished immediately, and that 100,000 Jewish refugees be admitted to Palestine at once.

However, this was only a committee. They could only "advocate." The British Foreign Secretary Ernest Bevin took it upon himself to reject the unanimous report. The White Paper restrictions would continue—despite the fact that even the scanty number of legal certificates were coming to an end, which meant there would soon be no more Jewish immigration to Palestine permitted at all.

When it became clear that the White Paper restrictions would, incredibly, continue to be enforced, the Yishuv exploded with fury.

Now they would fight! They would make things so tough for the British troops stationed in Palestine that Great Britain would be forced to give up its Mandate—and get out. After which, presumably, the new world governing body, the United Nations, would partition the country, giving the new Jewish nation at least part of Palestine.

The Haganah set down strict rules for this fight: no bloodshed. For example, on June 16, 1946, all bridges on the borders of the country plus numerous railroad tracks were blown up at once. Although four Jews were killed as they set the dynamite, not a single British life was lost.

In retribution, two weeks later, on a Sabbath day, a number of Yishuv leaders were arrested by the British and put in the detention camp at Latrun.

Golda's friends begged her to go into hiding. But Golda refused. "If they want me," she said, "they know where to find me."

She was not arrested. But Moshe Shertok was. He headed the Political Department of the Jewish Agency, the second most important position of leadership in the Yishuv. Ben-Gurion was head of the Jewish Agency. He was not arrested because he was out of the country at the time. He would, however, be arrested if he returned. Who, therefore, would head the Jewish Agency, the governing body of the Jews in Palestine?

There were many able leaders still at large. But Golda was chosen. She therefore became representative of the Histadrut *and* of all Jewish Palestine in all political negotiations with the British.

She was, in effect, for the time being, Labor Minister, Foreign Minister, and Prime Minister of the Yishuv.

Like virtually all of her countrymen she had always been a hard worker. As she once remarked, "The *halutzim* [pioneers] have not come here for a rest cure." But now the pace and the hours of her work day—and night— could only be regarded as astounding.

Her body rebelled. She was hospitalized several times. She would collapse from nervous fatigue. She had acute gall bladder attacks and other severe symptoms. Her friends and her children pleaded with her not to force herself up out of a sick bed for still another meeting. "Mother, you're killing yourself!" Menachem exclaimed as he tried to persuade her to rest.

The doctors said the same thing, in more medical terms. They warned her that if she continued at this pace she would not live.

To which Golda replied with a shrug, "A lot of us die around fifty."

She was in the hospital when she heard about the *Fede*.

This was one of the illegal ships—which were coming now with increased regularity to the shores of Palestine. With the war over, the British had an abundance of patrol ships and planes to devote to this "battle" against the incoming survivors. Although it was far easier now to get the illegals out of Europe, and easier to obtain ships, it had become virtually impossible to land the passengers undetected on Palestine's shores. The British announced that henceforth all captured illegals would be sent to internment camps on the island of Cyprus. The conditions in these camps were no better than those in the DP camps in Europe, perhaps worse. The refugees lived in tents or Nissen huts. The sun broiled down, yet there was no water for bathing or washing. Even drinking water was strictly rationed. "British soldiers," said Golda acidly, "stand guard on the walls as though they were watching over the most dangerous international criminals."

Yet Cyprus was closer to Palestine than were the DP camps of Europe. The organizers of the illegal immigration found it was far better for the morale of the survivors to be there than it was to sit in barracks which had so recently been part of the death camps.

Then, in April, 1946, the British captured an illegal ship, the *Fede,* before it had even left its European port. They promptly closed off the port and demanded that the refugees disembark.

The refugees refused. Furthermore, they declared that if any attempt was made to remove them, they would blow up the ship. This had already happened with the *Patria,* an illegal ship which was blown up in the harbor of Haifa. Two hundred survivors of the concentration camps had drowned. And the *Patria* had made world headlines. The British did not wish to risk a repeat of this with the *Fede.* Still, they would not release the ship.

On the fourth day of their detention in the Italian harbor of La Spezia, the *Fede* passengers unanimously decided to go on a hunger strike. They would not eat again until they were promised entry to Palestine.

Golda had just been released from the hospital. She proposed that the leaders of the Yishuv should also go on a hunger strike to help attract world attention to the present plight of Jewish survivors of the holocaust. The Yishuv leaders agreed.

Golda's doctor, however, forbade her to undertake the fast. She was in no condition to do so.

Calmly Golda replied that since the fast had been her idea she must of course participate. If the doctor refused her the certificate of good health (required by the Yishuv leaders) she would fast, privately, in her own home.

Knowing full well that his stubborn patient would do just this, the doctor issued the certificate. At least, by fasting in the open with the other leaders, she would be under constant medical supervision.

Golda later reported: "Thirteen of us decided that on that Friday at noon the strike would begin, and we would keep it up until the Jews came in. Just about ten minutes before the strike was to take place we decided to make one more attempt to see the Chief Secretary and plead with him to allow those people in. He very wisely and practically said to us, 'Mrs. Myerson, do you really and honestly believe, after all that has happened in the world, that the fact that you people are not going to eat is going to influence anybody?' I told him I did not, but we went on strike anyway."

The hunger strike was staged in the courtyard of the Jewish Agency building in Jerusalem, in full view of British officialdom, throngs of bypassers, and reporters. For the first two days the thirteen Yishuv leaders could be seen sitting on chairs, reading, talking together. By the third day they were weaker. Some, including Golda, spent much of the time reclining on cots. That third day was Passover, when every Jew is supposed to eat at the Seder dinner. So they did eat, each had a piece of matzah the size of an olive. And crowds outside the courtyard intoned the Passover prayer: "Let my people go." And it was all duly reported in the press of the world.

On the *Fede* itself—where 1,000 refugees were crowded onto a small cargo ship—more and more men, women, and children collapsed every day. Their increasing num-

bers were chalked up on a huge board which could be
seen from shore.

The Chairman of the British Labour Party flew to the
port, begged the refugees to return to the DP camps.
They refused. He then cabled the leaders of the Yishuv,
urging them to stop *their* fast. He was, he said, conducting
negotiations about the release of the *Fede*.

Golda was now so weak and ill that it was difficult for
her to speak. But she mustered her customary calm and
appearance of implacable strength. Informal promises, she
insisted, were not sufficient.

Then the hunger strikers aboard the *Fede* announced
that each day ten men and women would stand on deck
and, in full view of the crowds gathered on the pier—they
would kill themselves. The first ten had already volunteered.

At this the British said the ship could sail.

The strike on the *Fede* and in the courtyard of the
Jewish Agency building had lasted 104 hours. It had been
broken only by a glass of tea without sugar twice a day
and a tiny piece of Passover matzah.

The dramatic story of the *Fede* and other illegal ships
brought the hoped-for cries of outrage from that intangible
but powerful force: "world opinion." It seemed utterly
incomprehensible that the sick, suffering men, women, and
children who had somehow escaped Hitler's Final Solution
should still be housed in wretched camps when there was
a place for them to go and a people desperate to welcome
them home.

In Palestine itself, the sense of outrage reached such
heights that more and more people rebelled against the
restraining policies of the Haganah. They joined two
underground terrorist groups, the Irgun and the Stern
Gang—groups who felt the Yishuv would never get rid
of the Mandate by blowing up bridges and British installations. They would have to blow up some British soldiers
as well.

This they did, though Golda and other Yishuv leaders
tried hard to stop them.

Finally, there were 100,000 British troops in Palestine,

attempting, futilely, to keep order among 600,000 Jews. The situation was impossible—and growing worse every month.

That, plus the ever-swelling pressure of world opinion, finally made the British decide they'd had enough of the chaos. In January, 1947, they turned the matter over to the United Nations. Let *them* decide what should be done with this seething land called Palestine.

Chapter 14

Another Commission of Inquiry came—this time from the United Nations.

Golda, still Acting Head of the Political Department, was one of those chiefly responsible for showing the gentlemen around.

It was the most strategic time in the history of the nation—the nation ready and waiting to be born. These eleven gentlemen represented the world. If they decided against the emergence of a new Jewish state, the doors of hope would be slammed shut, perhaps forever.

And, as Golda later reported, "It could be said with certainty that when the eleven members of the United Nations Special Commission reached this country, there wasn't one among them who knew Palestinian affairs before he was appointed to the Commission.

"We had had our fill of ridicule and contempt for this hard and thankless task of ours, which has been to keep on explaining our cause over and over again to this body and that, to this Government and that, to try and get a hearing, to win people over—in the hope that perhaps somewhere in this chaotic world of ours a man of heart would arise and judge according to the dictates of his conscience. We were of the opinion that this time all the work of explaining and expounding our cause was wasted effort, that these outsiders, these Gentiles of the Commission, would never understand. . . . And, indeed, the members of the Commission showed lack of understanding in good measure—until they got to know our problems."

The eleven gentlemen of the commission carefully studied all aspects of the matter. Then they presented a comprehensive report—and a plan. Unanimously they recommended that the Mandate be ended and that Palestine be partitioned into equal halves; two new nations: one Jewish, one Arab, with an economic union between them. Jerusalem would be an international city, administered by the United Nations.

The Yishuv felt that a Jewish nation without Jerusalem would be like a body without a heart. Furthermore, two-thirds of the Jewish state was sun-scorched desert. (The Arabs had been allotted only a small strip of desert.) And some of the Jewish settlements would be in the Arab state.

Nevertheless, an independent Jewish nation of any size or shape would mean that the survivors of the Nazi holocaust could at last be freed from the barbed-wire imprisonment of the DP camps. All of them could at once be welcomed home.

So the Jews of Palestine immediately announced that they accepted the partition plan. And the Arab states immediately announced that they did not. In fact, they said, partition would mean war.

The Arabs went to Lake Success, then the home of the United Nations, certain that a mere war of words would be enough to kill the partition plan when it came to a General Assembly vote.

They already had eleven votes, for there were eleven nations in the Arab-Moslem block. To defeat partition they needed only six more votes. Whereas to *win* the Yishuv needed a two-thirds majority. That meant twenty-two votes merely to offset the Arab bloc's eleven. And from then on, two votes for every one the Arabs mustered.

And the Jews themselves, of course, had no vote at all. Indeed, to offset the eleven Arab nations, each with its official delegates, the Jews had only an eleven-man committee. The committee included Chaim Weizmann, Moshe Shertok, and others who were well practiced in, as Golda put it, "explaining our cause over and over, to this Government and that." Now the committee worked around the clock visiting delegates of this government and that.

But during this crucial period the Arab delegates were not exactly idle.

They used their powerful bloc as a bribe to many smaller nations. Vote against partition and you can count on our eleven votes when you need them. For the large nations there was the always effective inducement: Arab oil.

There were other powerful inducements. France, for example, was informed that if she voted for partition the Arabs in the French colonies of Algeria, Tunisia, and Algeria would rebel against the French yoke. And France listened—for these three colonies were already rumbling with unrest.

Greece was told by Egypt that the 150,000 Greeks living in Egypt would no longer find life very enjoyable should Greece vote for partition.

Great Britain needed no persuasion. She well realized that to keep her position of power in the Middle East she would have to see to it that the partition idea was put down —forever.

American foreign policy was closely tied to Britain's. How could the United States go against the wishes of its most respected ally?

And Russia? For twenty years Zionism had been outlawed in the Soviet Union. How then could they possibly vote *for* a Zionist state?

With the Russian vote went the Slav bloc.

With the British vote went the Commonwealth bloc.

With the Arab vote went the Afro-Asian bloc; the "nations of color" would stick together, the nations which had been so long oppressed by white imperialists.

And then of course there were numerous nations who were simply and traditionally anti-Semitic. They would vote against partition on principle.

A new Jewish nation had nothing to offer anyone—with the exception, of course, of a few million homeless Jews. But then, the Jews had been homeless since the year A.D. 70, when they were thrown out of their homeland by the Romans. The Wandering Jew was a traditional figure on the world scene. So why make changes now?

Would the United Nations vote be an "Évian" all over again?

The vote came on November 29, 1947.

Thirty-three nations voted for partition. Thirteen voted against. Ten abstained.

The United Nations had created a new Jewish state.

It was like a miracle. How had it happened?

Perhaps the most powerful bloc of all had been the six million murdered Jews. Perhaps their voices had finally been heard.

Golda was in Jerusalem when news of the UN decision came through on the radio—news which set the Jews of the city aflame with joy. As she looked out the window watching cheering, screaming crowds surge through the streets, watching stranger embrace stranger, tears streamed down her cheeks. It was going to happen. After all the centuries of dispersion and persecution, Jews were once again going to have their own homeland.

The emotion went far too deep for words. When she later recalled that day her sentences were stark and simple. "As head of the Political Department of the Jewish Agency in Jerusalem, it fell to my lot that day to address a huge demonstration there of our people and to appeal to the Arabs in Israel and in the neighboring countries: 'Our hand is offered to you in peace and friendship.' A few hours later we buried our first victims of Arab attacks."

During the following weeks newspapers throughout the Arab world bristled with gruesome statements from Arab leaders indicating the fate in store for the Jews should they dare to abide by the UN decision.

Said the Grand Mufti: *I declare a holy war, my Moslem brothers! Murder the Jews! Murder them all.*

Said Sheikh Hasan el Banna of the Moslem Brotherhood: *All Arabs shall arise and annihilate the Jews! We shall fill the sea with their corpses.*

Said Azzam Pasha, Secretary General of the Arab League: *This will be a war of extermination, and momentous massacre which will be spoken of like the Mongolian Massacres.*

And there were countless newspaper editorials such as that in Cairo's *Al Kulta: Five hundred thousand Iraqis prepare for this holy war. 150,000 Syrians will storm over the Palestine borders and the mighty Egyptian army will throw the Jews into the sea if they dare to declare their state.*

Did the Arab leaders mean what they said? Should the Yishuv take such statements seriously?

As she spoke at a meeting of the Western Galilee Regional Council, Golda put the answer this way: "I'm convinced that the newspapers are exaggerating, but I suggest you prepare yourselves as if every word in the papers were true. And if what the newspapers say should prove to be false, we'll survive the disappointment!"

The Yishuv was not "disappointed." History promptly began repeating—with a vengeance.

As before, Palestinian Arabs were not overly enthusiastic about fighting the Jews, with whom they had lived in peace and increasing prosperity for the past eight years, ever since the Mufti and his chief henchman, Fawzi el Kawkji, had left for Hitler Germany.

But now the two were back, operating out of Syria. They organized a huge army of well-paid volunteers, trained by officers of the regular Syrian Army and by numerous ex-officers of the ex-Nazi Army. Soon thousands of "liberation volunteers" were pouring over Palestine's borders, bombarding Jewish settlements, blowing up vital water pipelines, waiting in ambush on the roads, and attempting to foment a reign of terror throughout the countryside.

One chief center of attack was Jerusalem, a hilltop city surrounded by heavily populated Arab villages, a city connected to the Jewish centers of the country by a single road. The Arab strategy was simple. Cut the road and the water pipelines. Starve the city into submission.

The Jerusalem-Tel Aviv road became, consequently, the most consistently dangerous place in Palestine. And the Yishuv leader who traveled most frequently over this road was Mrs. Golda Myerson. Ben-Gurion had moved his staff headquarters to Tel Aviv. But Golda was in charge of the Jewish Agency in Jerusalem. Nevertheless, her presence was required in Tel Aviv several times a week.

She had numerous narrow escapes en route.

Once a bullet crashed through the window of the taxi in which she rode. Another passenger was wounded. But Golda was not hurt.

Once her driver took a wrong turn and she suddenly landed in the center of an Arab village, a village alive with snipers. As angry Arabs started to converge on the car, Golda suggested to her stunned driver that they leave at once. The car hurtled into reverse and they backed out before they were surrounded and seized.

On still another occasion her car was stopped by British soldiers, who had proved themselves remarkably efficient in searching and disarming Jews. However, being gentlemen, the British generally refrained from searching women. Consequently, the Haganah often used girls as gun-runners and bodyguards.

On this particular night—it was New Year's Eve—the girl accompanying Golda was asked to get out of the car. A gun dropped from her skirts. She was promptly arrested.

Golda asked where the girl would be taken.

"To jail in Faluga," she was told.

Faluga was a hostile Arab village which hosted many

of Kawkji's "liberators." Golda knew that the girl might well be lynched.

"If you take her," she told the officer, "then take me too."

When the officer looked at Golda's identity papers he radioed his commander, asking what to do.

"You've bitten off more than you can chew with that one," he was told. "Bring her here, to Hedera."

Hedera was a Jewish town. The police chief set out New Year's Eve drinks for Golda and the girl gun-runner. And he urged them to spend the night at Hedera, since the trip to Tel Aviv after dark was even more hazardous than in the daytime.

Golda regretfully declined. She was already late to a meeting in Tel Aviv.

She arrived at her meeting in style, with an impressive armed escort of British soldiers led by the Chief of Police himself.

That Tel Aviv meeting was important. The next one was even more so.

It was obvious that if they were to fight the war which was obviously coming, the Yishuv would need to purchase arms. The Haganah forces were currently fighting with an amazing collection of relics. Their total armaments consisted of a few thousand rifles, homemade Sten guns, four machine guns of World War I vintage, and a "secret weapon," the Davidka, a homemade mortar made of a six-inch drainpipe which fired off a "bomb" of nails. Its chief military virtue—it made a terrible noise.

With these weapons the Haganah had been able to cope with some 70,000 irregulars who had poured over the borders, for the Arab volunteers were of course not equipped with such military items as tanks and planes.

However, the British were scheduled to complete their withdrawal from Palestine by May 14, 1948. On that date, the new Jewish state would be declared. And the world had been warned by each Arab nation that *if* the Jews dared to declare their state, the official armies of Egypt, Iraq, Syria, Lebanon, and Jordan's crack British-trained

Arab Legion would invade the borders and drive the Jews into the sea. Strong fighting units from Saudi Arabia and the Sudan, plus the concerted Egyptian, Syrian, and Iraqi Air Force would join in the job. And the Yishuv had no reason at all to doubt the Arabs' word.

Without arms the new Jewish nation might well last only three days, as the Arabs predicted.

The procurement of arms was no simple matter. On January 14, the United States government had placed a strict embargo on the sale of arms to the Middle East. Great Britain, however, had been supplying arms to the Arabs and announced that she would continue to do so.

Furthermore, the Mandatory Power—though instructed by the United Nations to remain impartial until they withdrew—had adopted a strange definition of impartiality. Taking the Jerusalem-Tel Aviv road as one small example which applied countrywide: every Jewish convoy which tried to make its way along that road was stopped for an arms search. Every weapon found was confiscated— including pocketknives with blades over three inches long. Numerous Arab villages overlooked that road. Some had been cleared out by the Arabs so that the former homes of families could be used to house well-armed Arab snipers. As Golda put it: "It is quite remarkable that for weeks now the Government [the British] has not found it possible to go into those houses and arrest the snipers and confiscate, for a change, Arab arms."

It was obvious that if the British confiscated Jewish penknives—if they still were "confiscating" Jewish refugees who kept on coming to Palestine's shores, only to be shipped to Cyprus—the British Mandatory Power was certainly not going to allow shipments of Jewish-bought armaments into the country.

The Jews would have to wait, therefore, until after they declared their state before such items as tanks and planes could be delivered.

But the first and primary problem was to *buy* the arms and tanks—should any nation be found who was willing to sell them. Supplies for a new national Army and Air Force meant money. Millions of dollars. The Yishuv had already been taxed almost beyond capacity. They could give lives, but they had no more money.

There was only one source from which the needed millions might be derived: the Jews of America.

The January meeting of the Yishuv leaders had been called because Eliezer Kaplan, treasurer of the Jewish Agency, had just returned from the United States. At that meeting in Tel Aviv he made a lengthy report to the Executive. Although a minimum of $25 million was needed to buy arms, Kaplan had come to the inescapable conclusion that perhaps $5 million, and certainly no more than $7 million, could be expected from American Jews.

After all, he pointed out, American Jews had been giving and giving since the beginning of the Hitler era. Wartime prosperity had come to an end in the States. There was not that much money around any more. Gloomily Kaplan concluded that the Yishuv could not expect any salvation from dollars donated by American Jews.

But where else could the money come from? They all knew the answer. Nowhere.

When Kaplan ended his report, Ben-Gurion, fuming, jumped to his feet. "I will leave at once," he exclaimed, "for the United States!"

Whereupon Golda heard herself saying to B.G.—as his countrymen called him—"Let me go instead. What you can do here, I can't do. But what you can do in the States, I can do."

Brusquely B.G. turned down her offer. Raising money was obviously their most immediate and essential job. He, as the Yishuv leader, *must* go.

Whereupon Golda quite startled herself by saying, "Why don't we let the Executive vote on it?"

After a moment B.G. nodded. He sat down.

The Executive voted—that Golda should go. Furthermore, that she should leave at once. So Golda, carrying only a handbag as luggage, was driven directly to the airport.

On the way she was struck with sudden terror. What on earth had she done? Why had *she* volunteered? True,

B.G. could not be spared from Palestine during the coming months. But surely someone with more experience than she should be sent to the States. She had not been there for a decade. And then her job had been to win recruits to Zionism, not primarily to raise money. Fundraising was something special. An entire career. And to raise the funds on which a new nation depended for its survival! Had she—in the blunt phrase of the British Police Chief—bitten off more than she could chew?

Chapter 15

The terror did not leave her.

It almost overcame her as she stood on the rostrum to address a huge conference of the Council of Jewish Federations. These men and women were the leaders of organized Jewry in the United States. But they were not Zionists; they were not particularly concerned about a national homeland for the Jews. They had called their meeting to discuss the needs of Jewish communities in the United States: new hospitals, temples, cultural centers, and such. They might also discuss Jewish communities abroad. But not Palestine. Palestine was not even on the agenda. Not until Golda—a few hours after her arrival in the States—heard about this meeting to be held in Chicago and persuaded the organizers to let her speak.

She stood before them, a stocky middle-aged woman in a simple blue dress. Despite the paralyzing fear, her voice was firm. It was calm, but it somehow commanded that people listen. As always, she spoke without notes.

"I want you to believe me when I speak before you today that I came on this special mission to the United States not to save seven hundred thousand Jews. The Jewish people have lost during the last few years six million Jews, and it would be audacity on our part to worry the Jewish people throughout the world because a few hundred thousand more Jews were in danger.

"This is not the problem. The problem is that if these seven hundred thousand Jews can remain alive, then the Jewish people as such is alive and Jewish independence is assured. If these seven hundred thousand people are killed off, then at any rate for many, many centuries, we are through with this dream of a Jewish people and a Jewish home. . . .

"If we have twenty-five or thirty millions dollars—*in the next two or three weeks*—we can establish ourselves. . . . We are convinced that we can carry on. . . . We are not a better breed; we are not the best Jews of the Jewish people. It so happened that we are there and you are here. I am certain that if you were there and we were here, you would be doing what we are doing there, and you would ask us who are here to do what you will have to do. . . .

"You cannot decide whether we should fight or not. We will. No white flag of the Jewish community in Palestine will be raised for the Mufti. That decision is taken. Nobody can change that. You can only decide one thing: whether we shall be victorious in this fight or whether the Mufti will be victorious in this fight. That decision American Jews can take. It has to be taken quickly, within hours. . . ."

When her speech was ended, her audience rose and cheered. They did more than cheer. They pledged $25 million. To be made available at once. This was more than three times the amount Kaplan had predicted could be raised from all American Jews. And Golda had done it with a single speech. The professional fund-raisers were stunned. They had never heard of such an exploit. Golda was stunned herself.

She remained in the States two and a half months,

flying back and forth across the country, North and South, speaking sometimes in the morning when meetings could be mustered, always in the afternoon, always in the night —when she was not on a train or bus or plane. Every hour counted, and she made every hour count.

A Haganah agent in Europe had sent word to Palestine that he could buy ammunition if he had $10 million. Since he knew this was an impossible dream, he was coming home. Golda cabled: STAY. And sent the $10 million.

Another agent in Paris cabled that he could buy tanks if he could get $10 million at once. Golda telephoned. "Buy the tanks." And sent another $10 million.

Still another agent had found large stocks of captured German equipment in France—tanks, mobile artillery, even planes—which could be bought. But $25 million was needed. Golda got the $25 million.

Twelve fighter planes were ordered from Czechoslovakia —paid for by money which Golda had raised.

In all, she raised over $50 million.

Ben-Gurion was not a man given to grandiose compliments. But when Golda returned home, he said to her: "Some day, when our history is written, it will be said that there was a Jewish woman who raised the money which made the state possible."

It was not a grandiose compliment. It was the simple truth.

Munitions had been bought. But they could not arrive before the State was declared on May 14. Meanwhile, the ferocity of the Arabs' undeclared war had increased. And Golda returned home to find that a surprising move was taking place.

A new note had been added to the holy war tirades which poured out over the radio in mosques, cafés, and coffee houses. The Mufti and other leaders of the Arab Higher Executive were ordering Palestinian Arabs to leave their homes and move temporarily to a bordering Arab state. The reason was simple: as soon as the Jews officially declared their state, the official Arab air forces would bomb the country into submission. And the combined

armies of seven Arab nations would invade the 5,579
square miles specified, as the Jewish state. Since the invaders did not want to bomb or shoot their Arab brothers,
the simplest solution was for the Palestinian Arabs to
leave. If they did not, they would either be massacred by
the Jews, or, if they happened to survive, they would be
branded as traitors by the victorious Arab armies. It was
further pointed out that they would not have to leave their
homes for long. The war would be over in a few days.
Then the Palestinian Arabs could come back, select any
Jewish home or shop they wished, as well as any Jewish
woman—who happened to remain alive.

The exodus of the wealthiest Arabs had started early.
By the time Golda left for the States it was estimated that
some 20,000 had left. But this was put down as a normal
state of affairs. Many wealthy people with freedom to
move do so when they live in an area threatened by im-
minent war.

But by the time Golda returned, the propaganda was on
full blast. And Arab workers in the countryside and in
the cities were responding full blast. After all, why should
they stay and be bombed? Furthermore, they were told
—and this was true—that by leaving they would pull the
rug out from under the Jewish economy. What state
could exist if half its work force suddenly quit and left
the country? Therefore, the Arabs who fled would not only
be safe from bombs and bullets. They would be aiding
the Arab holy war as well.

In March, after the picking of the citrus crops, thousands of Arabs fled from the Sharon coastal plain. Jewish
farmers begged them to stay.

In early April the Arabs of Tiberias suddenly fled—in
long convoys of trucks provided by the British. The
Jewish Community Council of Tiberias, bewildered by the
mass departure, issued a statement: *We did not dispossess
them; they themselves chose this course . . .*

Months earlier, Golda, as acting head of the Political
Department, had called a meeting in her apartment in Tel
Aviv. It was on the eve of Yom Kippur, the Jewish Day
of Atonement. The subject of the meeting: to formulate

official policy regarding the Arabs who lived in the new Jewish State.

"Look," Golda said, "we shall have to show the world how we are 'making up' for our 2,000 years of suffering as a minority not by emulating what was done to us but by isolating every single method of making people suffer. And doing away with each of these methods, one after the other."

One of the first sections to be drafted of the new state's Proclamation of Independence contained the guarantees to its Arab citizens. They would have "full and equal citizenship and due representation in all its bodies and institutions." Their equal rights applied of course to men, women, and children. Consequently, the Arab women in the new Jewish state would become the only Arab women in the Middle East who were allowed to vote. Arab children in the new Jewish state would be the only Arab children in the Middle East who were guaranteed free, indeed compulsory education from the age of five through fourteen.

A team went to work drawing up pamphlets in Arabic explaining all the guarantees, giving eloquent reasons why the Arabs of Palestine should not leave their homes. Pamphlets pleading with the Arabs to stay were dropped from a Piper Cub plane over Arab centers such as Jaffa, Nazareth, Acre, and Haifa.

And thousands of Arabs did stay. But thousands more left. In late April the Haifa harbor was glutted with small boats: Arabs fleeing.

Ben-Gurion sent Golda to Haifa to see what could be done about the situation. She found the city plastered with posters: appeals by the Jews of Haifa to its Arab citizens:

For years we lived together in our city, Haifa, in security and in mutual understanding and brotherhood. Thanks to this, our city flourished and developed for the good of both Jewish and Arab residents. . . .

Do not fear! Do not destroy your homes with your own hands; do not block off your sources of livelihood; and do not bring upon yourself tragedy by unnecessary evacuation and self-imposed burdens. By moving out, you will be overtaken by poverty and humiliation. But in this city, yours and ours, Haifa, the gates are open for work, for life, and for peace, for you and your families.

Golda had a meeting with the Mayor of Haifa, Shabetai Levi, who was highly respected by the Arabs. On her suggestion Mr. Levi went down to the port and tried to convince the fleeing Arabs to stay, promising them that no harm would befall them or their property. He later reported to Golda that the Arabs said they believed him, but they had been told by the Arab Higher Command that Haifa would be bombed; it would therefore be better for them to leave and to come back later.

On April 26, the British Chief of Police in Haifa, A. J. Bridmead, reported: *Every effort is being made by the Jews to persuade the Arab populace to stay and carry on with their normal lives, to get their shops and businesses open and to be assured that their lives and interests will be safe.*

For days the British Police Chief kept issuing the same type of report. On April 28 he wrote: *The Jews are still making every effort to persuade the Arab population to remain and settle back into their normal lives in the town. . . . Arab leaders reiterate their determination to evacuate the entire Arab population, and we have given them the loan of 10 three-ton military trucks to assist the evacuation.*

But the vast majority of the Arabs who fled did not leave the land of Palestine. They merely moved to the sections of Palestine which had been allocated by the United Nations to the new Arab State. In most cases they moved less than fifty miles.

May came.

The brilliant British Field Marshal Montgomery was just one of the famous military experts who traveled to Palestine to evaluate the forthcoming military situation. Montgomery wrote a report saying that it would take the

Arabs eight to ten days to drive the Jews into the sea. The other experts issued similar pronouncements.

The land which the Jews had to defend was long and skinny, almost all border, surrounded on three sides by enemy nations.

But one of the borders was Trans-Jordan, and here there was some vague hope.

Golda was sent on a top-secret mission known to only three people in the country. She was to cross into enemy land disguised as an Arab for a dangerous meeting with King Abdullah.

In a previous secret meeting with the King, held at a house on the border, Abdullah had informed Golda that if the partition plan was ratified by the United Nations, he would annex the new Arab state, make it part of his own kingdom. And he promised friendship to the new Jewish state.

In the months which followed it seemed that Abdullah had forgotten his promise. But it was decided that Golda should try to see him once more—in the faint hope that the King could be persuaded to keep his country out of the forthcoming war.

Her only companion was Ezra Dannin, a Jew born in the city of Jaffa and an expert on Arab affairs. On Monday, May 10, Golda and Dannin drove to the border town of Naharayim, where the first meeting had been held. But Abdullah had declared that it was far too dangerous for him to come to the border again. He would send a car so that Golda and her companion could drive to his capital city of Amman, where they would meet in the home of a trusted friend.

Golda and Dannin arrived in the border town at nightfall. There Golda donned the Arab robes and veils she had brought with her. (She'd already had a "dress rehearsal" directed by Dannin, when she practiced moving as an Arab woman does in her exotic costume.)

The car arrived. As they crossed the border they were stopped by guards of the Arab Legion. Dannin presented their false identification papers. He was an Arab merchant traveling with his wife. Golda sat low in the back seat, her face hidden by veils.

They were stopped ten times by Arab guards before they finally arrived at their destination. Abdullah's friend then ushered them into a large room hung with rugs and drapes. They sat on a low sofa, before a coffee table topped by inlaid mother-of-pearl.

Within a few minutes the door opened and King Abdullah entered, a short regal-looking man with a dark beard. He wore a white headdress and long white robes.

Turkish coffee was served. The traditional amenities were spoken. And then Golda and the King got down to business.

Golda reminded Abdullah of the promise he had made her in November, that he would look with favor upon the creation of a new Jewish state.

Bluntly Abdullah replied, "Then I was alone. Now I am one of five."

It became bleakly clear that Abdullah would send his country to war against the infant nation. It was also clear that he did not want to. "I know you," he said. "And I believe in your good intentions. I believe with all my heart that Divine Providence has brought you back here, restoring you—a Semitic people who were exiled to Europe and shared in its progress—to the Semitic East, which needs your knowledge and initiative. Only with your help and your guidance will the Semites be able to revive their ancient glory. We cannot expect genuine assistance from the Christian world, which looks down upon the Semitic peoples. We will progress only as the result of joint efforts. I know all this and I believe it with all sincerity, but conditions are difficult. One dare not take rash steps."

The King then suggested that war could be avoided if the Jews did not declare a state on May 14. And if they agreed to stop immigration for several years. Why, he asked, should they be in such a hurry to declare a state?

Golda pointed out that a people that waited two thousand years could hardly be described as being in a hurry. Perhaps, she suggested, the Jews had been *too* patient.

After forty-five minutes the King left. Throughout the meeting Abdullah had seemed despondent and sullen. Even sad. Not like a man who wanted war. Like a man caught and tied by powers beyond his control.

On their drive back home Golda and Dannin saw the lights of Camp Mafrak, where troops of the Iraqi Army were massing for the war which would come in four days' time.

They were stopped so often by so many checkposts that when they reached no-man's-land, the Arab chauffeur refused to drive them on to Naharayim. He had been told who his passengers were. He was frightened and insisted they get out of the car.

It was just before dawn. They made their way over the dry river bed, Golda stumbling over the long Arab gown. Darkness was a threat. There were no paths. They could not even be sure they were heading in the right direction. Several times Golda felt a flash of panic. Were they, perhaps, walking back into Trans-Jordan?

But darkness was also a cover. When dawn came they would be seen by Arab patrols. For what reason was an Arab woman walking about in no-man's-land at this early hour of the morning? If they were sighted and questioned it could mean death.

Finally, after an hour they *were* sighted—by a Haganah scout who had been sent out to search for them. He told them his name was Abraham Daskal.

Golda's fear vanished. "I am very glad to meet you, Abraham," she said.

Golda as a young child, taken in Pinsk, Ukraine.

"Goldie was an attractive girl in every way," her school friend, *Regina*, recalls.

(Courtesy Embassy of Israel; Washington, D. C.)

Teen-aged Goldie Mabovitch (standing), with her oldest sister, Shana; her niece, Judith; and her brother-in-law, Shamai.

(Courtesy Pioneer Women)

Twenty-one-year-old Goldie in a Zionist pageant in Milwaukee.

On December 24, 1917, nineteen-year-old Goldie Mabo-vitch became Mrs. Morris Myerson.

(Courtesy Embassy of Israel: Washington, D. C.)

Golda hated chickens, but on the kibbutz she was assigned to run the hatchery!

(Courtesy Embassy of Israel: Washington, D. C.)

One of the supreme moments in Golda's life: signing the Proclamation of Independence, on May 14, 1948. With David Ben-Gurion and Moshe Sharett.

(Courtesy Pioneer Women)

As Labor Minister, Golda visited every corner of the country. Here she tramps through the searing hot Negev desert.

(Courtesy Embassy of Israel: Washington, D. C.)

Foreign Minister Meir made numerous trips to African countries. Here she is greeted by Ethiopia's Emperor Haile Selassie.

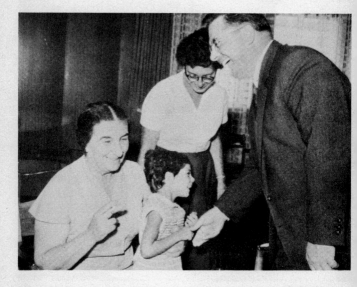

The Russian Ambassador to Israel took a shine to Foreign Minister Meir's granddaughter, Naomi. Golda's daughter, Sarah, looks on.

(Courtesy Pioneer Women)

After a long plane trip and many tiring meetings, Foreign Minister Meir often revived by joining the evening's folk dancing.

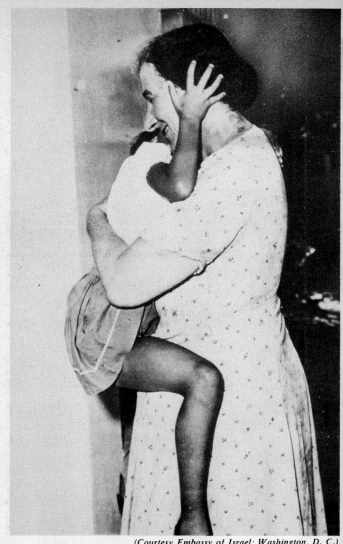

(Courtesy Embassy of Israel; Washington. D. C.)

Golda and her granddaughter.

(Courtesy Embassy of Israel; Washington. D. C.)

*An emotion-charged episode during the Six-Day War;
Golda visited the Western Wall, most holy place on earth
for Jews of the world.*

(Courtesy Embassy of Israel; Washington, D. C.)

Foreign Minister Meir meeting with President John Kennedy in 1958.

Israel's three top political figures: Defense Minister Moshe Dayan, Deputy Prime Minister Yigal Allon, and Prime Minister Golda Meir.

(UPI)

Golda's visit with President Nixon in December, 1971, established a new cornerstone in U. S.–Israel relations. The two leaders also enjoyed each other's company.

Mrs. Golda Meir, citizen of Israel, casts her vote.

(Courtesy Embassy of Israel: Washington, D. C.)

Chapter 16

It was ten minutes to four.

May 14, 1948.

She sat at a T-shaped table in the Tel Aviv Art Museum. Within the next half hour she, Golda Myerson, would be one of the thirty-eight men and women to sign the Proclamation of Independence of the new state of Israel. She remembered herself suddenly as a schoolgirl in Milwaukee staring at a list of names in her American history book: the signatures of the men who had signed the Declaration of Independence. Now, unbelievably, she herself was about to sign a document which—to her people—would be equally historic.

Israel, one of the oldest nations in the world, was about to become the world's newest nation. The only nation to have been reborn out of antiquity. The only nation to bear the same name, speak the same language, uphold the same faith, and inhabit the same land as it had 3,000 years ago.

And the first nation in the world to have been created —or re-created—by proclamation of the United Nations.

Eretz Israel—the Land of Israel—for centuries it had been a phrase in prayers and songs. Now, at last, it would be printed on world maps: *Israel*.

She looked out at the crowded hall. They had picked the Tel Aviv Art Museum for this historic event because it was small; the auditorium housed only 200 people. It would be easier to keep the meeting secret if the meeting place was small. And secrecy was essential, for if the Arabs learned the time and place of the event they might very well bomb the site. And the entire Yishuv leadership would be wiped out at once.

Obviously, however, the secret had leaked out, for as Golda and the others approached the museum they were startled to see a huge crowd of wildly cheering spectators awaiting them.

The auditorium was packed from wall to wall with prominent members of the Yishuv (they would soon be called Israelis!) and with reporters from newspapers around the world. And cameramen. Yet, with all this crowd the hall was strangely still. The silence was almost other-worldly, as though everyone realized that present and past were suddenly fused in this one momentous hour.

The heat was intense—added to by the arc lights of the movie cameramen and the flashbulbs of the photographers, which suddenly started popping and flaring around the room. For David Ben-Gurion had risen to his feet.

He usually wore shirt sleeves. He looked unfamiliar now in his dark blue suit and tie. The Proclamation of Independence was in his hand. A battery of microphones was before him. And behind him was the portrait of Theodor Herzl, hung against a background of blue and white: the colors of the new nation.

She remembered the words Herzl had written in his diary at the close of the First Zionist Congress in Basle, Switzerland:

> *If I were to sum up the Congress in one word, it would be this: at Basle I founded the Jewish State. If I were to say this today, I would be greeted with universal laughter. In five years, perhaps, and certainly in fifty, everyone will see it.*

The entry was dated: *August 29, 1897.*

At this moment—exactly fifty years and nine months later—Theodor Herzl's prophecy was coming true!

As the minute hand jumped to four o'clock Ben-Gurion

rapped the gavel on the table. "Let us stand to adopt the scroll of the Establishment of the State."

Everyone rose. And, spontaneously, they burst out singing, "Hatikva," the Hebrew word for "hope." "Hatikva," the national anthem of the new nation. This was not at all according to the planned program. It was as though the gathering could not help singing.

The aged Rabbi Moshe Fishman read the benediction in a voice which trembled.

And then Ben-Gurion, his face shining, read out the Proclamation of Independence.

As Golda listened, she fought back tears.

> *The Land of Israel was the birthplace of the Jewish people. Here their spiritual, religious and national identity was formed. Here they achieved independence and created a culture of national and universal significance. Here they wrote and gave the Bible to the world.*
>
> *Exiled from the Land of Israel the Jewish people remained faithful to it in all the centuries of their dispersion, never ceasing to pray and hope for their return and the restoration of their national freedom.*
>
> *Impelled by this historic association, Jews strove throughout the centuries to go back to the land of their fathers, and regain their statehood. In recent decades they returned in their masses. They reclaimed the wilderness, revived their language, built cities and villages, and established a vigorous and ever-growing community, with its own economic and cultural life. They sought peace, yet were prepared to defend themselves. They brought the blessings of progress to all inhabitants of the country. . . .*

The Proclamation was short—979 words.

Eighteen of those words—one single sentence—brought forth a sudden storm of applause.

The State of Israel, Ben-Gurion intoned, *will be open to the immigration of Jews from all countries of their dispersion.*

At last, the White Paper restriction would be ripped to shreds. The barbed wire surrounding the DP camps would be rolled back. Any Jew anywhere in the world would be welcomed home to Eretz Israel.

Then came the time for the signing. Each of the thirty-eight Yishuv leaders rose and came forward in alphabetical order. There had not been time to inscribe the Proclamation on parchment. This would be done later. The leaders signed at the bottom of the empty scroll.

Moshe Shertok held the parchment down flat as Golda wrote her name. She could barely see, for she could no longer hold back her tears. She was weeping openly.

At midnight the flotilla of the British Royal Navy, which escorted the departing British High Commissioner, reached the three-mile limit of Israel's territorial waters. The band on the aircraft carrier played "Auld Lang Syne." And the British Mandate ended.

Golda, standing on her balcony, watched them go.

Then she went inside. The radio was on. Kol Israel: the Voice of Israel. The news was electrifying. And completely unexpected. President Truman had just announced that the United States officially recognized the new nation of Israel.

Several hours later the wail of air-raid sirens shattered the silence of dawn over Tel Aviv. Egyptian planes roared low over the city, dropping bombs.

And by dawn, as duly promised, seven Arab nations officially declared war on the new state. Their armies invaded Israel's borders.

It was David against Goliath. The purchased Israeli arms were on the way but would not arrive for weeks. Meanwhile, the Jews fought back with weapons which could well be likened to the slingshot.

Fighter planes and bombers of the Egyptian, Syrian, and Iraqi air forces flew low and leisurely over cities and farm settlements, dropping highly destructive twentieth-century bombs. The Jewish Air Force consisted of a few tiny Piper Cubs. Their bombs were grenades, mostly hand-made, which they tossed out the window.

On the first day of the war the Egyptian fleet sailed in, bent on destroying Tel Aviv. One of the Piper Cubs swooped down on the lead ship and hit it. Whereupon the

Egyptian fleet turned around and sailed back home. But
the Piper fell, and its pilot and bombadier were killed.

The remaining Pipers were soon shot down. So were
three Egyptian bombers—downed by kibbutzniks who
fired from the ground with machine guns.

The Jewish population in Israel was less than 700,000.
The Arab population in the seven invading states was
more than 50,000,000. As Ibn-Saud, King of Saudi
Arabia, put it: "With fifty million Arabs, what does it
matter if we lose ten million people to kill all the Jews?
The price is worth it."

The Arab territory was 300 times that of Israel. The
Arabs could therefore retreat endlessly. But the Jews in
their long, narrow, little land could lose only once.

Golda summed up the military situation succinctly:
"We have our backs against the wall. We don't even have
a wall. We have a sea. The only friendly neighbor we have
is the Mediterranean."

And even the sea would not prove overly friendly,
should the Arabs succeed in their loudly proclaimed war
aims of driving the Jews into it within three days' time.

On the third day of the new state's existence, Golda was
asked to leave at once for a repeat mission to America.
More money was urgently needed for more arms. And
once again she took off with only a handbag—which still
contained the long Arab veil she had worn on her Abdullah visit. This item, along with her lack of luggage,
puzzled New York customs inspectors no end.

The telephone was ringing as Golda entered her hotel
room. She picked up the receiver. "A person to person
call for Mrs. Golda Myerson," the telephone operator said
in a matter-of-fact voice. "From the Minister of Transport
of the State of Israel."

Mrs. Golda Myerson gasped. Emotion flooded through
her. *The State of Israel!* Those simple words spoken by
the telephone operator brought the full realization for
the first time. Israel actually *existed!*

Soon friends were crowding into her hotel room. Golda
was fairly glowing with happiness. Even as she described

the perilous conditions engulfing the four-day-old nation, she would interrupt herself to exclaim: "We have a country! Imagine! We have our own country!"

Golda was the first official of the new state to arrive in the U.S.A. As one of her visitors put it: "She came with a new nationality, which she herself helped to create!"

Now, fund-raising was a far easier matter. The Jews of America responded with joy—and with checks—to the unbelievable reality. Finally, after 1,878 years, there was once again a Jewish nation.

And they responded to the crying need. For the nation was already in dire danger of extinction. Furthermore, that nation was fighting three wars at once.

At the same time as she was combating seven Arab armies, *another* army was descending upon the land. Thousands of Jewish refugees were arriving each day from the detention camps of Cyprus. Thousands were flooding in from the DP camps on the continent. And tens of thousands more were already on their way.

Furthermore, this army brought nothing with it—except disease. Which immediately engulfed the new nation in its third war, against every conceivable type of infectious disease. Tuberculosis, infantile paralysis, dysentery, trachoma. . . . Never before in medical history did a country have to deal with so many different and drastic medical problems in so short a space of time.

Almost every other nation had strict health restrictions: no would-be immigrant with a contagious disease was permitted to enter. But on the first day of her nationhood, Israel had announced her first law: the Law of Return. Her gates would henceforth be open to any Jew who wished to come. There would be no restrictions whatsoever!

To fight the three wars at once, three ingredients were needed in massive quantities: courage, determination, and money. The Israelis had ample amounts of the first two. Golda addressed herself to the third. Again she worked night and day, back and forth across the country. She put facts starkly before her public. And she pulled no punches.

"Jews cannot come into Israel and the country cannot

be established by speeches and by resolutions and by declarations and by applause. . . . You people have to make up your minds. . . . We must have your answer. . . . Is what is happening in the Jewish world today something that is so important and so vital that you here too are prepared to change your way of life and your way of thinking for a short period, for a year or two or three, in order to have this thing put on its feet? . . . We know that we couldn't have done what we have done until now without the help of American Jews. And we certainly can't go on from here without your help. . . . Believe me, my friends, that's all we ask of you—to share in this responsibility with everything that it implies—difficulties, problems, hardships, but also joy—a lot of joy. This responsibility I ask on behalf of the people of Israel and on behalf of those who want to be people of Israel tomorrow."

And American Jews responded, to an extent neither they nor anyone else—Golda included—had ever imagined possible.

One day as she was about to leave her hotel room for yet another fund-raising function, a cable arrived from Israel's new Foreign Minister, Moshe Shertok. Would Golda accept the appointment as Minister to Soviet Russia?

She stood looking down at the cable, frowning. What was wrong with her? She should feel pleased. This was a great honor. Yet, she had been looking forward with almost childlike excitement to returning to Israel. She wanted above anything else to *be* there in these desperate but exciting days. At least in America she felt that what she did had direct effect on what was going on at home. Her words were translated into dollars, which were turned into guns and tanks and tents to house the thousands of homeless immigrants who arrived at Israel's ports every day. But what could she do in Moscow that would be of any immediate help? It was like being exiled.

Yet she had always gone where she was asked to go,

done what she was asked to do. This was not the time to start rebelling.

The appointment was officially announced on June 7, 1948. Mrs. Golda Myerson would leave at once for Israel. After a short visit she would depart for Russia and her new post as Minister.

Golda said her good-byes. She was on her way to Brooklyn to see an old friend, when suddenly a car crashed into her taxi. A crowd gathered, an ambulance clanged to the scene, and Golda was rushed to the Hospital for Joint Diseases.

The hospital switchboard was soon flooded with calls. Golda's room became an instant flower show, overflowing with baskets and bouquets—many from people who had never met her but who felt that they knew her after hearing her speak.

She had a fractured leg and phlebitis, blood clots. The treatment included complete and absolute rest, otherwise the situation could become dangerous. If a clot moved into her heart or her brain it could mean death.

Somehow a rumor got started, chiefly in the Communist press. This was a "diplomatic illness." Israel was snubbing Russia. Daily phone calls and telegrams came from the Israeli foreign office. *When* would she be able to leave? Yet, her doctors insisted she must not move until the blood clots dispersed. She wired home: appoint someone else. The suggestion was rejected. But could she not leave *soon*? After all, Russia had been the second of the great nations to recognize the new state of Israel. They could not afford to offend her.

As if to apologize for their pressure, the Israeli Foreign Office asked Golda whether she would object to having her daughter join her Moscow staff as radio operator.

Sarah Myerson had left home at the age of seventeen to live on a kibbutz. She was now in Revivim, one of the first three settlements to be established in the Negev desert. When she moved there, Revivim was merely a cluster of tents surrounded by a stone wall. Now there was a cement-block children's house, which could serve as a fortress if necessary. And it *had* been necessary. During the first weeks of the war, Revivim was one of the isolated desert settlements in the path of the Egyptian Army. They had been subjected to frequent attacks by Egyptian infantry, armored cars, artillery, and aircraft. They had fought back with hand grenades and Molotov cocktails.

But Revivim had not only meant hardship, hard work, and danger for Sarah. She had fallen in love with a handsome young man named Zacharia Rechavi. He loved her. And they wanted to marry. When the Foreign Minister heard of this further development, Zacharia was asked to go to Moscow as a code and radio expert.

Golda, and her children, had always shied away from special privileges which her position might have brought. But this assignment somehow seemed too special to turn down. Mr. and Mrs. Rechavi—to honeymoon in Moscow!

But first there must be a wedding.

Golda, still lying in a hospital bed, was now doubly anxious to get up and out and on the move, for reasons of state and reasons of motherhood. Finally, despite the dire predictions of her doctors, she insisted that she was well enough to travel. (But she was not. Her too-hasty departure led to much suffering and an operation on her leg a few years later.)

She arrived home in time for the wedding. It was held in the garden of Shana's cottage in Holon. (A truce in the fighting had been called by the United Nations. Consequently, bird song replaced the sound of shelling as background music.) There were not many wedding guests. Only a few close friends had been asked. "Otherwise," said Golda, "we'd have to invite half of Israel."

But all the family was there, with the exception of Aunt Clara. Tzipka (or Clara, as everyone, including Golda, now called her) had planned to move to Palestine with her parents. But in the summer of 1925, she had met a young man named Fred Stern. They fell in love. Since both were in college, they decided to marry, to graduate, and then move to Palestine. But after graduation David was born. They did not want to risk the long and difficult boat trip with the newborn infant. They would go when he was a year old. But that year, 1929, Arab riots broke out. They would wait till things calmed down. Then Fred was offered an excellent job in Cleveland, Ohio. And when they were again all set to leave for Palestine, an even more exciting job offer came along. So they moved instead to Bridgeport, Connecticut, where Fred became and remained Executive Director of the Jewish Family Society. Clara, a sociologist, also went to work and soon became active as well in the United Jewish Appeal. And Clara, Fred, and David became "the American branch" of the family.

Bluma and Moshe had come to Palestine in 1926, and the proud grandparents were, of course, at the wedding. Shana was there with Shamai (who had also arrived in 1926) and their three children. (The youngest, Jonah, was a *sabra*—he had been born in Palestine.)

Menachem came home on leave to be at his sister's wedding. And Morris was there to give his daughter away. Though he and Golda had been officially separated since the children were teen-agers, there was still deep affection between them. All tensions and conflicts had vanished. Morris was able to say, with something of a smile, "What happened? Well, you might put it like this: I came to Palestine for one reason only. To be with Goldie. But she was never there."

The years had also given Menachem perspective on his mother's constant meetings and traveling. "If we really needed her," he said, "she was always there." Then he added, "The last thing you would call my mother is a career woman. She did these things because she felt it was her duty."

Sarah put it this way: "For such a mother it was worth it."

The wedding held under the plum trees in Shana's garden was, in its way, symbolic of the nation's future. Two native-born *sabras* were joining in matrimony. But it was more than that. There were now deep divisions of culture, of language, of background between the so-called Oriental Jews, who came from Arab lands, and the European Jews, who had thus far been responsible for reclaiming the ancient Jewish homeland.

Zacharia was an Oriental Jew. His parents had come from Yemen. At the wedding they sat shy and separate, apart from the Westerners whose language and customs they did not understand.

But their son, Zacharia—handsome, slender, olive-skinned—was marrying the blond and blue-eyed Myerson girl, whose parents had come from Russia. And the children of Zacharia and Sarah would be a blend of both. Their backgrounds would fuse into the new nationality: Israeli.

Regina was one of the few family friends invited to the wedding. She came alone from Jerusalem—a city which had somehow lived through a four-month siege.

At the wedding Regina filled her plate high with food, which Golda had prepared. "Goldie," she said, "I'd hate to tell you how much time I spent during that four months dreaming of a feast like this!"

For weeks Regina and her young son, Ronny, had lived on a single piece of bread and four olives a day. Sometimes they added vine leaves which they had picked.

"It's strange," Regina said. "During that time no one reported in for the sick fund. Everyone was just too busy trying somehow to stay alive."

Yet, despite starvation and severe water rationing, the Jews of Jerusalem had gone on with their lives. Children went to school. Adults went to work. Regina still worked at the Jewish Agency. Her office faced the Old City, which had fallen to the Arabs on May 28. "We didn't *go* to work," she recalled. "We crawled to work. Stooping, then running. Because they were shelling all the time. When B.G. proclaimed the state, we were in the office, under the table, listening to the proceedings over the radio. While bullets and shells kept exploding outside."

As Regina was leaving, Golda asked about her eighteen-year-old daughter who was an Army nurse.

"We haven't heard," Regina said flatly. "Not where she is or how she is. It's been almost six months now, and we haven't heard a word."

On September 3, 1948, Golda, her daughter, and her new son-in-law drove to Lydda Airport, which had recently been recaptured from the Arabs by a unit whose leader was the eye-patched Moshe Dayan.

When she left Russia at the age of eight, Goldie Mabovitch had scarcely imagined that forty-two years later she would be returning as Minister to Moscow representing the new Jewish state.

Chapter 17

Moscow's severe housing shortage extended to diplomats. So, while the Israeli delegation waited to be assigned an official legation building, they were allotted suites in the splendid Hotel Metropole.

There were twenty-six members of the legation, including children. And Golda promptly organized life along kibbutz lines. No salaries were paid. All adults were given equal amounts of pocket money. The chauffeur received the same as Madame Minister. And neither received very much.

Since expenses were paid by the Israeli Treasury—which had virtually no money—the legation staff usually ate in their rooms, preparing the food themselves. And Golda took her turn shopping, cooking, and washing dishes.

The setting, however, hardly matched the kibbutz lifestyle, for the rooms at the Hotel Metropole were immense and lushly furnished: huge glittering cut-glass chandeliers, thick Oriental carpets, bathrooms large enough to house an entire family.

There were also an unending number of waiters and chambermaids who kept popping in at all hours. Each of them, the legation had been warned, was undoubtedly a member of the secret police. And every room was undoubtedly wired, every phone tapped. Since such courtesies were even accorded to tourists from other Communist countries, it was inconceivable that an official legation should receive anything less.

To further add to the general sense of unease, there was on each landing a huge stuffed Siberian brown bear rearing up on his hind legs. And on each floor sat a stern-faced, middle-aged housekeeper, obviously an agent of the secret police.

A week after her arrival, Golda was summoned to present her letter of credentials to the President of the Soviets. The question came up which many women utter many times a year. But it was a question quite unknown to Golda. What shall I wear? She was accustomed to dressing in a manner which was simple, to say the least. The only necklace she owned was a ten-dollar strand of fake pearls given to her by an American friend. The only hat she owned was a black velvet turban—which she had never put on.

Golda had been informed by the chief of protocol that when presenting credentials men wore uniforms or tails. Mere tuxedos were regarded as far too informal. When asked what Minister Myerson should wear, the protocol chief only shrugged.

At eleven o'clock on the morning of September 11, Golda—garbed in a long-sleeved black evening dress, pearls, and her black turban—presented her credentials. At the ceremony she spoke in Hebrew, a language which had been banned in Russia since the days of the Revolution.

Indeed, since the Revolution a concerted effort had been made to stamp out Judaism. And aside from a few hundred elderly Jews who attended the few remaining synagogues, it certainly seemed as though the government had succeeded in eradicating all sense of Jewish identity from Russia's three million Jews.

As Golda later put it: "When we set out for Moscow we wondered whether—under such a regime with its power and cruelty—any trace of a link between the Russian Jews and the Jewish people remained."

Although she was not notably religious, Golda decided it would be suitable for the legation to attend synagogue. So, on the first Saturday after presenting her credentials, they went. There were, reportedly, 500,000 Jews in Moscow. Of these, less than 300 were in the synagogue. Most of those were old men. Only the rabbi had been told that the Israeli legation would be among the worshipers.

As usual, the rabbi offered a prayer for Stalin and other Soviet officials. Then he said a prayer for Golda Myerson, Israel's Minister to Russia. A visible wave of emotion rose below as the old men turned to stare up at Golda, who sat in the women's section.

When she left, they followed her, swarming around her. Golda became separated from the rest of the legation. She started out alone walking toward the hotel, but she was uncertain of the way. An old man passed by her and murmured in Yiddish, "Don't talk to me. I'll walk ahead. You follow."

When the hotel was in sight, the old man turned and said, in Hebrew, "Blessed are we that we have lived to see this day." Then he disappeared.

Several weeks later the Israelis went to synagogue again. It was Rosh Hashanah, the Jewish New Year. As Golda emerged from the hotel, she gasped. Some momentous event must have occurred—and no one had informed her about it. The streets were a sea of people. Indeed, no streets could be seen at all. No traffic. Nothing but a surging swarm of humanity. She was immediately engulfed in the crowd. And then she saw that all the faces were turned toward *her!* Smiling faces, most of them men, of all ages. Men wearing worker's caps. Some in Army uniforms. And they were calling out to her. In Yiddish. *"Golda shelanu!* [Our Golda!] *Goldele, leben sollst du. Shana tova* [Goldele, long life to you. Happy New Year]."

These masses of smiling, cheering men were Jews! They had come to greet her, as the symbol of the new Jewish nation.

She was swept along to the synagogue. There, in the packed women's gallery, worshipers pressed close to her, to see her, to touch her. Most of the women were weeping. And below, the men were crying, shrieking, wailing, as they gazed up at her.

Golda sat, staring straight ahead, too overcome with emotion to show any reaction at all.

When she came out of the synagogue she was practically submerged by the crowds. It was obvious she could never reach the hotel on foot. So, despite the holiday edicts against riding in vehicles, several men from the legation formed themselves into bodyguards and got her somehow into a taxi. But the taxi could not budge, for the ecstatic throngs pressed close around it.

Golda put her head out the window and, with effort, she managed to utter a sentence. She spoke in Yiddish. *"A dank eich wos ihr seit geblieben Yiden.* [Thanks that you have remained Jews]."

Her words were passed on, block after block, as one Jew reported to another what *Golda shelanu* had said.

Finally, somehow, all the legation members made their way back to the Metropole. And they all went to Golda's room.

Later, Mrs. Lou Kaddar, Golda's close friend and personal assistant, recalled that scene. "We just sat. Somebody was pacing back and forth. Back and forth. We couldn't talk. It was too terrible to talk. I was crying. I never knew that I could cry so much. Golda just sat there, like a stone."

And later, Golda said, "I am sure that not only I, but everyone who was a member of this first mission, inwardly asked forgiveness a thousand times from these Jews for having dared to doubt their spiritual strength and their Jewish ties with the whole past, present, and future of the Jewish race."

The legation went again to synagogue on Yom Kippur Eve. The crowds were estimated at fifty thousand. Now, however, the officials had been forewarned, and police surrounded Golda, pressing the throngs back.

The climax came on the day of Yom Kippur, the Day of Atonement, when at the conclusion of the services the worshipers recited the prayer, *L'shanah ha-baah biYerushalayim* (Next year in Jerusalem).

"The words shook the synagogue as they looked up at me," Golda said. "It was the most passionate Zionist speech I had ever heard."

Although nothing was mentioned of this matter in the Soviet press, the authorities had quite obviously taken note. And, quite obviously, word went out. The next time the Israelis went to synagogue, there were no crowds at all. And when they attended the Yiddish Theater, no one came up to them during the intermission.

Five months later the Yiddish Theater was closed by the Soviet government. The Yiddish newspaper *Einigkeit* was shut down, as was the Yiddish publishing house.

Since Russia had officially recognized the state of Israel, the Jews of Moscow had naïvely believed that they would be free to "recognize" the head of the Israeli legation. Their massive, emotional response had caused the authorities to clamp down on the last remnants of organized Jewish expression in the Soviet Union. Only a few synagogues were permitted to remain open. And no one dared to attend the services except the same scattered hundreds of *davening* old men and women. The government obviously was not concerned about their loyalties, since they soon would die.

A few months later a permanent residence was found for the Israeli legation. They moved into a large, two-story stone villa which had once belonged to the world-famed conductor Serge Koussevitsky.

Golda got down on her hands and knees to help lay the carpets, climbed up on ladders to hang the drapes. She had always rather enjoyed housework as a relief from other pressures. But now she longed for the "other pressures."

What was she doing here hanging up drapes when her country was fighting for its life?

Over and over like a terrifying refrain, the words of Yigal Yadin ran through her head, Yigal Yadin, Chief of Staff of the Israeli forces. She had been at a meeting two days before the state was declared. A meeting called by Ben-Gurion. A meeting of Yishuv leaders, called to decide whether they would dare to declare a state. B.G. had asked Yadin what Israel's chances were if they waited three more months before declaring statehood, three more months which would give them time to buy more arms, to become better prepared. Slowly Yadin had replied, "Even if we wait, even if we get more arms, we have only a fifty-fifty chance."

Fifty-fifty.

And here she was a million miles away; a minister plenipotentiary serving coffee, tea, and cakes to members of other embassies and legations. Making courtesy calls. Giving and attending receptions. *A fifty-fifty chance of survival!*

Incredibly, the nations of the world who had voted to establish the Jewish state, who had already officially recognized the Jewish state, were now refusing to sell arms to the Jewish state so that it could fight for its life. While the Arab countries were able to get unlimited supplies.

Coded communiqués came through to Minister Myerson describing the strange feats Israelis had to undertake in order to secure arms. For instance, they set up a film company in Great Britain (which had imposed an arms embargo on Israel). The first sequence of the script called for an air battle. The cameras whirred. The planes took off, flew out of camera range—all the way to Israel.

Personal contacts were also important. For instance, the brilliant and charming Ehud Avriel, Israel's first appointed and youngest Ambassador (to Czechoslovakia) had made friends with the Czech Minister of Defense. The first result of this friendship, a shipment of rifles which arrived in Israel in time to be issued to virtually weaponless troops en route to the front.

A fifty-fifty chance.

And here she was holding open house in Moscow every Friday night.

Then, in January, 1949, the impossible happened. Israel won the war.

Golda sat in her suite reading the dispatches—ecstatic and astounded.

This tiny sliver of a country, almost submerged by an ever-increasing flood of sick, helpless, maimed refugees, had somehow managed to fight off the well-equipped forces of seven Arab nations.

Soon daily communiqués started coming in on the armistice negotiations between Egypt and Israel which were held in the splendid Hotel des Roses on the island of Rhodes. The United Nations had sent Dr. Ralph Bunche as mediator. And, at first, Golda read incredulously to her legation staff reports that the Egyptians had refused to meet in the same room with the Israelis. They wanted Dr. Bunche to run back and forth from one floor to the other as some sort of super messenger boy. But Bunche put an end to this by announcing: "It was my understanding that we had come here to negotiate, and to do this, gentlemen, one side must talk to the other."

Whereupon, the Egyptians agreed to meet with the Israelis in Bunche's sitting room, where—after weeks of negotiations—members of the two delegations became quite friendly, even played billiards together in the evening. When the armistice agreements were finally signed on February 24, both parties attended a gala festivity to celebrate.

Dr. Bunche then invited delegates from Jordan, Lebanon, and Syria to join Egypt in signing the agreements. Which they did.

According to the armistice agreements, the lines of the troops on the cessation of the fighting became, in the main, the new borders. At least, they were the borders until the official peace settlement was signed. And that, said the Arabs, would come "soon."

Israel had lost 4,486 soldiers—men and women. Over 2,000 civilians. Thousands more had been wounded. But

she had also gained—in territory. The Jews now had, at
least, half of Jerusalem. The other half belonged to the
new Arab state, which King Abdullah subsequently absorbed into his domain, retitling the two merged countries
Jordan. Jerusalem, Jordan and Jerusalem, Israel were
separated in many places by strands of barbed wire, a
block of bombed-out buildings, or a narrow street.

Israel itself was now 7,933 square miles. It stretched
260 miles from tip to toe, 70 miles at its widest point in
the triangular-shaped Negev. But north of Tel Aviv it was
a mere 10 miles wide. One could drive from the Mediterranean Sea to the Arab border in ten minutes.

Now that Israel could stop fighting for her life, she
could start putting some order into her life. The first
national elections were held. As had been the case in the
provisional government, which had led the country since
the signing of the Proclamation of Independence, Dr.
Chaim Weizmann was President (with duties more cere-
monial than political). Ben-Gurion was Prime Minister
and the nation's leader. Moshe Shertok was Foreign Minister. (He soon Hebraicized his name to Sharett, meaning
"servant.")

Then Ben-Gurion announced his Cabinet appointments.
There would be one woman among many men. She would
be the nation's first Minister of Labor and Development.
Her name was Mrs. Golda Myerson.

On April 20, 1949, Golda left Moscow to assume her
new post. She was very glad to go. It was only later that
she was to fully realize what those eight months in Russia
had meant to her.

"What more can anyone Jewish ask for," she said,
"when one has been privileged to be the first to reach that
Jewry which had been for decades so completely cut
off? . . . Whoever has had the privilege of hearing the
words, 'Next year in Jerusalem' from the lips of those
Jews in the synagogue—will remain indebted forever."

Chapter 18

Golda's new job was an impossible one.

When she was sworn in as Labor Minister one out of every three Israelis was a brand-new immigrant. They came from different civilizations. Different cultures. Different centuries. And they spoke a babel of different languages.

There were swarthy, turbaned Kurdish Jews who spoke Aramaic, the language of Jesus. There were nomadic Hadhramautic Jews whose women painted their faces blue and yellow. There were dark-skinned Jews from Afghanistan, Abyssinia, Libya. There were Tunisian Jews and Turkish Jews, Hungarian Jews, Bulgarian Jews, Austrian and Bukharan Jews. They came from seventy-two different lands.

And they kept on coming, at the rate of a thousand a day.

"Sound the great trumpet for our freedom, raise the banner for gathering our exiles, and gather us together from the four corners of the earth into our land."

Three times daily, for over two thousand years, millions of Jews throughout the world faced the direction of Jerusalem to chant this prayer. And now they *were* coming— from the four corners of the earth. There were even Jews from India, dignified men in white dhotis and their obedient sari-clad wives. And slant-eyed Chinese Jews from Kai-Fung-Foo.

Never before in history had so many, and so many different types of people descended in so short a space of time onto so small a section of the globe.

Some people thought the government should establish quotas. When the first hundred thousand new immigrants were housed and had jobs—the chief dual responsibilities of the new Minister of Labor—*then* allow in another hundred thousand.

But, as Golda bluntly put it, "We don't need a Jewish State that stops immigration. So that solution is out!"

Israel, in fact, did more than welcome in every Jew who wanted to come. She—and Jewish philanthropic organizations—brought those who could not afford the trip. And over ninety percent of the new immigrants fell into this category.

Those who had spent ten years in Europe's camps of course had no funds. Nor did the hundreds of thousands who now came fleeing from the Arab countries. For years they had lived in their own communities, in peace with their Arab neighbors. But when the war began in 1948, pogroms broke out in Arab lands. Some Arab countries let Jews leave—if they left all their possessions behind.

Over 50,000 Yemenite Jews were air-lifted into Israel. In Yemen they had been forced to live in ghettos. Every Jewish orphan became the property of the state and was forced to become a Moslem. Most of the gentle, pious Yemenite Jews had never seen a fork or spoon, a tin can, a water faucet. When they reached Israel and were allotted tents, many crawled underneath the cots, believing them to be for protection. They had come straight from the twelfth century. Yet, strangely, they had all boarded the twentieth-century aircraft with absolute assurance, for had Isaiah not said, "But they that wait upon the Lord shall mount up with wings as eagles"? Indeed, when they landed at Lydda Airport, many of them looked around for the Messiah. They expected Him to be there to greet them in person.

Operation Ali Baba rescued 122,000 Jews from Iraq, for that government, having failed to win on the battlefront, turned her full vengeance on the Jews in her country.

And thousands of Jews were brought in who had lived in caves in Libya and on the remote island of Djerba.

In all, some 500,000 Jews fled out of the Arab countries into Israel (which was, coincidentally, about the same number as the Arabs who fled out of the Jewish section of Palestine).

As Golda put it: "For the most part, the new immigrants come destitute, many of them broken in body and spirit. They have to be fed, clothed, given a physical examination, their sanitation needs attended to, their sick cared for. They must be given food, shelter, a roof over their heads. All in one day, the first day. Afterwards, we need schools, hospitals, work, houses, especially houses."

Of the 500,000 Jews who had fled from the Arab countries, less than one percent had worked on the land, less than two percent in the buildings' trades. A large percent were illiterate.

How could the new Minister of Labor and Development possibly get housing and jobs for this diverse, largely untrained, and ever-increasing flood tide of new immigrants?

Such a task had never been faced by anyone before, in Israel or out of it.

When Golda took over, some 250,000 new immigrants were living in tent cities. After the treasury-draining War of Independence, there was no money to erect permanent housing.

Golda's job therefore was threefold. She put it this way: "My ministry not only has to present a program, and execute it. Into the bargain, it has to raise the needed capital."

It was soon agreed that no other member of the Israeli government worked as hard at fund-raising and raised so much as Minister of Labor Myerson. To do so, she traveled not only to the United States but to South America and Europe as well.

Now, fund-raising was far more difficult. The life-and-death drama was gone. As Golda said when addressing a luncheon of the Allied Jewish Appeal, "Why do people tell me it is not the same as last year? True, there was a war on. I love American Jews too much, I respect them too much, to believe that they can become excited only when Jewish boys and girls in Israel are being killed, that only bloodshed and death are dramatic. I refuse to believe that the reconstruction of life is not exciting."

In that same speech, made in June, 1949, Golda illustrated one of the main methods through which her Ministry brought hundreds of thousands of new immigrants out of tents into their own new homes, and supplied them first with job training and then with jobs, all at the same time.

"I went to Parliament two weeks ago last Tuesday," she told the gathering of American Jews. "I presented a project for thirty thousand housing units by the end of this year. Parliament approved it, and there was great joy in the country. I did a strange thing: I presented in Parliament a project for thirty thousand units of one-room houses, for which I didn't have the money.

"The plan is that we will give each family a luxurious apartment of one room. And that room is not finished. We are going to build it of concrete blocks. We are not going to plaster the walls. We are going to give them a roof, but not a ceiling. We are hoping that since these people will be learning the trade as they build their houses, they will finish the houses, and eventually add on another room. In the meantime, we will be happy, and they will be happy, even though it means putting a family of two, three, four or five into one room. Today in the camps of Israel, there are four, five and six families in one tent!

"I finished the debate in Parliament on Wednesday night two weeks ago, and left for the United States on Thursday morning, hoping that these thirty thousand units and many more tens of thousands of units will be paid for by you.

"It is an awful thing to do—to forge a signature to a check—but I have done it. I have promised the people at home and the people in the camps that the government is going to put up these thirty thousand units. We have already started with the little money we have at our disposal. But we have not enough even for these thirty thousand units. It is up to you either to keep these people in camps and send them food packages, or to put them to work and restore to them their human dignity and self-respect. They are entitled to it."

The 30,000 units were built. As were hundreds of thousands more—under what was called "the Myerson Plan." Indeed, by the end of Golda's seven-year "reign" as Minister of Labor and Development, there was not one single new immigrant family in Israel still living in a tent. Over 200,000 attractive, balconied, low-income apartments had been built.

But the check which paid for them did not come entirely from "rich Jews" outside the country. To help finance their most immediate needs—housing, medical care, and defense—Israelis underwent the most severe type of rationing of clothing and food. Indeed, for a long time the only food items not rationed were eggplant and frozen fish. And even the fish was often impossible to obtain.

The spectacular housing program was also paid for in large measure by the spectacularly high taxation, which kept rising all the time. As one wry Tel Avivian put it at the advent of a new tax rise: "Two thousand years we waited for our nation to be reborn—and it had to happen to me!"

During her years as Labor Minister, Golda's public life absorbed so many hours of each day and evening that she had little time left for any private life. But matters of birth and death and marriage always supersede matters of state. And during her years as Labor Minister there were five such matters.

In 1950, she returned home from the United States to be told that her daughter was dying. Sarah, still plagued by kidney trouble, had been warned by doctors that if she became pregnant there was little likelihood she would live. But Sarah had chosen to disregard the warnings. One night she became violently ill and went into convulsions. No doctor could be found there in the depths of the Negev desert. So Sarah, in agonizing pain, was rushed in a kibbutz truck over the rocky road to the Hadassah Hospital in Beersheba.

When Golda reached the hospital she was told by the doctor, "I'm sorry, Mrs. Myerson, I can give you no hope."

She had heard the same words before, when Sarah was six years old—words which filled her with terror and frantic despair.

The recovery was a miracle. But the doctor warned that miracles could not be expected too often. Sarah must not get pregnant again. Furthermore, he strongly advised the girl to move from Revivim, for there still was not adequate drinking water on this pioneer kibbutz. Settlers on Revivim had only salt water to drink. And this was hardly a cure for a chronic kidney condition.

But Sarah had evidently inherited her mother's stubbornness and her total lack of concern about her own physical well-being. As soon as she was well enough she went straight back to Revivim. And two years later, in a Jerusalem hospital, she gave birth to a beautiful, healthy baby girl.

Golda's first grandchild was named Naomi.

In 1951, Golda was in the United States on another fund-raising mission. She received a telephone call. Morris Myerson had died.

They had been separated for years. But she was shattered by his death. She flew home at once to attend his funeral.

In that same year, her beloved mother, Bluma, also died.

In June, 1956, came a memorable day of happiness.

Menachem, now a professional cellist, had studied at the Juilliard School of Music and with the world-famous Pablo Casals. He had played with the Israeli Philharmonic, and had given numerous private recitals in Israel and abroad. But now he had come home to teach at the Tel Aviv Conservatory of Music.

One evening in Jerusalem he decided to look up a girl he had known years ago. They had gone to Beithachinuch, the School for Workers' Children. And they had been very good friends in the eighth grade.

Her name was Ayalah, which in Hebrew means gazelle. Everyone called her Ayah. She had large dark eyes, wavy dark hair, and she was beautiful. She had now, he was told, graduated from the Jerusalem Medical School. She was a child psychiatrist.

They remet. Shortly afterward, Menachem proposed. And they were married.

The wedding was simple—family, a few close friends. And all the food homemade by Golda.

The setting, however, was spectacular. The wedding was held on a huge terrace overlooking the brooding beauty of the Hills of Judea, with the town of Bethlehem in the distant background.

This was Golda's terrace. It was the only special personal request she had made as Minister. She wanted a home with a view.

She had found two small laundry rooms on the roof of an old house on David Marcus Street in a suburb of Jerusalem. Here, she decided, she wanted the residence of the Minister of Labor built.

It was pointed out to her that this exposed location was dangerously close to the Jordan border. But Golda was in love with the view.

Consequently, the two laundry rooms became the Minister of Labor's kitchen. A small bedroom was added, plus a large living room with many windows. And a huge terrace. From her various windows Golda had a varied panorama. She could see the Old City of Jerusalem, in Jordan. And from the opposite side of the apartment, she could see the New City of Jerusalem, in Israel, with its new office and apartment buildings, all faced—by law—with the golden stone of the ancient city.

She could see the mountains of Moab in Jordan, the swelling slope of Mount Zion in Israel, and on a clear day she could look halfway down both countries to the Dead Sea shimmering under the desert sun.

In June, 1956, Ben-Gurion asked Golda to become Foreign Minister of Israel.

Not only was it the second most important job in the Government. But who ever heard of a *woman* Foreign Minister? Many people asked B.G. the question. His answer was simple: "She's the best man in my Cabinet."

(When Golda was asked by a journalist how it felt to be a woman minister, she told him tartly, "I wouldn't know. I've never been a man minister.")

She accepted the position of Foreign Minister with fear, with uncertainty, with excitement—and with regret. She later called her seven years as Labor Minister "the most beautiful years." She had been doing what she loved most—something constructive, something concrete. Seeing thousands upon thousands of new houses going up. Seeing thousands of miles of new roads being laid. Roads which led to the isolated outlying farm settlements. And beautiful, broad main roads lined with newly planted trees. *Goldene wegen,* her countrymen called them in tribute to their Labor Minister. Golden roads.

No matter where she traveled in this land she loved, she could look around and see what she and her ministry had accomplished.

But to be Foreign Minister—it was a totally new realm. One of terrifying responsibility. Yet, Ben-Gurion had said he needed her. And she had thus far always responded to this call and this challenge.

She would move now into the official mansion of the Foreign Minister on Rehov Smolenskin. It was perhaps the most splendid residence in all of Jerusalem. But one of her chief regrets upon accepting the post of Foreign Minister was the fact that she would have to leave her beloved rooftop apartment which had been built to order for its panoramic view.

Chapter 19

In July, Golda moved into a new house and a new life. She also had a new name.

Ben-Gurion had always felt strongly that since ancient Hebrew had been revived as the language of the newly revived nation, it was fitting that Israelis should follow through by adopting Hebrew names. Hebrew was, he insisted, the single most important factor in unifying the multifarious and multilingual Israeli citizens. Their old names were like name tags connecting them to their old country and their old life.

Many Israelis did not take to this policy. But there was great pressure put on government officials to Hebraicize their names. Golda was one of the last holdouts. Now, however, since she held the second most important position in the government, she must, B.G. insisted, drop the "Mrs. Myerson."

With a shrug of her hands and her shoulders Golda acquiesced. But she came as close to Myerson as she could. She selected Meir (pronounced May-EAR), which in Hebrew means "illuminate."

The Foreign Minister's residence was an impressive government-owned mansion, guarded by two impressive policemen.

The ground floor, where official functions and dinners were held, had a large formal dining room replete with thick carpet, crystal chandelier, and three glass doors opening onto a patio and rose garden.

Golda's private apartment was upstairs, furnished with her own belongings. The small marble-floored sitting room was lined with bookshelves at either end. There were some books in Hebrew, some in Yiddish. But most were in English, volumes which included Proust, Churchill, Truman, Schweitzer, Dylan Thomas, and *The World's Best Jokes*. (This worthy tome is found in the library of many noted speechmakers. But no one had ever known Golda to include one of its entries in any of her speeches. She had no need to. Her own original brand of dry wit was ever-present and widely quoted.)

In her small bedroom photographs of Sarah and Menachem as children were hung on the walls, with a large framed picture of Morris Myerson on the bed table. There was also a guest room and a small kitchen.

It was in this simply furnished apartment that Golda spent most of her time when at home. But she was at home far less than she had been in any of her previous jobs, for, as the title of her Ministry implied, her territory now was the world.

She was even away on moving day. She came home from a trip to the United States to find she had been "installed"—her furniture arranged, her pictures put up, her curtains hung, her plants set out. Not as she would have done it herself. But, somehow, she never found time to redecorate.

On the night of September 28, 1956, the new Foreign Minister took a trip which, unlike her other voyages abroad, was top-secret. She did not fly on a scheduled airline, but on a French bomber of World War II vintage. There were only three other passengers: the Minister of Transport, Moshe Carmel; the Director General of the Defense Ministry Shimon Peres; and Army Chief of Staff General Moshe Dayan.

The Minister of Transport spoke fluent French and had come along in part as interpreter. However, he almost didn't make it. He opened a door to what he thought was the toilet. But it was the bomb bay, half open. He fell in.

His body dangled half in the plane, half in the night sky. Finally, with great effort, he managed to pull himself back. He said nothing of the matter when he returned, for his companions were embroiled in heated discussions concerning the forthcoming conference in Paris. It seemed hardly the appropriate time to mention his misadventures.

The conference had been called by the French Foreign Minister, Christian Pineau, who had just returned from another secret meeting in London with the British Foreign Minister. Subject: the Suez Canal.

Egypt had suddenly nationalized the Suez Canal, which was owned by a group of shareholders, primarily French and English. The Canal had been closed to Israeli ships since the first day of Israel's statehood—a fact which had never particularly troubled the French or the British. Now, however, they were mightily concerned about what might happen to *their* shipping, with Colonel Nasser directing traffic. They had, consequently, set up a joint command, under the title Operation Musketeer. Their aim: to take the Suez Canal, then force Nasser—or his successor—to internationalize it again.

Why had Golda, Dayan, and the other Israeli ministers been invited to the Paris meeting? For good reason. Indeed, for three good reasons, any or all of which might erupt into war at any moment. And, if this happened, the French and the British wanted to coordinate their "piece of the action."

The first reason was the *fedayeen*.

In a speech before the United Nations, Golda described ". . . the *fedayeen* campaign unleashed by Colonel Nasser in the summer of 1955. You know who these *fedayeen* are. They are gunmen, trained by Egyptian army officers, and recruited chiefly from among the Arab population in the Gaza stirp. . . . *Fedayeen* gangs have been planted in Jordan, Lebanon and Syria. With very heavy concentrations in the Sinai desert. These terror squads cross our borders at night with the sole objective of indiscriminately shooting or bombing any Israel house, or any man, woman, or child. The slaughter of six children and their teacher in the agricultural village of Shafrir . . . the bombing of a wedding in the Negev village of Patish—these are examples of the kind of heroic exploits so lustily applauded by Colonel Nasser. . . . The people of Israel demand the protection which every state owes its citizens; protection against wanton and indiscriminate murder which strikes not at military targets, but solely at civilians. . . ."

Before the advent of the *fedayeen* there had been other terrorists. Indeed, barely six months after the armistice agreements were signed in 1949, the Arabs began—and continued—guerrilla warfare along Israel's borders. They had dynamited schools, bridges, buses, reservoirs, railroad tracks, and irrigation pipes carrying water to the desert settlements. By now they had succeeded in seriously disrupting civilian life in Israel.

The second factor which augured war was the sudden massing of the Egyptian Army on Israel's borders—Egyptian forces armed and aided by the Soviet Union and other nations of the Soviet bloc.

The third factor was the matter of the waterways. Not only had Nasser barred Israel's ships from the Suez Canal, but he had, equally illegally, blockaded the Gulf of Aqaba so that no Israeli ships—or ships carrying Israeli goods —could enter or exit from the Red Sea, the international waterway to Africa and Asia. Unlike many of her Arab neighbors, Israel had no oil or other notable natural resources. She could, however, develop important overseas trade with agricultural produce and manufactured goods. She could—if her ships were allowed past the imprisoning Egyptian guns which seriously cut into her economy and cut off her future growth.

The guns must be removed.

These were the three-pronged dangers and dilemmas discussed by the ministers en route to Paris.

They were also, incidentally, the reasons Golda was now flying to Paris as Foreign Minister, instead of Moshe Sharett—whom she had replaced.

Sharett had been widely criticized as being "too cautious" about the Prime Minister's policy of "active defense" against the *fedayeen*. Sharett's general approach was to try to overcome obstacles by patient persuasion, whereas Golda, though no extremist, preferred to tackle obstacles by head-on attacks. And it was this direct, simple, straightforward approach which Prime Minister Ben-Gurion needed now. In these days which were becoming more critical by the hour, he needed a Foreign Minister who was with him all the way.

Coincidentally, Golda's appointment to replace Sharett came almost ten years to the day after she first filled in for him when Sharett, then head of the Jewish Agency's Political Department, was arrested by the British.

Golda's direct approach came into action at once, in the secret meeting held on Sunday morning in a Montparnasse mansion. She turned to French Foreign Minister Pineau and asked whether it was his understanding that the British planned to encourage Iraq to send troops into Jordan. If so, Golda pointed out, Israel would suddenly find itself in double jeopardy. Egypt, Jordan, Lebanon, and Syria had at least signed armistice agreements with Israel after the 1948 war. But Iraq had refused to do so. She therefore regarded herself as still at war with Israel. Consequently, any minor border flare-up could explode into war, in which combined Iraqi and Jordanian armies, aided perhaps by British forces, could descend upon Israel's northern sector where the country was less than twelve miles wide.

In his recent meeting with the British Foreign Minister, Golda asked, had Monsieur Pineau been told whether they planned to underwrite the security of Jordan and Iraq by a military guarantee?

Monsieur Pineau evaded this strategic question. He kept coming back to the subject of Nasser, whom he called a dictator, one who might one day plunge the world into war as Hitler had done.

The talks lasted through an elaborate luncheon and into the late afternoon. When they ended, the Israelis had won agreement on two vital points. The French agreed to sell more arms to Israel, in order to help equalize a situation which was now thrown so off balance by the constant supplies of weapons and planes, particularly bombers, which the Russians were giving to Egypt.

The foreign ministers also agreed on future joint consultations as events developed.

The Minister of Transport translated ably all during the session. Golda noticed, however, that he seemed rather pale and pained. It was only later that he told her about his fall through the bomb bay. He went to a doctor and discovered that he had broken three ribs.

Golda returned to Israel on October 1. She returned to find that Arab terrorists based in Jordan had increased their activities. A mother and daughter had been shot . . . a tractor driver murdered . . . three watchmen killed . . . six students murdered . . . five young Israelis slaughtered at night in the Negev . . . and four prominent Israeli archeologists killed. All within two weeks' time. One of the archeologists was well known to Golda. She had seen him last at Menachem's wedding. He was the father of the bride.

On October 9 and 10 there were more murders by Jordanian terrorists. And Israel troops moved into Jordan to demolish the terrorist police fort. Heavy fighting broke out. Jordan's King Hussein appealed to the British to send in the Royal Air Force and appealed to Iraq to send in troops.

Golda received a telephone call in the middle of the night. Britain was seriously considering sending planes to Jordan under the terms of the Anglo-Jordanian Defense Treaty. The next morning Golda was informed that Iraqi troops would start moving into Jordan on October 15, and Britain would go to the aid of Jordan and Iraq if their troops were attacked by Israeli forces.

Foreign Minister Meir issued an official statement pointing out that the entry of Iraqi units into Jordan constituted a direct threat to the territorial integrity of Israel. The government of Israel would "frustrate this hostile design."

On October 22, the Egyptians, Syrians, and Jordanians signed a military alliance, putting their armies under

Egyptian command. Their sole objective: to encircle Israel with a steel ring and then annihilate her.

It seemed inevitable that Israel must fight to prevent her own destruction. But fight whom? And when?

Foreign Minister Golda Meir was involved in crucial meetings which seemed to go on nonstop. Would Israel fight Jordan? Or would it be Jordan and Iraq, backed by Britain? Or would Israel be fighting *with* Britain against Egypt on the western front, at the same time as she was fighting *against* Britain and Jordan on the eastern front? And should Israel wait till she was attacked, her cities bombed? Or should she attack first—and risk being branded aggressor by the United Nations?

During the long tortured meetings answers were finally arrived at. But would the answers mean salvation for Israel? Or national suicide?

Since the promised quantities of French armaments had not yet arrived, the greatest weapon the Israelis had was—surprise. But could a nation be mobilized in secret?

Only a few key people in the country knew of the plans. Golda, of course, was one of them.

On a Friday morning she was driven down to Revivim. The car hurtled along the *goldene wegen* built under her auspices as Minister of Labor. Would Egyptian troops soon be traveling up these broad, convenient roads en route to Tel Aviv?

Golda was on her way to see her new grandson, Shaul, born the month she became Foreign Minister. The little boy was now six months old. Would his life be over in a few more days? If all did not go according to plan, the Egyptian Army would sweep through the Negev, and Revivim would be one of the first kibbutzim to be overrun.

If only she could on some pretext take Sarah and the children back with her to the relative safety of Jerusalem. But the thought was immediately banished. She had never asked or accepted special privileges because of her position. She would not do so now. Her children must fight—or fall—like the children of every other mother in the land.

As she sat in the sand before Sarah's one-room cabin

and played with her grandchildren, the Foreign Minister showed no hint of tension or worry. Smiling, she watched little Naomi, who was an exquisite blend of East and West: huge, dark eyes, high cheekbones, olive skin, and a flashing smile. "You'll have to watch out for this one," Golda warned Sarah. "She'll be a real heartbreaker when she grows up."

As the Foreign Minister was leaving the kibbutz, the young man in charge of Revivim's security came up to her. He had heard something about the mobilization orders. "I'm not asking any questions," he said to Golda. "But —should we dig trenches?"

"Well," Golda permitted herself to say, "if I were you, I would."

Some 200,000 Israelis were secretly mobilized in three days. The "Regular Army" was startlingly small. It consisted only of several hundred officers and an unlisted number of young draftees. All eighteen-year-old boys in the country were drafted for two and a half years, all unmarried eighteen-year-old girls for two years. The exception was Israeli Arabs, who were not drafted but could volunteer.

The rest of Israel's Army was composed of "fighting civilians." Every able-bodied man in the country served two to four weeks a year in the Active Reserves till age forty-nine. All unmarried women and childless wives were in the reserves till age thirty-four.

Also mobilized were milk trucks, intercity buses, taxis, and family cars and trucks to help transport the array of sudden-soldiers (many of whom lacked uniforms) to the front—which most thought would be Jordan.

On October 29, 1956, this motley army went to war— one of the most extraordinary wars in military annals.

Within 100 hours, the Army of Israel slashed from Sinai to the Suez Canal. They destroyed all the *fedayeen* bases. They knocked out Nasser's Sinai Army, one-third of the Egyptian Regular Army. Vast quantities of Soviet arms and equipment were either destroyed or captured. And some 4,000 Egyptian officers and men were taken prisoner. (The Egyptians captured 4 Israelis.)

The campaign to smash the blockade of the Gulf of Aqaba took longer. Two days longer. An entire Israeli infantry brigade hauled and pushed their trucks and jeeps along an impassable route—the narrow strip of rock and sand of the Sinai desert edging the Gulf of Aqaba. They captured the Egyptian fortress of Sharm el Sheikh, from which Egyptian coastal guns had blockaded the Gulf of Aqaba to Israeli ships.

There was some fierce fighting in all the campaigns, but the Israeli losses were relatively light: 172 killed, 817 wounded.

What, meanwhile, had happened to the British and French and *their* plans to regain control of the Suez Canal?

Twelve hours later than scheduled, they bombed Egyptian airfields. Eight days after the start of the Sinai Campaign, their troops landed around the Port Said area, captured the airfield, and took Port Fuad.

On that same day Golda was handed a message signed by Soviet Prime Minister Nikolai Bulganin. Israel was pointedly informed that Russia had ballistic missiles capable of reaching any specified spot on the globe. Immediately, Golda left for Paris, acompanied by Director General of the Defense Ministry Shimon Peres. They went straight to Christian Pineau at the Quai d'Orsay and asked the crucial question. What would the French do, if the Soviets intervened against Israel?

Monsieur Pineau frowned. He shrugged. He said that although France would back Israel "with everything we've got," the inescapable fact was that Russia was far more powerful than France. And Russia had the missiles. "I am sorry," said Monsieur Pineau.

Golda and Peres flew back home. As they stepped out of the plane at Lydda Airport they were greeted with further sobering news. President Eisenhower had curtly demanded that Israel stop fighting and withdraw her forces at once. He had sent the same message to England and France, replete with threatened sanctions. Britain and

France immediately accepted the American ultimatum. A mere twenty-four hours after they had landed, Anglo-French forces started withdrawing from Egypt. Control of the Suez Canal remained firmly in Colonel Nasser's hands. He was still free to blockade and boycott at will.

Israel held out longer. After an emergency Cabinet meeting, Ben-Gurion went on the radio at three o'clock in the morning. He announced to the listening, sleepless nation that "the campaign had been brought to a successful close." However, Israel insisted that she would not withdraw her troops until the United Nations stationed Emergency Forces along the Gaza Strip to prevent further *fedayeen* activities and until further UN forces were stationed at Sharm el Sheikh to ensure the passage of Israel's ships to and from her port of Eilat on the Red Sea.

The United Nations agreed. And on November 8— eleven days after the so-called Weekend War began— Israel promised to withdraw its forces from Egyptian territory "as soon as satisfactory arrangements can be made with the United Nations in connection with the United Nations Emergency Force."

The next day staged troop withdrawal started.

Several weeks later Golda flew down to the waterless, desolate Sharm el Sheikh. "It was astonishing to observe," she later reported to the United Nations, "the elaborate installations, the ammunitions depots, the airstrip, the spacious accommodations which the Egyptians had established, with the sole aim of obstructing the free passage of commerce between two parts of the high seas."

Golda also visited Gaza, a strategic strip of territory 26 miles long, 6 miles wide, its northernmost tip only 35 miles from Tel Aviv. The strip—originally part of Mandated Palestine—had been captured by Egypt during the War of '48. And during that war, some 200,000 Palestinian Arabs had fled to the strip. For eight years they had been supported by the United Nations Relief and Works Agency (UNRWA). Egypt had done nothing for the refugees or for the 95,000 local residents of Gaza, some 65,000 of whom were virtually starving and had to be supported by the Israeli government as soon as Israel's troops moved into the area.

"I went through the city," Golda reported, "and found it quiet and peaceful. I heard of what has been accomplished in the few short weeks that Gaza has been under Israel's administration. Local councils have been established in Gaza and in the other towns in the area. Educational and health services are running smoothly. Plans are being considered by our government for the development of the area in order to create employment for the tens of thousands of the Gaza inhabitants who have been idle and destitute since the Egyptian occupation. Plans for agriculture, public works and industry are already underway.

"And the Jewish settlements in the area are now experiencing for the first time a feeling of security and peace. The nightmare of years of constant shelling and shooting from across the border is becoming a thing of the past."

The United Nations sent out a special inquiry unit to Gaza. They came back and published a lengthy and enthusiastic report detailing the amazing results the Israeli government had achieved in Gaza within a few months' time.

Bending to the will of the United Nations and the United States, Israeli troops had quickly withdrawn from all the Egyptian territory they occupied with two exceptions—Sharm el Sheikh and the Gaza Strip. "These two areas," as Golda told the United Nations, "touch the question of Israel's security at its most sensitive point."

Israel wanted to make very sure that the United Nations Emergency Forces would and could see to it that the strategic strip did not once again become a base for Egypt's armed aggression against Israel. She also wanted to make very sure that the United Nations forces could guarantee freedom of passage for Israeli ships sailing in and out of the Red Sea.

Finally seventeen nations—including the United States, Great Britain, France, and Canada—banded together to guarantee that they would protect Israel's right of passage on the Red Sea.

Whereupon, on March 1, 1957, Foreign Minister Golda Meir went before the General Assembly of the United Nations. She felt deeply troubled.

In virtually every speech she had made as Foreign Minister she had spoken of Israel's desperate longing for peace. In virtually every speech she had turned to the Arab countries with a plea for friendship and cooperation. Only three months ago she had concluded a speech to the General Assembly by saying:

> "Mr. President, the countries of the Middle East are rightly listed in the category of the 'under-developed.' The standard of living, disease, illiteracy of the masses of people, the undeveloped lands, desert and swamp, all these cry out desperately for minds, hands, financial means and technical ability. Can we envisage what a state of peace between Israel and her neighbors during the past eight years would have meant for all of us? Can we try to translate fighter planes into irrigation pipes and tractors for the people in these lands? Can we, in our imagination, replace gun emplacements with schools and hospitals? The many hundreds of millions of dollars spent on armaments could surely have been put to a more constructive purpose.
>
> "Substitute cooperation between Israel and her neighbors for sterile hatred and ardor for destruction, and give life and hope and happiness to all its peoples."

Never, Golda felt, had the possibilities for peace in the area been so close as directly after the Sinai and Suez campaigns.

Had it not been for the intervention of the United States and the USSR, Nasser might have been toppled from his throne. His realization of this fact, coupled with the shattering defeat of his armies, might well have induced him to sign a treaty of peace with Israel—had the community of nations insisted that he do so!

Instead, incredibly, the community of nations had

insisted upon no such thing. Their only worry seemed to be how quickly Israel would withdraw her troops.

The brief, hopeful shock of realism Colonel Nasser had undergone was already giving way to fantasy. He was busy persuading his people that Egypt had emerged from the Sinai and Suez campaigns as a victor. Any losses they had incurred were due to the powerful Anglo-French armies, which they had roundly defeated within a few days. The fact that the United Nations was displaying such good will towards Egypt was "proof" enough to turn fiction into fact in the minds of the Egyptian people.

And *why* was the United Nations insisting with such fervor that Israel give up the two minuscule strips of land which were so vital to her safety and to her future? Israel, after all, had done more to better the lot and the life of the Arabs of Gaza in four months than Egypt had done in eight years. Indeed, it was Egypt which had acted in Gaza like a foreign conqueror. Why then this frantic world worry to get Israel out of the thirty-five mile strip? And how assured could Israel be that the United Nations Emergency Forces would actually uphold UN guarantees should Nasser decide once again to mass his armies in the Gaza Strip or to retake Sharm el Sheikh and close the Gulf of Aqaba to Israeli shipping?

Golda felt little optimism as she contemplated these questions.

But Israel had agreed to comply every step of the way with the dictates of the United Nations. And their Foreign Minister had been sent to make the statement.

She managed to erase conflict and concern from her voice as she spoke the opening words of her speech. "The Government of Israel is now in a position to announce its plans for full and prompt withdrawal from the Sharm el Sheikh area, and the Gaza Strip."

Unfortunately, as soon as the United Nations Emergency Forces replaced Israeli troops in Gaza, the Egyptian Army marched in. They immediately declared martial law, released all the *fedayeen* from prison, and announced they would punish every Arab who had "collaborated" with the Israelis during the four months' occupation. They fired every official who had not resigned when the Israelis came in. But those who merely lost their jobs were fortunate. Many Arab residents of Gaza—including the directors of health clinics, teachers, and civil servants— were dragged from their homes and murdered.

The United Nations Emergency Forces did nothing about any of this.

Golda was later to exclaim: "To stand before the United Nations and say we will withdraw—that was not my finest hour."

And, as events bore out, she had very good reason for making such a statement.

Chapter 20

It was a sultry October afternoon, exactly one year after the start of the Sinai Campaign.

Golda, sitting in the Knesset, was turning through some papers. From time to time she whispered to Ben-Gurion, who was next to her.

Suddenly came an ear-splitting explosion. And a scream.

Golda shoved Ben-Gurion to the floor. Other Cabinet members clambered under the table. But there were no more shots.

Ben-Gurion had been wounded. Moshe Shapira, the Minister of the Interior, lay groaning. Then she noticed that her leg was bleeding badly. She looked up at the balcony where bedlam had broken loose. The guards had captured someone.

She felt dazed with pain as she was carried out to an ambulance.

The next morning in the hospital she read about it. A grenade had been thrown by a madman, who had been apprehended. Fortunately, no one had been killed. The Prime Minister was expected to leave the hospital in several days. Special mention was made of the fact that the Foreign Minister had not screamed or uttered so much as a groan.

Golda was forced to remain in bed for two weeks. But two weeks in bed did not mean two weeks of rest. For she was hard at work developing what was to become the most important achievement of her Foreign Ministerial reign.

Since the Sinai Campaign the young nation knew peace and tranquillity for the first time. Aside from the shelling of settlements from the Golan Heights on the Syrian border, there were no more terrorist attacks or raids. And Israel's ships sailed, for the first time, to ports in Asia and Africa.

But Foreign Minister Meir was resolved that commerce should not be the only connecting link between her country and these two great continents.

Israel, a small, poor nation, was in the process of solving many problems which other small, poor nations were facing. "We must," said Golda, "carry out our responsibility to share the knowledge we have gained through our own economic and social development."

Thousands of Israeli experts were sent to African and Asian countries: engineers, teachers, doctors, specialists in agriculture, sanitation, port management, social welfare, irrigation, transport, conservation, cooperatives, civil administration. . . . Golda's advice to the experts going abroad was: "Tell them about the mistakes we made. So they won't repeat them." She well knew that the way in which information was imparted could be, in its own way, as important as the information itself.

And thousands of government leaders and students from Africa and Asia came to Israel to take special courses the Israelis had set up for them. Many of them came on

Israeli-funded fellowships. Some lived on and studied the
workings of kibbutzim, which they then adapted to the
needs of their own nations. Others studied the many
unique facets of Israel's national labor union. Still others
studied the successful methods Israel had used to train
thousands of unschooled immigrants in the use of advanced techniques in agriculture and industry.

Golda also set up, in a splendid new building in Haifa,
an International Center for Community Development for
Women, in which women from newly developing nations
took courses which helped them span the centuries.

Three months after she emerged from the hospital,
Golda set off for her first trip to Africa.

Her countrymen worried. Was she well enough? Golda's
popularity was unbounded. She had become a sort of
collective grandmother figure. She was almost sixty years
old. Was this any age to go sporting about amid the
steaming jungles of Africa . . . visiting tribal villages . . .
arriving at makeshift airports?

Her countrymen, however, did not know the half of it.

In Liberia, for example, Golda was made Honorary
Paramount Chief of the tribe of Gola, after which she was
admitted to the secret Zoe Society of Women. Her traveling companion, Mrs. Lou Kaddar, recalled the scene:
"Golda was taken into a little round hut made of reeds.
The hut wasn't much taller than she. Somehow twenty
women of the tribe managed to crowd in there with her.
We heard music, chanting, drums. It was the hottest day
I can remember. There were no windows in that hut. We
felt certain she'd suffocate. Golda was in there for half an
hour. Finally, she came out—in African robes—looking
radiant. As though this was the greatest day of her life.
She was the first foreigner ever to be admitted to the Zoe
Society. And since the initiation was secret she would
never tell us a word about what had gone on inside that
hut."

At a party given in Golda's honor in Ghana, the or-
chestra suddenly struck up the strains of the *horah,* Israel's
traditional folk dance. Suddenly her traveling companions

were startled to see their Foreign Minister whirling about in a circle of dancers including members of the Israeli embassy and Ghanaians who had learned the dance when they visited Israel.

In the years which followed, Golda made many trips to the newly emerging nations of Africa and Asia, including even Moslem countries in the Arab bloc. Government leaders were won by her simplicity, her sincerity, her charm. "You are like a mother to us," one African official said, when introducing her at a formal dinner. "You should change the name of your ministry," another told her, "from the Foreign Ministry to the Friendly Ministry." But perhaps the most notable tribute to her popularity were the thousands of letters she received from African and Asian mothers informing her that she had a new god-daughter whose name was Golda or Golda Meir.

The Foreign Minister also made many trips throughout South America and Europe for in her mind the most important part of her job was the establishment of better understanding with nations throughout the world. And, as far as one person could succeed in this, Golda succeeded. No matter what the official policy of the country she visited happened to be, the people she met in that country always responded with warmth and respect to Mrs. Meir. They trusted her. She was one world figure who said the same thing in public as she said in private. She became a symbol of down-to-earth honesty.

And the people of Israel stopped worrying about the health of their widely traveled grandmother as they read with pride about her journeys around the globe. Each minor happening was well reported, for, as the world's only woman foreign minister, Golda made "good copy." The following item in the Philippines *Herald* is typical of thousands of news stories written about Israel's most popular and peripatetic minister:

> *Davaoenos say that the only ray of sunshine to hit their city over the past few weeks was Israel's cheerful and tactful Foreign Minister Golda Meir. When Mrs. Meir waded ashore at the Davao airport, our citizens*

*were embarrassed by the fact that they could offer their
distinguished visitor only a waterlogged reception.*

*At a luncheon-banquet in her honor Mrs. Meir smiled
her grandmotherly smile at the assembled throng and told
her gratified listeners that they "must never apologize for
rain. In Israel we constantly pray for rain, and we greed-
ily hoard every drop of water we can get to moisten the
desert. You should be happy to have all this wonderful
rain and not complain that the sun is not shining. Back
home, we have just too much sunshine."*

*The audience roared and protocol was thrown out of
the window as Davaoenos gave Mrs. Meir a standing
ovation.*

Protocol was often "thrown out of the window" when
Israel's Foreign Minister entertained at home. There were,
of course, the required number of formal dinners, when
Golda was aided by her housekeeper and several waitresses
specially hired for the evening.

During formal dinners Her Excellency received her
guests with ease and graciousness. But there were no airs,
no affectations. Golda was simply Golda, whatever the
company, whatever the setting. Presidents, ministers, ambassadors were greeted with the same warmth and human
interest as she accorded her chauffeur. Indeed, if it came
to it, the chauffeur might receive special preference.

On one occasion, for example, Golda was entertaining
in a manner and a setting she preferred to the formal
dinners. A group of notables had been invited to tea in
her private apartment upstairs. An American diplomat was
delegated "to pour." Itzhak, Golda's Rumanian-born
chauffeur, happened in and she invited him to stay. A few
minutes later she interrupted herself in the midst of a discussion on world affairs to whisper to the American, "Give
him a white cup." She indicated the chauffeur, and she
spoke in English, which Itzhak did not understand. During
her intense political discussion, she had taken time to note
that the "good white cups" were running out. She realized
that Itzhak might feel slighted were he handed a pink
plastic household cup, whereas if one of the distinguished

guests received the plastic cup he would not regard it as a personal matter.

Perhaps the only role in which the Foreign Minister felt vaguely uncomfortable was that of "lady of the house," when it came to asking someone to do chores which she felt, as a basic kibbutznik, she should be doing herself. Consequently, she always shined her own shoes, always washed her own hair, and usually washed the dishes if she had company after the maid went home.

Often, if Madame Minister was home alone for lunch, Esther, or Yehudith the housekeeper, or Lea the cook, or all three, sat down at the kitchen table with her to eat. Since all three were union members, worked an eight-hour day, and usually departed at 3:30 in the afternoon, Golda, when she ate alone or with family or friends, would warm up the dinner Lea had prepared and later would do the washing up.

"On one occasion," Lou Kaddar recalled, "one of many, Golda had a large late-night meeting in her house. As usual, she washed up all the cups and saucers and put them away. Then she noticed that, since it had been a rainy night, the floors were streaked with mud. 'Esther' [the cleaning woman] 'left me a nice clean floor,' she said. 'I can't give it back to her like this!' So Golda got out the mop and did the floors at 2 A.M. in the morning."

In June, 1963, Ben-Gurion suddenly resigned, two years before the close of his four-year term. "The old man," as they called him, had resigned once before, in 1953. Moshe Sharett had taken over for a two-year term as Prime Minister—until B.G. decided to return. But this time it looked as though Ben-Gurion really meant it. He'd been the leader of this nation long before it was a world-recognized nation. He was in his late seventies. He was tired. He wanted to retire to his kibbutz in the Negev, to tend sheep, to study the classics, to write his memoirs.

Who would succeed him?

Israel holds a countrywide election every four years in which every citizen over eighteen may vote (and usually does). They vote not for a prime minister but for a party

and its list of candidates. There are 120 members of the
Parliament, or Knesset. And each of the many parties sends
to Parliament a number of candidates according to the
proportional share of the total national vote the party has
received. (Since one out of every ten Israelis is an Arab,
there are generally some seven Arab members of Parliament. And, though debates are carried on in Hebrew—
usually in heated Hebrew—there are simultaneous transla-
tions into Arabic.) The party which garners the most votes
in the national election selects the man it wishes to be
prime minister.

Thus far Mapai had always been the winning party, and
they now chose as Prime Minister the man B.G. had
designated: Levi Eshkol, the likable and levelheaded
Minister of Finance.

Eshkol asked Golda to remain as his Foreign Minister.
And she agreed.

But, as the 1965 elections approached, Golda let the
party chiefs know that she too would retire at the end of
the term. She too was tired. She had worked for the
government—pre-state and post—well over thirty years.
Furthermore, her health was failing. She had been hospitalized many times, for pneumonia, phlebitis, kidney stones,
cardiovascular complications, and numerous collapses from
sheer exhaustion. In addition, she was plagued by migraine
headaches which descended suddenly and with knockout
pain.

Like Ben-Gurion, she wanted time to relax and enjoy
her life. "I want time to read a book," she would say.
"Time to enjoy my grandchildren." She now had five, for
Ayah and Menachem had three handsome, bright, and
charming little boys: Ammon, age seven, Daniel, age five,
and little Gideon, age three.

Golda had a small two-story cottage on Baron Hirsch
Street in Ramat Aviv, a suburb of Tel Aviv. Menachem
and his family lived next door. She would become a full-
time *savta*—grandma—or almost full-time, for she agreed
to retain her seat in the Knesset. (For many people this
alone could be considered a full-time job.)

One of the most difficult parts about leaving the Foreign

Ministry was packing up. Her Jerusalem apartment had become a veritable museum overflowing with gifts she had received on her world travels. African statues and masks, intricate carvings of jade and ivory, figurines from the Far East, Royal Copenhagen china. Her closets were filled with keys to a worldwide assortment of cities; and honorary degrees, plaques, and scrolls abounding with high-flown tributes to "The Founding Mother of Israel" . . . "The Heroine of the Jewish Renaissance" . . . "The Modern Deborah" . . . "The Greatest Woman of Our Time."

She selected a limited number of items for her Ramat Aviv cottage. The rest she gave to museums, including a splendid collection of valuable gold necklaces and bracelets presented to her in Africa.

The morning after her official retirement, she stood in the middle of her Jerusalem apartment, surrounded by cartons and suitcases as she supervised the packing. Her chauffeur came in. Almost tearfully he begged to be allowed to serve her in Ramat Aviv.

Golda shook her head. "Not one day," she told him firmly. "I'm no longer the Foreign Minister. I'm a citizen of Israel. And like every other citizen, I will take the bus."

She did. The first bus she took was in Tel Aviv. It was a rainy day. She climbed aboard, paid her 22 agora (6 cents). The passengers suddenly became aware that the former Foreign Minister was in their midst.

"Going home?" the bus driver called to Golda.

She smiled and nodded.

Her home was several blocks from the bus stop. But she did not have to walk in the rain. The bus driver departed from his customary route and deposited Golda at her own front door.

Chapter 21

Mrs. Golda Meir, citizen of Israel, rested.

As she hung out her wash in the backyard . . . as she played with her grandsons who kept dashing in and out to visit *Savta* Golda . . . as she answered letters and read books and made plans to visit many friends she had so long neglected, Golda could reflect with some satisfaction upon the final years of her career.

She had achieved her objective of reaching "better understanding" with numerous nations around the globe. And perhaps no other foreign minister of a small country had ever faced so difficult a job—for since the day the state of Israel was declared, the Arabs had engaged in a campaign to cut the country off so far as contacts with other nations were concerned.

The Arabs permitted no communication whatever between their nations and Israel. It was even impossible to make a telephone call or mail a postcard from Jerusalem, Jordan to Jerusalem, Israel though in many sections one was merely across the street from the other.

Any foreign company which did business with Israel was blacklisted by the Arab bloc. Consequently, any businessman who decided to deal with Israel, population 2.5 million, would have to write off eighteen Arab states or sheikhdoms with a total population of some 90 million.

Cargo ships of other nations which called at Israel's ports were blacklisted by all the Arab countries. Planes which landed at Israel's Lydda Airport were not only forbidden to land at any Arab airfield but were forbidden to fly over Arab territory. Since this was an area covering some four million square miles, the stipulation proved a considerable inconvenience to those international airlines which had decided to service Israel.

The Arab nations' boycott even extended to such subtleties as banning all Elizabeth Taylor movies because the actress, when married to Eddie Fisher, had decided to adopt her husband's religion and become a Jew.

Many nations in Asia and Africa were predominately Moslem, their religion providing deep-rooted ties with the Arab countries surrounding Israel. Also, during Golda's term as Foreign Minister the newly emerging "nations of color" felt especially called upon to stick together on the international scene. Israelis were considered "white Westerners"—which again had not made Golda's job any easier. And then there were the dual weapons of Arab oil and the Suez Canal.

The Egyptians had never allowed an Israeli ship through the Suez Canal. But the Israelis circumvented this by sending their cargo through the Canal in ships of other nations. However, eighteen months after the Sinai Campaign the Egyptians blacklisted foreign vessels carrying cargo to or from Israel; frequently such cargo was confiscated. Not only had the United Nations failed to reprove Egypt for such violations, but the World Bank had promptly approved a loan of $56 million to Egypt for the improvement of the Canal. As Golda had pointed out in a speech to the Knesset, Nasser was "bound to regard this as an encouragement to him to take similar action in the future."

The Suez boycott hurt. As Golda put it: "Supposing the Philippines, or Japan, or Ceylon want to buy orange juice from us, or cement. We are not the only country in the world that produces these products. . . . What the Egyptian Government wants is to make things so difficult, so complicated, that it becomes virtually impossible for other countries to buy from us."

By the time of Golda's retirement in 1965, Israel had slid into a severe recession, replete with marked unemployment and a new set of government austerity measures. One rueful saying making the rounds was: "Let the last man leaving Lydda Airport not forget to turn off the lights."

Furthermore, there were crucial political problems. Ben-Gurion had turned against Eshkol, and formed his own party, seriously disrupting the solidarity of the Labor coalition. A new political setup might emerge which would put Mapai, the leading party, out of office.

One month after her retirement Golda was in her kitchen making coffee when a group of Mapai officials entered unannounced. They sat down. They had some hot coffee. And they asked Golda to take on the top political job of Secretary General of Mapai. They assured her she was the only person in Israel who could reunite and restore the country's confidence in the party. Who else was *applauded* when walking down the street? Golda must "stump the country," bring the Labor Party's message before the people, and reunite the nation's quarreling political factions.

Golda was thoroughly enjoying her first real relaxation in forty years. About the last thing she felt like doing was stumping the country. But she agreed it was essential to form a powerful coalition so that Israel would not be torn into internal shreds politically. She took on the job.

As Labor Minister she had visited virtually every nook and corner of the nation. But as Foreign Minister she had spent most of her time abroad or in Jerusalem and Tel Aviv. Now, as she spoke at farm settlements, in union halls, in village squares, now as she crisscrossed the country, she found verdant new woodlands where, on her last trip, there had been barren hillsides. She found networks of villages where, on her last trip, there had been empty desert. She found all the recent man-made miracles which she had read about in government papers, which she had spoken about in official speeches. Now she was seeing the country again, in closeup. She went to bed every night exhausted but inspired and excited by this land—her country—where every day men's dreams were brought to life.

While the Israelis were fighting unemployment, recession, and political upheaval, the Arabs were preparing for, as Nasser put it, "another round," which the Russians cheered on with military, diplomatic, and economic aid.

When Britain and France beat their hasty retreat from Suez in 1956, Russian rubles, Russian military experts, and Russian warships had entered the Mediterranean to fill the vacuum. The Soviets' three chief protégés were Egypt, Syria, and Iraq. Emboldened by their generous and mighty Big Brother, the Arabs' terrorist attacks across Israel's borders gradually increased. By now shells rained down almost daily from the Syrian-held Golan Heights onto Israeli settlements which lay, like sitting ducks, directly below.

On a Friday evening, for example, the kibbutzniks of Gadot were sitting in the sun on canvas beach chairs reading or playing with their children when Syrian shells exploded in their midst. The residents of Gadot raced into trenches and shelters. They were used to this. The eighty children of Gadot slept in the crowded underground shelters every night. But this attack was the worst of all. Over 350 shells exploded within thirty-five minutes. Crops were set aflame. Houses were burned. The kindergarten and two of the children's nurseries were completely destroyed.

The next day volunteers from nearby settlements moved in to help the settlers rebuild their small kibbutz. But how long could people go on living in the eye of Soviet cannon which could lob shells from a distance of twenty miles?

Two months later, Israel celebrated her nineteenth Independence Day. Chief of Staff Yitzhak Rabin stood beside Prime Minister Eshkol reviewing the troops. When the two men left the stand, Rabin told Eshkol that he had just received some news. Egyptian troops were massing on Israel's border in Sinai.

The following day Eshkol ordered a limited mobilization.

Two days later Nasser bluntly informed U Thant, Secretary General of the United Nations, that he wanted the UN Emergency Force troops removed from the Gaza Strip. Before U Thant could so much as reply, Egyptian troops were sent to reoccupy Sharm el Sheikh. And Cairo Radio's *Voice of the Arabs*—the unofficial voice of the government—proclaimed: "All Egypt is now prepared to plunge into total war which will put an end to Israel."

At 7 A.M. on the morning of May 18, Golda's alarm clock rang. She snapped it off. Immediately, like a loud echo of the alarm, the telephone rang. It was Adi Yaffe, Political Adviser to the Prime Minister. "Golda? Can you join the Cabinet meeting in the PM's office at nine this morning?" He hung up without waiting for a reply. He was obviously a man with many calls to make.

At the meeting, Prime Minister Eshkol announced that U Thant had complied with Nasser's orders. He had directed all UN Emergency Force troops to leave Gaza at once. He had also directed them to leave Sharm el Sheikh. He had done this entirely on his own, without pausing to ask for UN debate or vote on the matter—despite the fact that it was the UN Security Council which had voted to send the Emergency Force troops to the two strategic areas in the first place. Now, incredibly, the forces sent to preserve the peace were being rushed out at the very first sign that the peace was threatened!

With an almost physical stab of pain, Golda remembered the terrible doubts she had felt on the day, eleven years ago, when, as Foreign Minister, she stood before the United Nations General Assembly to announce that her government would comply with the UN directives and would return to Egypt the two strips of territory Israel had taken during the Sinai Campaign: the two strips most vital to Israel's security and her future: Gaza and Sharm el Sheikh. Now all her doubts had become realities.

But there still was hope. After all, in addition to the UN guarantees, seventeen nations had also guaranteed Israel's freedom of navigation into and out of the Red Sea.

At the early morning meeting in Eshkol's office it was decided that Foreign Minister Abba Eban should leave at once to visit the capitals of the most powerful of these guarantor nations.

Eban departed.

In Washington, London, Paris, he was told to wait, to be patient, while the guarantor nations "worked things out." De Gaulle then imposed a strict embargo on French arms to Israel. It would now be impossible for Israel even to get replacement parts for the French planes she had purchased for vast sums.

Meanwhile, on May 22, with his troops once again in Sharm el Sheikh, and with the UN troops safely out, Nasser closed the Gulf of Aqaba to Israeli ships and to ships of any nation carrying strategic materials to Israel. "If Israel wishes to threaten war," he announced to his army, "we tell her, 'You are welcome.'"

A few hours later, the United States' President Lyndon Johnson went on television to reaffirm the commitment to Israel. Johnson also proposed "an international flotilla" which would sail through the Straits of Tiran accompanying an Israeli ship. It seemed likely that Egypt would allow this colorful flotilla flying an assortment of flags to sail through to the port of Eilat and back again. But would all these international ships be on hand to chaperon each subsequent Israeli ship wanting to sail in or out of the Red Sea? The Israelis could not see much of an answer in this endeavor. Still, they were asked to wait until it was organized.

Golda was reminded of a remark she had made as Foreign Minister to the late President John F. Kennedy when he assured her: "Mrs. Meir, nothing will happen to Israel. We are committed to you."

"Mr. President," she had replied, "I believe you one hundred percent. I just want to be sure we're still there by the time you come to honor your commitment."

By May 26, Nasser had massed 80,000 troops and nearly 1,000 tanks along Israel's border in Sinai. *We are ready,* he wrote in the newspaper *Al-Ahram, to undertake total war with Israel.*

Four days later Jordan's King Hussein, grandson of King Abdullah, came to Cairo to sign a defense pact with

Nasser. An Egyptian general was put in charge of Jordan's army. And Iraqi troops and pilots were sent to Jordan. "This is the day of the battle and of revenge," the Iraqi President told his troops. "We will meet in Tel Aviv and Haifa."

And Nasser announced, "The armies of Egypt, Jordan, Syria, and Lebanon are stationed on the borders of Israel. . . . Behind them stand the armies of Iraq, Algeria, Kuwait, Sudan, and the whole of her Arab nation. . . . The Arabs are ready for the fray. The hour of decision has arrived."

On June 1, the President of Iraq summed it up simply: "The clear aim is to wipe Israel off the map."

Perhaps the seventeen "guarantor nations" did not believe these threats. They were still talking futilely about the flotilla.

But the Israelis believed the Arab threats. They had no reason not to. Every day dire warnings came charging over the radio in ever-mounting intensity. Israelis were warned they would soon be hacked to pieces. Dayan was warned, "We are coming to put out your other eye." The gruesome manner in which Eshkol would meet death was described in vivid detail.

Day by day tension increased. And day by day mobilization increased. Soon the city of Tel Aviv, which ordinarily pulsed with life and bright lights and traffic, was eerily empty and quiet. It seemed a city populated only by old people, women, and children.

Schools were closed so that youngsters could fill in for mailmen and merchants who had been mobilized. They helped housewives dig trenches in backyards. They filled sandbags. And they dug trenches in the parks. Civil defense officials in Tel Aviv were told to prepare for 40,000 deaths.

In the government there were, again, virtually nonstop meetings. And Golda attended most of them. Again the agonizing questions were posed: What should Israel do? The flotilla idea had by now fallen flat. Yet none of the guarantor nations had come up with any other plan. All they seemed prepared to do was to ask Israel to wait. To wait for what? For more thousands of troops and tanks to be massed on all her borders? How long *could* she wait? Most of her able-bodied men under fifty were mobilized by now. How long can a small country function without its men?

Between all the meetings, Golda—like other mothers and grandmothers throughout the nation—made worried telephone calls to friends and relatives.

Her daughter-in-law, Ayah, recalled, "She would telephone to ask, 'Have you got the ditches dug? Have you filled the sandbags? Have you rehearsed the children in running to the shelter?' I never in my life," said Ayah, "saw such tension as we knew in Israel during those days. The feeling was that Nasser was preparing a great massacre. The hospitals in Tel Aviv had thousands of additional beds ready—in the corridors, in the cellars. The tension became unbearable."

Chapter 22

Early on Monday morning the fifth of June, 1967, Israel went to war. But virtually no one in the country— Golda included—knew what was going on. The newly appointed Minister of Defense, Moshe Dayan, hero of the Sinai Campaign, had learned many lessons during that campaign. One was that the Egyptian leaders, unable to trust the glorified reports of their own commanders, had tuned in to Kol Israel, the Israeli radio station, to learn what was happening on the battlefields. This time, Dayan determined, he would offer no such services to the enemy.

Consequently, Kol Israel played music throughout most of the day, interspersed with such brief announcements as: "Battles in the southern sector . . . still going on. The next newscast will be at 10 A.M. Be calm."

Radio Cairo, however, was full of announcements. The Egyptians were bombing Tel Aviv . . . Jerusalem . . . Attacking by land and by sea. Fantastic victories were described.

On the morning of June 5, Prime Minister Eshkol sent a message to Jordan's King Hussein through the United Nations' General Odd Bull. *We shall not initiate any action whatsoever against Jordan. However, should Jordan open hostilities we shall react with all our might. And he [Hussein] will have to bear the full responsibilities for all the consequences.*

General Bull delivered this message. But the King received another message that morning. From Nasser. *I have destroyed seventy-five percent of the Israel Air Force.* Nasser urged Jordan to enter the war.

King Hussein promptly gave his answer—by shelling the area around Israel's Hadassah-Hebrew University Medical Center. By noon Jordan had launched a full-scale offensive against Israel's settlements along the entire West Bank, and against Jewish Jerusalem.

A United Nations Security Council Emergency Session was called. The Russians were silent. No one asked for a cease-fire. The meeting was adjourned after five minutes.

That evening—at 9 P.M.—a press conference was called in Tel Aviv. The journalists gathered. But no one came to announce anything.

Finally, at 1:30 A.M., Army Chief of Staff Yitzhak Rabin and Commander of the Air Force Mordechai Hod arrived at the press conference. They reported that in the space of three hours, the Israeli Air Force had wiped out almost the entire Egyptian Air Force which was far superior to the Israeli Air Force in the number of its planes and airfields. In addition, most of the Egyptian airfields had been put out of action.

Israel had lost 19 of her planes. She had destroyed over

300 Egyptian planes and, during the course of the day, over 100 Jordanian, Iraqi, and Syrian aircraft.

It seemed to Israelis as though a miracle had come to pass. Yet, they knew they would need a few more miracles. The tremendous military might which Nasser had massed along the Egyptian-Israeli border had somehow to be smashed. The Jordanians and Syrians were dangerous. But the Egyptian threat was deadly.

Israel was fighting for her life. And for the next five days Golda was among the first of the nation's leaders to be apprised of the battles.

General Israel Tal's men fought the first strategic battle. Golda read the general's report: *My men knew that on this battle depended the outcome of the war—possibly the fate of Israel. More than ten years had passed since we had last clashed with the Egyptians. We could not tell what effect the Russian training, the modern Russian equipment, and the new morale of the Egyptian army would have on their fighting capacity. We knew that we would be fighting forces whose equipment was superior both in quality and quantity to our own. For its size the Egyptian army is probably the richest in the world, after the U.S. army.*

In the first day of fierce fighting General Tal's men cut off the Gaza Strip, trapping the Egyptian troops who were there. One of the towns the Israelis took was Rafiah, at the southern end of the strip. Egyptian prisoners later complained that the Israelis had not played fair, since the Egyptians were expecting them to come from the north instead of sneaking up from behind in the south.

Then General Tal's men and other Israeli troops under the overall command of the soft-spoken, gentle General Yeshayahu Gavish, fought their way through the first line of Egyptian fortifications. Gavish's three general objectives: to break through Egyptian fortifications, to encircle and destroy large sections of Egyptian armor, and to press on across the scorching desert toward the Suez Canal.

The troops had arrived at the desert in tanks, half-trucks, jeeps—and in city buses, station wagons, milk wagons, delivery trucks, laundry vans, ice-cream trucks.

Israeli children had been told to cover these vehicles with mud. "Not for camouflage," said General Ariel Sharon, "but to make them look a little military." However, the mud fell off in the baking sun, and the motley array of vehicles entered the war in their work-a-day colors.

By dawn on Friday Israeli forces had reached the Suez Canal.

The UN immediately called for a cease-fire. Egypt agreed. And, after four days of desperate battles, the war on the Egyptian front was over.

Israel's forces had gained control of the Sinai Peninsula, the Gaza Strip, the Suez Canal and Sharm el Sheikh.

But, on her western borders, Israel was still engaged in momentous battles with Syria and Jordan. The most impossible of the objectives was the Golan Heights. Golda was at the all-night Cabinet meeting at which a delegation from the kibbutzim and other settlements pleaded: "We can no longer live the way we have lived for nineteen years. . . . We can no longer work in our fields and be shelled. . . . If you can't send the army up the Heights, we'll go up ourselves." They also mentioned a television program they had watched that day, beamed from Damascus. They had seen Syrians murder two captured Israeli pilots and hack up their bodies.

At 4 A.M. on Friday morning, the Israeli forces started up the Golan Heights. Some of the rocky hills soared up almost a mile high. Bulldozers went first, clearing a rough path for the tanks and tractors which then lumbered upward, sometimes almost on their sides. They were slow, easy targets, and one by one they were shelled by the Syrians. The Israelis jumped out of their burning tanks and kept on shooting upward until they ran out of ammunition or were killed. It was a suicide mission. When their officers were killed, the soldiers clambered on, even without orders, crouching, running, scrambling on hands and knees. As the Syrians in their concrete bunkers blasted away, the Israelis kept coming. They had an invisible secret weapon—Golda had named it during the War of Independence. *Ein brera*. No alternative. Each Israeli was fighting for the survival of his own home and his own homeland. It was a weapon the Arabs lacked. It was a weapon which helped the Israeli soldiers scale the Golan Heights and rout the Syrian Army.

The Israelis then discovered that the Syrians had built themselves three solid lines of concrete bunkers with walls five feet thick, sunk into the cliffs. These virtually indestructible bunkers had underground labyrinths replete with large dormitories, separate officers' quarters, supply rooms of ammunition, sensitive communications equipment, and carved slits in the walls through which Syrian soldiers could keep constant watch on the tiny Israeli settlements in the valley below—the settlements which had stubbornly stuck it out year after year, despite the constant shelling.

The Israeli commander looked through the slits. Then he sent a message down to the kibbutzim, *Only from this height can I see how big you are.*

On the Sabbath afternoon of June 10, another message went out to the people in the settlements below. *No blackout tonight. The Heights of Golan are ours.* And that Saturday night the children slept in their beds above the ground.

The most unexpected battles in the war were fought in Jerusalem. Israeli intelligence had reported that, whereas the Arabs planned a holocaust in Haifa and Tel Aviv, the Holy City of Jerusalem would not be attacked. Like Paris and Rome in World War II, it would remain an open city.

Instead, through the first two days of the war, Jordanian troops of the crack Arab Legion sat safe in their strongly fortified position on the Old City wall and blanketed Jewish Jerusalem with tens of thousands of mortar bombs and a steady rain of machine-gun fire. Over 500 civilians on their way to shops or offices were rushed instead on stretchers to hospitals. Over 900 apartment buildings were shelled. The Hebrew University, the Israel Museum, and numerous other public buildings were damaged. The Knesset, however, was not hit. The government held its customary session, after which all the leaders moved to Tel Aviv for the duration.

That night the air-raid sirens wailed in Tel Aviv. Golda, Ayah, and her three little boys hurried to the air-raid shelter—the cellar of one of the larger apartment buildings up the street. Ayah later recalled: "We had mattresses, chairs, pillows in the shelter. And fresh water. We brought along crackers and cheese. Golda sat up all night on a kitchen chair. She exuded calmness. She was like the mother of us all."

By Tuesday Israeli troops had taken the offensive in Jerusalem. The Israeli High Command gave orders that buildings and sites holy to the three religions should not be damaged. The orders were obeyed, though the Israeli army sustained heavy casualties because it refrained from artillery attack or bombing, and instead captured the Old City in hand-to-hand street fighting.

Golda read a dispatch sent by Colonel Mordechai Gur. *The fighting was of a sort I had never experienced both as to intensity and duration. We had to penetrate fortifications of nineteen years. We had to break through five fences of barbed wire, kilometers of underground tunnels, kilometers of trenches, hundreds of bunkers.*

The fighting raged on—the fiercest hand-to-hand fighting of the war—from room to room, cellar to cellar, rooftop to rooftop, and through the ancient twisting alleys of the Old City. It was early on Wednesday afternoon that Colonel Gur's men reached the Western Wall. This was the last remnant of the Holy Temple which had been rebuilt by King Herod in 63 B.C., rebuilt on the site of the magnificent Holy Temple constructed by King Solomon, son of King David, who had founded the Jewish city of Jerusalem around 1000 B.C.

Throughout the centuries of their dispersion, the Western Wall had been the holiest place on earth to the Jews of the world. They had often called it the Wailing Wall, for the story was that the dew which formed on the massive stone blocks was tears wept by the wall for the Jews who had been driven from their capital city of Jerusalem.

For the past nineteen years no Jews had been permitted to worship at the Western Wall, for it was situated in Jerusalem, Jordan. But now the blue and white Jewish flag was raised over the sacred wall. And by the end of that day, for the first time in nineteen centuries, the whole of Jerusalem was under Jewish control.

On the fifth day of the Six-Day War, Golda left for the United States to fulfill speaking engagements made many months ago, engagements which, it was hoped, would result in essential money for the nation which once again was fighting for its survival—and paying heavily for the fight.

On her way to the airport Golda made a long detour—to Jerusalem. To the Western Wall.

Golda had sometimes been criticized for crying. There were those who felt it was highly unseemly for a high-ranking government personage to be seen weeping. Perhaps it was for this reason that she always shied away from speaking of her personal emotions.

It was Lou Kaddar who reported on Golda's visit to the Western Wall that Friday morning.

"Look, she just cried."

For a long moment Lou Kaddar said nothing more. Then she went on. "She was recognized by a bunch of soldiers who were dirty and dead tired and they cried with her."

Chapter 23

By the time Golda's plane put down at Kennedy Airport, the war was over. It had lasted six days. In one of the swiftest and most shattering feats in all of military history, Israel had overcome three heavily armed nations and was now almost four times her former size.

She controlled the territories most strategic to her future security: the Golan Heights, the Gaza Strip, and Sharm el Sheikh on the Red Sea. And she controlled the territory most strategic to the heart and soul of the nation: Jerusalem.

In addition, she occupied all of the Sinai Peninsula to the Suez Canal and all of the West Bank to the Jordan River.

Golda was driven straight from the airport to Madison Square Garden, where she was scheduled to speak. Her plane had been delayed; she had no time to stop at the hotel to freshen up. As she stood before the huge audience of 18,000, it was obvious that she had not even paused to comb her hair, for stray graying wisps escaped from the usually neat bun she wore at the back.

Her voice was strong, her tone somber. She did not reflect in any way the ecstatic ebullience of her audience.

"Again, we won a war—the third in a very short history of independence. The last thing Israelis want is to win wars. We want peace."

She spoke, as usual, without notes. She did not need them.

191

"Our boys did not fight for territorial expansion. They were not sent to battle like the Egyptian soldiers in a holy war to destroy and annihilate. They were sent by a government ready at any moment for cooperation with its neighbors so that people should *live*."

She spoke of the agreements broken by the United Nations and by the Egyptians in Gaza, in Sinai, in Sharm el Sheikh. And she spoke of her visit to the Western Wall. "Paratroopers in uniform put down their guns and stood before the wall, kissing its stones. They wept . . . because they stood again in this holy place as Israelis in Jerusalem." She did not mention her own tears.

Then she surprised her audience, and she shocked many of them, by prognosticating with bitterness about the immediate future, when Israel's friends as well as her enemies would demand that she retreat at once to her former borders.

"A wonderful people these Israelis! They win wars every ten years whatever the odds. And they have done it again. Fantastic! Now that they have won this round, let them go back where they came from so that Syrian gunners on the Golan Heights can again shoot into the kibbutzim, so that Jordanian Legionnaires on the towers of the Old City can again shell at will, so that the Gaza Strip can again be a nest for terrorists, so that the Sinai Desert can again become the staging ground for Nasser's divisions.

"Is there anybody who can honestly bid the Israelis to go home before a real peace? Is there anyone who dares us to begin training our ten-year-olds for the next war?"

Throughout the vast stretches of Madison Square Garden the word *"No . . . NO!"* rose in a swelling wave.

Golda nodded. "You say no. I am sure that every fairminded person in the world will say no. But, forgive my impertinence, most important of all—the Israelis say no!"

She made more speeches in more halls in more states. Then she went home. Her original job, that of reuniting the Labor Party, still had to be completed.

Six months later, on January 21, 1968, she was able to

announce the birth of a new coalition to be called the Israel Labor Party. And she was promptly elected Secretary General of this new party.

The formation of the new party barely rated an inch of news space outside of Israel. But within the country it was recognized as an essential and strategic achievement.

It had not been accomplished, of course, without considerable opposition. But even Golda's most ardent opponents seemed to regard her, in the main, with a high degree of wry tolerance. As one of them put it. "She comes clumping along with that sad, suffering face drawn with pain from her varicose veins and God knows what-all. You rush to help her to your seat. She thanks you kindly. And the next thing you know you're dead."

Six months after the birth of the new party, Golda announced that now, at the age of seventy, she would retire. For good. It was high time to relax and enjoy a private life.

"It's this little book that kills her," said Golda's personal assistant, Lou Kaddar, as she held up a fat, green, government-issued appointment book. "That's what she wanted to be rid of. She wanted to know that when she got up in the morning, her day would not be directed by this book. She wanted to be free to go to concerts and museums. To accept invitations to marriages and bar mitzvahs. She's very gregarious. She loves people. And she wanted to put some order into her papers. She has the most fascinating things stuffed away into drawers. She wanted to travel in the country. To stay at kibbutzim. To visit friends. She wanted not to be always hurried. She wanted to be able to sleep late in the mornings without feeling guilty. And she wanted, above all, to spend more time with her children and her grandchildren."

All those things Golda did. Friends—and political enemies—watched, waiting. She could not survive, they predicted, without politics. Without participating.

But Golda survived very well. Indeed, she reveled in her retirement.

Then, abruptly, eight months later, at 10 A.M. on February 26, 1969, it all came to an end.

Golda was in a car driving to Tel Aviv when she heard a news report on the radio. Prime Minister Levi Eshkol had just died of a sudden heart attack.

Immediately, Golda reversed her direction and drove to Jerusalem. She was one of the first to arrive at the Prime Minister's residence; one of the first to embrace and to comfort Eshkol's young widow.

A recent poll had been taken in the nation. Israelis were asked who they thought would become the next prime minister. Three percent had put down Golda Meir, who was deep in retirement at the time. Highest on the poll was Defense Minister Moshe Dayan. Deputy Prime Minister Yigal Allon had also received a substantial number of votes.

The regular national election would be held in October. In the meantime, because of Eshkol's sudden death, it was necessary for the leading party to appoint an interim prime minister who would serve until the elections were held.

Six members of the Party Bureau of the Labor Party met day and night. It seemed obvious that, come election time, the two chief contenders for the seat-of-power post would be Dayan and Allon. It was decided to postpone the showdown between these two brilliant men until the normal election time. Meanwhile, a dark horse compromise candidate would fill in to run the nation for the next nine months.

What better compromise candidate than Golda, who had recently succeeded in the difficult job of forming a coalition party based on compromises? "I don't see why we have to quarrel among ourselves," she had proclaimed tartly. "As long as the Arabs are still at war with us, I am opposed to a Jewish war!"

Perfect views for an interim prime minister to hold.

Golda was consequently proposed. The idea was met with some astonishment and some no-holds-barred opposition. The country, it was claimed, needed something more than a sick old grandmother. And Golda had indeed been very ill, very recently. One newspaper even went so far as to publish a medical report detailing how many times she had been hospitalized over the past years and why. There was also religious opposition, particularly from Agudat Israel, a party whose members adhere to the religious law counseling Jewish men not to so much as shake hands with a strange woman.

There was someone else who opposed the proposal. Golda herself. She *was* retired. She *was* seventy. She was *not* seeking to reenter the political fray; especially not in the most momentous job of all: prime minister.

But the Party Bureau persisted. They insisted that she was the ideal interim candidate. Her country needed her. She *must* agree.

Once again, though with some reluctance, Golda heeded this call. And accepted.

The Party Bureau then put their proposed candidate up before the Party Secretariat, which met to vote on the matter. There were forty votes in favor of Mrs. Meir. None against. And seven abstentions.

The press reported to the populace: *Her selection as interim premier postpones a showdown in Israel's leadership until the October 28th elections.*

Golda took over full of "awe, and trepidation and endless doubts." The nation fully reflected her feelings.

The country was faced with problems Israel had never even envisioned. For example, there were now one million Arabs in the territories Israel had occupied during the Six-Day War. Since there were only 2,841,000 Israelis (including 406,000 Israeli Arabs) this meant that over one out of every four people in the Prime Minister's domain had—for the past twenty-one years or, in many cases, for their entire lifetime—been fed an unremitting diet of hatred for Israelis.

The week Golda was sworn in as interim Prime Minister, Arab *fedayeen* commands had enlisted the aid of Arabs in the Occupied Territories—who had blown up a supermarket, exploded a bomb in the cafeteria of the Hebrew University, and hurled a grenade into an Israeli bank. The day after she was sworn in, a five-hour shelling duel erupted on the Suez Canal. The Arab press was filled with derisive cartoons and epithets about the new Israeli

Prime Minister. The least objectionable of the names they called her was Golda Lox.

Could Golda cope? No one seemed to have an abundance of confidence in the interim Prime Minister. Including the lady herself.

After her inauguration, Golda said, "I have always carried out the missions the state placed on me, but they have always been accompanied by a feeling of terror. The terror exists now."

The statement was understandable—but somewhat disconcerting to a nation in need of a strong and powerful leader.

Soon, however, it became evident—even to her most ardent opponents—that the nation *had* a strong and powerful leader. Golda continued the policies of the Eshkol government, but with more decisiveness than her predecessor had shown.

Furthermore, though Golda had accepted the job of Prime Minister with tears in her eyes, saying, "I did not want this heavy responsibility," it seemed that she now was thriving in the role. Though she had recently been very ill, doctors now reported that her health had never been better. As to her age, Golda remarked tartly: "Seventy is not a sin!"

And when a correspondent inquired as to which of the two men, Allon or Dayan, she thought would become Prime Minister in the October elections her brows went up as she exclaimed, "Oh, I didn't know there was a time limit on *my* term in office!"

Within a matter of weeks Golda had won the complete confidence of the nation by her unique combination of qualities, which, in her role as Prime Minister, were able to come to full fruition. Not only did she have tremendous skill at negotiation, coupled with a realistic understanding of when and how to compromise. But she had, at the same time, a striking capacity for firm and resolute decision-making and action.

As one correspondent reported, "She runs her Cabinet like a front-line officer, thumping the table for order, and making blunt and rapid decisions."

"She listens to everyone," an aide said, "but she interrupts if they ramble. She has an open mind, but it's like arguing before a judge. When she makes a decision, it's made."

Her political adviser, Simcha Dinitz, summed up her most unique combinations of leadership attributes in these words: "She has the best qualities of a woman—intuition, insight, sensitivity, compassion—plus the best qualities of a man—strength, determination, practicality, purposefulness. So we're lucky. We have double qualities—in one person."

Two further incidents concerning Mr. Dinitz illustrate a few of these qualities "in action."

When Golda had been appointed Foreign Minister, she looked around for an assistant to run her office. Someone recommended Dinitz, who was at the time running the Director General's office. Golda phoned the Director General to ask about Simcha. Said the Director General, "Why do you need Simcha? There's a fellow coming from one of our embassies abroad. He's very good."

"Do you like him?" said Golda.

"Oh, *very* much!" said the Director General with high enthusiasm.

"Then," said Golda, "*you* take him! I'll take Simcha."

Later, Simcha Dinitz recalled his first meeting with Golda. "She was always, to me, an ominous-looking woman. I was scared stiff when I went to the first interview. Golda said, 'Why do you want to work with me?' I told her, 'I don't!' 'When can you start?' said Golda."

A genuine affection developed between them during the years they worked together. "She's very human," said Simcha. "And she has a tremendous sense of humor. To me," he added, with something of a twinkle, "the greatest sense of humor is being able to appreciate someone else's sense of humor. Which she does! If I can't relax with someone, I can't work with them. But we—well"—he shrugged and smiled—"we have a real rapport."

When Golda retired as Foreign Minister, Simcha went on to another government department. And when she was asked to become Prime Minister, he was in Washington.

"I'd been in the States a year," said Dinitz. "I'd rented a house. My kids were in school. I felt I'd just gotten set up. Then one day I got a letter from Lou Kaddar. The letter said, *The Boss wants very much for you to come. Why do I think she wants? Because she told me so. But she also told me not to tell you.*

"I wrote back, *Tell the Boss I'll be in Israel in a few weeks on vacation and I'll come to the kitchen and we'll discuss it.* So I came in two weeks and I said to the boss, 'Look, it's very nice of you, all these exercises in politeness. But why?'

"Golda said, 'I thought maybe it would be an imposition on you. Just when you're all settled in over there.' Then she smiled. 'When do you think you can come?' "

After he had recounted this brief tale, Simcha Dinitz said, "I appreciated it. Her delicateness. Her thoughtfulness. She's like that."

Dinitz' remark, "I'll come to her kitchen and we'll discuss it," reflected the fact that he well knew Golda would remain Golda though she now had become the most important woman in the world. And—historically speaking—one of the three women to head the Jewish state in the 2,000 years Jews had ruled in the Holy Land.

"Decisions cooked in Golda's kitchen" had been a byword ever since her Labor ministerial days. Numerous conferences at the highest level were held with the participants seated on high-backed kitchen chairs, and Golda getting up every so often to make sandwiches and tea or coffee.

There were many conferences. These involved all the normal affairs in running a nation: affairs which keep the leader of any "normal" nation fully occupied, full time. In addition, there were all the unpredictable, ever-present crises arising from the fact that the country was surrounded by enemies, all of whom abided by the politics they had officially adopted at the Arabs' Khartoum Conference in September, 1967. *No peace with Israel, no recognition of Israel, no negotiations with Israel.*

For example, in a single week in August, 1969, the Prime Minister was forced to deal with the following "extra-curricular" crises: a fire in Jerusalem's Al Aksa Mosque which nearly incited a severe Arab riot (until it was proved that the fire had been set—not by Jews, as the Arabs claimed—but by an insane Christian tourist from Australia) . . . a major rocket attack on Jerusalem . . . the hijacking of a TWA aircraft over Israel by Arab terrorists . . . a steady increase of border incursions by Arab guerrilla bands . . . And the mass public execution of nine innocent Iraqi Jews, whose bodies were left hanging in the crowded Liberation Square, each with a sign on it: "Jew."

Although Egypt alone had lost two and a half billion dollars' worth of planes, tanks, missiles, and munitions during the Six-Day War, by September, 1969, she had been fully reequipped by Russia—including, this time, super-dangerous surface-to-air missiles, nicknamed SAM's, or—more specifically—SAM-2's.

Egypt had received most of the replacements free of charge. A small percent was to be paid for in Egyptian cotton or by low-interest, long-term loans—which would effectively keep the country in the Soviet's long-term economic grip.

Israel's arms came almost exclusively from the United States. But she had to pay for each item in full either on delivery or on a high-interest "installment plan." This was a drastic drain on her treasury. Forty percent of Israel's total national budget was now allocated for defense spending, and the effect was felt by every man, woman, and child. Thousands of children stood on street corners after school shaking little boxes which said, in Hebrew, *Pennies for Phantoms*—for the fifty Phantom jets the United States had agreed to sell Israel cost some $3,500,000 each. Israel had had no direct gifts of U.S. aid, military or otherwise, since the early 1960's.

On the other hand, in its attempt to pursue a policy of neutrality, the United States had given direct gifts of military equipment and other forms of economic aid to numerous Arab nations. For example, hundreds of thousands of dollars had been given by the United States to Jordan in an attempt to keep King Hussein propped up on his rather shaky throne. (Hussein's chief military op-

ponents, the Palestinian terrorists, were being backed by
the Russians and the Red Chinese. Consequently, during
the Six-Day War, Israel—a country smaller than the state
of New Hampshire—had found herself a sudden arena for
the world's great powers. To the west, Israeli troops were
met by Russian-made tanks. But in Jordan, Israeli troops
were fired upon by tanks made in the U.S.A. Meanwhile,
terrorist groups from all sides were busy firing in grenades
and missiles made in China.)

Ever since interim Prime Minister Meir had opened the
summer session of the Knesset on May 5, 1969, the shelling and terrorist attacks from Israel's Arab neighbors had
mounted in severity. As Golda put it, two months later,
"Thousands of shells have been lobbed across the lines at
Israel Defense Forces' positions as well as at peaceful villages and at farmers working in the fields. There can be no
doubt as to who initiated the firing. Witness thereto are
the reports of the U.N. observers along the Suez Canal,
who have determined the true facts . . . We shall act along
the cease-fire lines on the basis of reciprocity. Anybody
who fails to honor the cease-fire agreement and shoots at
us cannot claim immunity from the results of his aggression. Those who attack us should not be surprised if they
are hit sevenfold in response, since our main purpose in
retaliating is self-defense and deterrence. Once again I
wish to declare that Israel desires that the cease-fire arrangements be complied with fully, but he who violates
them should not expect Israel to stand idly by."

The new, sophisticated Russian-made missiles—SAM-2's
—were, however, making it increasingly difficult for Israel's Air Force to retaliate. These missiles did not require
any great degree of accuracy on the part of Egyptian anti-
aircraft crews, since the missiles were designed to pursue
a flying plane, home in on it, and explode it in midair.

Only Israeli planes which flew dangerously low could
escape the dreaded SAM-2's. In addition, Egypt kept up
almost constant shelling of Israeli defensive positions along
the Suez Canal.

In September, 1969, shortly after a pro-Nasser regime
came to power in oil-rich Libya, Nasser made a further

announcement: "We can now wage a hundred-year War of Attrition against Israel. We have an inexhaustible supply of manpower for protracted conflict. With Libya and the Sudan we have privileged sanctuaries for our aircraft. And with Libya alone we have the resources to pay for the effort."

During the six-month period Golda had been in office, 73 Israeli soldiers and airmen had been killed and 255 wounded by the Egyptians. As an Israeli Cabinet member put it: "For Israel to lose twenty men is comparable, in population ratio, to the U.S. losing eighteen hundred men in Vietnam."

Golda put it another way: "In Israel, we do not hide facts. Each military death is recorded. Each one who falls defending the country—his story is told, his picture is in the daily press. We count each one. And each sorrow is not only of the mother, but of all mothers, of everybody in the country. They're everybody's sons."

This was not merely the political jargon of a Prime Minister.

According to Golda's close political adviser Simcha Dinitz: "When Mrs. Meir knew soldiers were going out on a military operation, she would say, 'Phone me when the boys come home.' I'd be called by the army—and then I'd call Golda—at two, three or four in the morning. She always answered at the first ring. At such times she never slept."

Meanwhile, as the military noose was once again tightening, the powerful Arab lobbies and propaganda forces in the United States had begun to pay off. As Golda had predicted in her Madison Square Garden speech directly after the Six-Day War, some of Israel's friends had now joined her enemies in insisting that she now give back the territories she had occupied during that war.

Golda felt strongly—as did virtually every Israeli—that the Occupied Territories were the best "weapon" the country had; they would be a weapon aimed not at war, but at peace.

As she had said time and again, and again, Israel was

not interested in acquiring territory. Before the Six-Day War 60 to 70 percent of the Israeli population was within range of Arab guns. After the war this had been reduced to 10 percent. Before the war the Knesset and the Prime Minister's Office—the buildings in which most of Israel's top leaders met most often—were within one mile of Jordanian guns. Now the Knesset was beyond the range of Jordan's heavy artillery. Before the war Tel Aviv had a two-minute warning time in case of Egyptian air attack. Now she had twenty minutes. Before the war there had always been the danger that the narrow-waisted country would be cut in half at its 10-mile width near Tel Aviv. Now she had lost her waistline. The western border had been stretched some 50 miles, straightened, and now ran along a natural boundary, the Jordan River.

But despite all this, Israel insisted she had no interest in keeping the territories she held, with a few strategic exceptions such as Sharm el Sheikh, the Gaza Strip, the Golan Heights. And, of course, unified Jerusalem.

What Israel *did* want, had wanted desperately, since the first day of her existence, was peace with her neighbors. And secure, defensible, and recognized borders.

This could come about only if the Arabs agreed to sit down with the Israelis for peace talks. The Arabs certainly did not seem disposed to do this, even after losing three wars. But at least the prospect of getting back their vast captured territories might eventually offer them some incentive to sit down and talk. If the territories were obligingly given back—as they had been, to the last square inch after the Sinai Campaign—the incentives for sitting down would evaporate. As would any remote chance for peace.

In October, 1969, with tension running high in the country and munitions and morale running low, Golda decided to make a trip to her former homeland, the U.S.A.

She would go with, as she put it, a "shopping list," which included twenty-five more Phantom jets and eighty A-4 Skyhawks. These planes were now more essential than ever, for three days before the Six-Day War France had embargoed all military sales to Israel. This included delivery of 50 Mirage fighter-bombers, for which Israel had already paid in full.

The United States, it seemed, was the only ally the tiny nation had left. But how staunch an ally?

This was the second essential purpose of Golda's trip. She would do what she could to present to the U.S. public Israel's problems and point of view.

Chapter 24

Madame Prime Minister Meir was well received.
Nixon. There was an elaborate formal dinner at the White
In Washington, D.C., she was met with full military honors, a nineteen-gun salute, and a smiling President House (with Golda garbed, for a change, in a long evening dress, but wearing—as usual—not one whit of makeup). There was a meeting with the Secretary of Defense, two meetings with the Secretary of State, a session with 60 Senators on Capitol Hill, and two private meetings with President Richard Nixon.

Golda asked not only for the planes but also for a reduction of the seven percent interest on the Phantoms Israel had already bought. And for loans including $400 million worth of U.S. credit in the years ahead.

Golda made it quite clear that *all* her country wanted was the opportunity to purchase U.S. planes and munitions. Israel had never asked for a single soldier of any other land to help her in her fight. Nor did she ever plan to.

Israel had, furthermore, important collateral to offer.

If, for example, the nation of Israel were destroyed, Russia would take over control of the oil-producing Arab countries upon which the economy of Western Europe was dependent. (The United States gets only five percent of her oil from the Middle East.)

If Israel fulfilled the Arab dream and disappeared off the map, Russia would soon have both military and economic control in the Middle East. Syria and Iraq were already within the Russian sphere of influence. As for Egypt, Golda put it this way: "Nasser was very proud that he chased the British out of Egypt. Now he's opened the door wide to the Russians. And we have yet to see a country where the Russians came in—and *left!*"

If President Nixon made any promises to Prime Minister Meir they were not officially announced. But Nixon, thereafter, spoke far less about his "policy of an even-handed approach" to the Middle East.

A Washington correspondent summed up Golda's effect on U.S. leaders: *She demonstrated the qualities that statesmen dream of in a beleaguered ally: she was resolute but not belligerent, uncompromising but not overbearing, and all she asked was arms for self-defense.*

In New York, Golda was given one of the largest catered dinners ever served by the city—with a guest list of 1,200. The elaborate event was held in the huge Grand Hall of the Brooklyn Museum against a background of ancient Egyptian antiques, and valuable paintings. "I promise not to stand in front of any work of art," Golda assured the museum curator, "in case I get shot."

In Philadelphia, the Prime Minister was met at the airport by the Mayor, who kissed her as she stepped off the plane. Menachem and his family were temporarily in the States, and Golda's eight-year-old grandson was among those in the waiting crowd. "It's not very nice of Grandma," he commented flatly, "to kiss a man she doesn't know!"

Golda stayed in the States for ten days. But the stop she enjoyed most was Milwaukee, where she returned to her old elementary school. The students—all of whom were now black—greeted her with high enthusiasm. They wore handmade headbands decorated with the Star of David. They waved Israeli flags. And they sang "Hatikva," in Hebrew.

One of her old teachers presented her with a report card which remarked that Golda Mabowehz was "talkative."

When it came Golda's time to speak she said, "I really —despite the fact my teachers called me talkative—I am at a loss for words to say to you." She was, in fact, very close to tears. It was difficult for her to talk at all.

Elsewhere, however, her customary eloquence was at its best. She spoke on radio and television. There were numerous newspaper interviews. She had never before had such "coverage." And Americans soon found that they were first intrigued, then impressed, then genuinely moved by this plainspoken Jewish grandmother.

Her acid comments were widely repeated. Of Jordan's King Hussein she said, "When I saw him speaking on television in the United States I was reminded of the story of the man who had killed his parents and was up for murder. He pleaded with the judge, 'Have pity on me; I'm an orphan.'"

Of Nasser she said, "We're told over and over that he is humiliated. Humiliated as a result of what? He wanted to destroy us, and—poor man—he failed. Somehow I just can't bring myself to feel too sorry for him."

Of the general situation she said, "We intend to remain alive. Our neighbors want to see us dead. This is not a question that leaves much room for compromise."

Of friends she said: "God knows Israel needs friends. But sometimes it seems as though our friends will stand by us only if we do—not only the possible—but the impossible."

Of war she said: "What we hold against Nasser is not only the killing of our sons, but forcing them for the sake of Israel's survival, to kill others."

Of peace she said: "We don't know how to explain this very simple thing—we want peace for ourselves, peace for our neighbors. Is that so difficult that it can't be explained?" As she spoke these words a note of urgent desperation shook in her voice. (Outside, Arab demonstrators set fire to a batch of Israeli flags. And others shouted, "Long live Al Fatah. Israel is a death trap for the Jewish people.")

But perhaps it was what Golda said when speaking of hope for the future which remained most indelibly in the minds of Americans. She expressed this memorably in a speech she made on October 6, 1969, before a vast audience of workers and union executives at the AFL-CIO convention in Atlantic City.

"For two thousand years our people were in exile; always the candidates to be massacred, to be discriminated against, to be second- and third- and tenth-class citizens in all parts of the world. But they had the courage to dream a big dream. 'One day, we will come back to the land from which we were driven twice before. We will establish there again our sovereignty. We will work with our hands, create everything in that country. We will live at peace with our neighbors and at peace with the entire world.'

"My friends, at least part of that dream has come true. I believe that the first thing that is necessary for people in the world is the courage to dream great dreams, and then the reality to face difficulties in order to accomplish and make these dreams come true. And I believe in this as sincerely as I believe that the day must come when there will be real peace between us and the Arabs. I have said over and over again I do not believe, I refuse to believe, that Egyptian mothers in the Nile Valley are giving birth to their children and have them for the great glorious ideal that when their boy reaches the age of eighteen or seventeen or nineteen, he will go off to war and fight the Israelis and who knows whether he will come back. But maybe he will be very successful in killing the son of a Jewish mother in Israel. I do not believe that this is what Egyptian mothers are giving birth to their children for. I do not believe that Egyptian and Syrian and Iraqi and Jordanian mothers are prepared to see their infants die because of lack of medical care, and just for the great future that lies before them—maybe they will finally succeed in killing the children of Israeli mothers. I refuse to believe it.

"Once their leaders realize this and once the masses among the Arab people dare to stand up and say to their leaders, 'There is no glory in having our sons killed. We gave birth to them in order that they may be alive,' I see a future for friendship, peace, cooperation between our neighbors and ourselves.

"Israel has sent thousands of men and women to the African continent, to the Asian continent, the Latin American continent, to bring them the results of our experience, to work with them as brothers, to help them in their development plans. It will be a great day when the young Jew from this side of the Jordan on his farm will cross the Jordan not with tanks, not with planes, but with tractors and with a hand of friendship as between farmer and farmer, as human being and human being. A dream? Maybe. I am sure it will come true."

On October 28, 1969, an amazing eighty-three percent of all eligible voters in Israel went to the polls to vote in the country's seventh national election.

A poll had been taken just before the election. People were asked to put down their choice for the next prime minister. The result: within eight months Golda's "rating" had zoomed from three percent to eighty percent. Consequently, no one was very surprised at the election returns. Of the sixteen political parties, it was the Israel Labor Party—with Golda at its head—which would lead the nation for the next four years.

Within a month Golda presented to the Knesset the largest Cabinet in the country's history. It was promptly dubbed a "wall-to-wall Cabinet," for it was composed of a coalition representing nearly ninety percent of the electorate. In fact, so large was the Cabinet that new, smaller chairs had to be ordered so that the twenty-four ministers could all fit around the government table in the parliamentary chamber. Among the most important posts: Abba Eban would continue as Foreign Minister, Moshe Dayan would continue as Defense Minister, and Dayan's brother-in-law and nephew of the late Chaim Weizmann, Major

General Ezer Weizman (he dropped the second *n* as a measure of independence), was made Transportation Minister. Weizman had headed the Israeli Air Force since 1958. He now proclaimed, "For the love of me, I do not know why we can have one of the best air forces in the world—sorry, *the* best—and one of the worst train services. But you just watch this wagon move from now on."

Aside from the train service, constant complaints about the telephone system, the difficulties of obtaining apartments, and other such civilian headaches heard in most nations around the globe, life within the country was, in the main, devoid of crises. Indeed, were it not for the constant drains, tensions, and sorrows resulting from "the neighbors"—as Israelis generally called them—life for the new Prime Minister would have been deeply satisfying.

Although Golda had to warn her people that some belt-pinching was in order, she was able to put this in positive terms: "There is no doubt the people in Israel will have to forego some of their easy way of living." This was largely accounted for by the heavy expenditures in foreign currency necessary to pay for military equipment.

But the recent recession was over. The country had full employment. Indeed, despite the disadvantages imposed by the Arab boycotts and blockades and the constantly increasing military budget, the nation's economic growth could well be considered phenomenal.

For example, when Israel was officially reborn in 1948, her industrial exports could be listed in a very short sentence: citrus by-products, pharmaceuticals, textiles, and false teeth. Now the mere listing of industrial exports took pages. New products were constantly being added, replacing the need for imports and conquering new export markets. One tiny entry which specially pleased the Prime Minister: Revivim, the desert kibbutz which her daughter had helped to found, was no longer a struggling, arid settlement whose inhabitants had only salty water to drink. Now, with the piping in of fresh water, Revivim had become a peach, pear, and gladiolus growing oasis. At Christmastime the kibbutz exported flowers by air to Italy, the land of flowers.

Other statistics were equally inspiring. Israel's free and compulsory education had now been stretched from age five to age fifteen. The country now had five fine universities, three of them of worldwide repute, with two more currently being built.

Israel's health statistics now bettered those of most Western nations, including the United States. Particularly noteworthy were the health improvements among Israeli Arabs. For example, their death rate dropped from 20 per 1,000 in 1948 when Israel became a state, to 5.9 at the last census in 1968—one of the lowest death rates in the world.

Indeed, all the statistics concerning Israel Arabs were noteworthy. They had a far higher standard of living than any Arabs in any other Middle Eastern country. This included such factors as education, housing, health, land-ownership, electricity, running water, and political and individual freedom. Israeli Arabs, of course, received the same pay as Jews for equal work and the same benefits. They had been given every opportunity to maintain their own culture and traditions. Hebrew and Arabic were the two official languages in Israel. There were now two Arabic daily papers, several weeklies, other periodicals, and regular Arabic programs on Israeli television.

One out of every ten Israeli citizens was an Arab. They might have become a dangerous fifth column within the state. But despite the fact that Arab leaders and Palestinian guerrillas outside the country were constantly provoking Israeli Arabs to commit acts of sabotage, the Israeli Arabs had always remained basically loyal to the Israeli government. During the Six-Day War, for example, Israeli Arabs were not involved in any hostile activities whatever.

Among the most surprising statistics were those about Israel's tourist industry. When other nations were beset by dangerous border incidents, their hotels generally stood empty as tourists stayed away in droves. In Israel, however, tourism had remained a constantly flourishing industry. Indeed, since the Six-Day War it had become the country's prime foreign currency earner—bypassing its chief competitor, citrus exports, for the first time.

The country had some 300 hotels ranging from kibbutz guest houses to 20 luxury hotels—so consistently crowded that another five luxury hotels were currently under construction.

The nation's chief new tourist attraction was the unified ancient city of Jerusalem, which—since the Six-Day War—had been fully open to tourists and Israeli citizens of all denominations for the first time in nineteen years. Though the Armistice agreements had provided that Jordan would assure—among other things—*free access to the Holy Places and cultural institutions and the use of the Mount of Olives,* this agreement was never honored. The Jordanian government had refused permission to Israeli Moslems to enter the Old City so that they might pray at the holy Mosque of Omar, Islam's third shrine after Mecca and Medina. Israeli Christians, and tourists, were permitted to enter the Old City only at Christmas and Easter. And Jews of course were denied all access to their Holy Places: the Western Wall, Rachel's Tomb, and the ancient cemetery on the Mount of Olives, where Jews have buried their dead for 2,500 years.

In order to promote tourism in Jordan, King Hussein permitted a road to be built from the new Intercontinental Hotel across the Mount of Olives Cemetery. Hundreds of ancient Jewish graves were destroyed. The gravestones of rabbis and sages were used in the construction of walls, pavements and latrines of a nearby military camp. The ancient Jewish quarter in Old Jerusalem had been completely destroyed, including all the thirty-five synagogues, some of which were centuries old.

Since the Six-Day War, however, a renaissance had overtaken the unified city of Jerusalem. Archeologists, architects and city planners had joined forces to rebuild the historic quarters of the Old City with careful concern for the ancient architectural integrity of the area. Slums had been torn down; the inhabitants relocated to newly built apartment houses on the outskirts of Jerusalem. Important excavations were going on at many sites, including the Western Wall, from which centuries of earth had been removed, revealing twice as much of the wall's stately splendor. And a new national park was being built, which would encircle the entire Old City in a belt of green.

But of all the statistics submitted to the Prime Minister by the various ministries and government departments, perhaps the most striking of all were those concerning the Occupied Territories, or, as Golda preferred to call them, the Administered Territories.

The official Israeli policy concerning the Territories was: *to allow the population of the areas to carry on their life and activities just as they had been used to till the 5th June 1967*. This meant that it was Arab policemen—not Israeli soldiers—who patrolled the streets to keep law and order. (Israeli troops were concerned only with security, and were stationed on high ground outside the cities.) In fact, few Israeli officials of any variety were seen in the Occupied Territories.

It also meant that any Arab in the Territories could visit any Arab country. And many Arabs, mainly those from Jordan, could obtain a special pass which enabled them to visit the Territories and, from there, to go into Israel.

At the beginning there had been some trouble in the Territories, particularly in the West Bank, which was notorious for its instability. But more than 2,000 terrorists had been rounded up and put in jail. And by now general peace prevailed.

Although some of the imprisoned West Bank terrorists had been found guilty of murder, and although the death sentence did exist in Jordan, it did not exist in Israel. Consequently, none of the terrorists had been put to death —even though the people in the Occupied West Bank Territory still lived, in the main, under Jordanian law.

The 1,000,000 Arabs in the Territories fully expected to be returned to their original states and status when the territories were returned to Egypt, Syria, or Jordan. In the meantime, the general feeling seemed to be that they would relax and enjoy the "fruits of being occupied."

Early one morning in January, 1970, a fat manuscript of typed pages was delivered to Golda's desk. It was en-

titled: *Three Years of Military Government, 1967–1970,*
and it would shortly be printed by the government. As she
turned through the pages, Golda saw in the typewritten
facts and figures a bridge of hope to the future. The Territories were divided into four Administrative Sections.
The first of them, Judea and Samaria, was typical of the
others.

The harvest there had improved in three years by 50 to
100 percent because of new methods introduced by the
Israelis. With the help of irrigation, crop rotation, agricultural research stations, the volume of production of field
crops had increased 95.6 percent. In addition, 2,250,000
new trees had been planted.

Since June, 1967, the road system had been repaired
and renewed and a number of new roads constructed.
Seventeen new bus routes had been added to villages which
previously had had no public transportation at all.

Golda turned to the section on education. A sentence
stared up at her. *The authorities supply free textbooks to
all government schools.* She remembered suddenly the
American Young Sisters Society which she had organized
in Milwaukee at the age of ten to provide textbooks for
needy schoolchildren—for books were not then supplied
free of charge.

The textbooks supplied free to the schools in the Territories made no attempt to change what and how the
Arab children learned—with a single exception. Hatred
was deleted from the pages. Outside the Territories, Arab
children were, for example, still learning subtraction with
printed problems such as: *If there are eleven Israelis and
four are killed, how many are left?*

Golda read on: *The educational institutions in the area
are generally housed in old buildings from the times of the
Turkish rule or of the Mandate. The Jordanian government neglected school construction, and, in light of the
serious lack in this area, the administration began a building plan. . . . This aid will amount in the next two years to
five million Israeli Pounds and will thereby markedly re-
lieve the situation.*

Seventeen vocational training schools had been started,

including schools for training mentally handicapped boys in building skills. All students received free training manuals, free food allotments, and a daily allowance for each study day.

Golda turned to the section on *Health Services* which were free to the Arabs of the Occupied Territories. In three years the government had doubled the budget allocated by Israelis to pay for such items as new medical equipment for hospitals and clinics in Judea and Samaria; 20 new rural clinics; 2 new mobile clinics serving twenty-two villages; 91 government clinics; 23 mother-and-child welfare stations; large-scale campaigns for the immunization of children and adults against smallpox, infantile paralysis, dysentery, typhoid, typhus, and cholera. (This often included free immunizations given on the Jordan bridges to residents of Jordan or other Arab lands.)

In addition, all the health services in Israel itself were open to the population of the Territories.

And so it went on, as she turned through the pages headed: *Welfare . . . Rehabilitation . . . Community Development . . . Summer Camps*—which were held in Israel for children of the Territories. Thus far, 4,100 Arab children had *met with the Israel population and with the children of Israeli summer camps. Tours and rambles were also held in various places.*

All this required a good many Israeli pounds. During the coming year Israelis would foot the bill of 94 million pounds—or $27,260,000—appropriated to cover the costs of governing and bettering the lives of the 600,000 Arabs living in the 5,500 square kilometers of Judea and Samaria. Each of the other three Administrative Sections had its own hefty budget. And each of the four budgets had increased substantially every year.

Golda and her government firmly believed that this was money well spent. She remembered a story told her recently by the Israeli diplomat Ehud Avriel who had been invited for dinner to the home of a prominent Arab family in the occupied Judea territory. At the end of the meal, Avriel had asked his host: "If you could have your wish come true concerning the Occupied Territories, what would it be?"

After a long moment of consideration, the Arab answered, "With our hearts we wish we could wake up in the morning and find that Israel had vanished into thin air. Then there would be no problems. With our mouth we are for a return to Jordan. With our mind we want the present situation to continue."

Golda agreed with Avriel that this attitude was probably fairly typical of Arabs in the Territories. And she agreed with Avriel's conclusion: "This is the first time that they feel they have a government which is not using them for a political football. We must win their friendship because whatever the political solution, they will be our neighbors for all time."

Another Israeli official had put it this way: "We know we cannot make the West Bank Arabs love us, but our hope is we can show them means to improve their own lives so that one day when our occupation ends in some form of settlement they will want to retain contacts and peaceful relations with us."

In the Administered Territories Israel was putting into practice ideas and ideals that Golda had expressed in so many speeches through so many years.

Chapter 25

The following month Golda attended a funeral.

It was a mass funeral. She had been asked to say the eulogy.

She stared down at the pinewood, flag-draped coffins lined up one by one on the wooden structure which had been hastily erected in the courtyard of Jerusalem's Town Hall.

Were the coffins empty? Had they found any remains at all? Forty-seven passengers had been blown up in mid-air. Dr. Hanoch Milwidsky was one of them. She had known him well. A man of gentleness, wisdom, compassion. The head of cardiac surgery at the Hadassah-Hebrew University Medical Center. He was fifty-eight years old. He had so much to live for. He had so much to give.

Forty-seven lives, suddenly ended.

The shofar was blown; its mournful sound seemed to echo back through the tragedies of centuries. Then there was silence. They were watching her. They were waiting for her to speak. She put both hands over her face. She could not say any words. She could only weep.

However, on Monday morning she spoke.

She stood at the speaker's rostrum on the stage of the Knesset beneath the portrait of Theodor Herzl and in a voice flat and firm she spoke the words that had been written down.

"Members of the Knesset. . . . Grief and anger have overcome all of us ever since Saturday when we received the terrible tidings of the dreadful disaster to the Swissair plane en route to Israel, in which the lives of the forty-seven passengers and crew were lost. . . .

"Immediately after the disaster, at seven ten P.M. on Saturday night, Radio Beirut broadcast the announcement of the Popular Front for the Liberation of Palestine General Command, claiming responsibility for the explosion of the Swissair plane. This announcement was also broadcast by Radio Amman . . . The BBC's Arabic broadcast from London at ten forty-five that evening quoted an Amman spokesman to the effect that the Swiss plane had been blown up because the Popular Front for the Liberation of Palestine proposed to strike blows everywhere. . . . On the same day of the Swiss plane disaster, an explosion occurred in an Austrian plane en route from Frankfurt to Vienna, carrying mail destined for Israel. It was only by sheer miracle that passengers and crew were saved from a horrible death. The West German police are searching for two Arabs who handed in a parcel at the Frankfurt post office on Friday morning containing a radio receiver in which there were explosives. . . .

"About a fortnight earlier, Arab terrorists ran wild at the Munich Airport, causing the murder and wounding of innocent passengers on their way to an El Al plane and of people at the airport. It was thanks only to the resourcefulness and bravery of the plane's captain and one of the passengers, the late Arieh Katzenstein (who threw himself on the grenade, paying with his life) that large-scale slaughter was avoided. It has been reported that the perpetrators of this crime had arrived from Damascus to carry out their design. A further band of armed Arab terrorists equipped with Iraqi and Jordanian passports was caught in Munich the following day. According to local authorities, this group, too, had designs against air traffic.

"The Zurich airport, from which the Swissair plane departed on Saturday afternoon, had been the site of trouble in the past as well. On February 18, 1969, a band

of Arab terrorists opened fire on a passenger-full El Al
plane prior to take-off. The terrorists murdered one of
the crew members and doubtless intended to set plane
and passengers on fire. Thanks to Mordechai Rahamim's
bravery, a grave disaster . . . was averted. The assailants,
members of the Popular Front for the Liberation of
Palestine, were arrested. . . .

"Acts of air piracy on the part of the Arab terrorist
organizations began on July 23, 1968, with the hijacking
to Algiers of an El Al airliner en route from Rome to
Israel. For five weeks, the Algerian government held the
Israeli passengers as hostage . . . and demanded the
release of Arab terrorists in ransom for the Israelis.
Proposals made by international organizations to impose
a boycott and sanctions came to naught. Quite possibly,
the helplessness displayed at that time in the reaction of
the international community served as a source of encouragement to the terrorists to continue their criminal
attacks against international air traffic.

"On December 26, 1968, an El Al plane was attacked
in Athens and an Israeli passenger was murdered by members of the Popular Front. . . . On August 29, 1969, a
TWA plane en route from Rome to Tel Aviv was hijacked
by the Popular Front . . . forced to land in Damascus.
After the landing, an explosive charge, placed in the
plane by the terrorists during the flight, went off. The
Syrian government imprisoned the Israeli passengers and
released the hijackers. . . ."

She went on, detailing more incidents of murder and
bloodshed. And she concluded: "The Arab governments
are the only ones in the world providing encouragement,
immunity, and protection for these criminals and their
crimes. These terrorist organizations act from within the
Arab states . . . where their bases are located, from which
they depart on missions, and to which they return. . . .
The President of Egypt himself testifies to the close ties
between the terrorist organizations and the Arab governments. In his speech on July 23, 1969, broadcast over
Radio Cairo, Nasser stated, 'We, for our part, provide
them with everything we have in the military, political,

and technical spheres. We shall do this without counting the cost and without reservation.' "

Then Golda looked up from the typewritten page. She looked at her audience, and beyond it. "If the states of the world do not curb terrorism, the terrorism will destroy civil aviation."

Who were these terrorists? Where had they come from? Why was their hatred so implacable?

The answers to these questions had their genesis in 1947 when most of the terrorists were small children and some had not even been born.

Abiding by the directives of Arab leaders outside the country, some 600,000 Palestinian Arabs fled from their homes in the territory which had been designated by the United Nations as the new Jewish state. Some fled to the Gaza Strip, which Egypt acquired under the Armistice Agreements of February, 1949. Some fled to Lebanon, some to Syria. But most fled less than 50 miles to another part of the land which had been known historically as Palestine.

In the first partition in 1922 three-quarters of the original Mandated Territory of Palestine had been given by the British to Feisal's brother Abdullah so that he could reign as King over a sovereign Arab state, which he named Trans-Jordan.

As for the second new Arab state called for in the UN Partition resolution: "Why," said Golda, "did those Palestinians who remained in the western bank after the 1948 war—why did they not set up their Palestinian state? They could have done it. They could have called it Palestine. Instead, they did nothing—so in April, 1949, King Abdullah annexed this land to his own kingdom of Trans-Jordan, with," Golda added, "no great cries of courage heard anywhere in the world."

Since King Abdullah now had land on both sides of the Jordan River, it was necessary to change his nation's name, for Trans-Jordan meant "over the Jordan." He might at that time have given his country its centuries-old appellation: Palestine. Instead, he chose to retitle it the Hashemite Kingdom of Jordan.

And many of the Arabs who might have become Palestinians in their own Arab state became, instead, refugees.

On September 6, 1948, the secretary of the Palestine Arab Higher Committee said in an interview with the Beirut *Telegraph:* "The fact that there are these refugees is the direct consequence of the act of the Arab states in opposing partition and the Jewish state. The Arab states agreed upon this policy unanimously, and they must share in the solution of the problem."

But the Arab nations did nothing whatever to "share in the solution of the problem." Instead, they segregated the refugees into huge camps, refused to feed them, house them, or pay for their upkeep. Although Jordan was reluctantly willing to incorporate refugees into the state, she did nothing to encourage them to leave the camps. In Syria, Lebanon, and Egypt the refugees were, in the main, forbidden to work. And Egypt kept "her" Palestinians as virtual prisoners, not permitting them to travel outside the narrow Gaza Strip.

The Arab nations consistently refused international offers to pay all costs of resettling the refugees in under-populated Arab lands where they might become self-supporting citizens with—as the late Dag Hammarskjöld put it—"benefit to the economy of the whole population of the area."

The Arab nations did, however, permit the international community to pay for the upkeep of the Palestinian refugees in the camps. More than a half billion dollars was expended by the United Nations Relief and Works Agency to feed, clothe, house, train, and educate them—including some university scholarships. More than 60 percent of this was paid for by the U.S. taxpayer. The USSR contributed nothing—except propaganda.

The New York *Times* summed up the situation in an editorial titled "Subsidizing Subversion":

> *The camps have become recruiting and training grounds, and in some cases headquarters, for extremist groups bent on destroying all efforts by the U.N. and others to achieve an accommodation between the Arabs*

and Israelis. . . . What began as a noble humanitarian effort has been prolonged and perverted until it has become an instrument for sabotaging the work of the world organization.

Over 500,000 Jews had fled from the Arab countries into the new state of Israel. Although most of them were penniless, many were illiterate, and all differed in background, culture, language, and customs from the European Jews who founded the state, they had been integrated into the working life of the nation—at no cost whatever to the international community.

After World War II there were some 40 million refugees throughout the world: Koreans, Hindus, Moslems, Sikhs, Chinese, Vietnamese, Sudeten Germans, and Jews. In every case, resettlement, and not repatriation, had proved to be the answer. The refugees had found new homes in new lands, usually among their own people and, in most cases, at no cost at all to the international community.

The only remaining refugee problem in the world was that of the so-called Palestinian refugees. Why were the Arab nations so intent upon keeping them separate, secluded, and suppressed?

Because they were using the refugees as a huge human weapon in the ongoing war against Israel. For nineteen years the refugees were fed by the Arab nations—not with food, but with virulent anti-Israel propaganda. After years of idleness and exploitation by political agitators, there were only two goals which gave their lives a sense of purpose and direction. To return to the home from which they had been "driven" by the Jews. (And this home, more often than not, had been blown by dreams and imagination into a flourishing orange grove or a splendid mansion.) And to drive the Israelis into the sea.

Among the most vehement about their return to the homeland were the young men and women who had been born in the camps. They charged the word "Palestinian" with a fanatical ferver. As Golda put it: "From 1948 until 1967 nobody heard of a Palestinian entity. What makes them now more Palestinian than they were until 1967?"

What had perhaps made them "more Palestinian" was the shattering defeat the Arab countries suffered in the '67 Six-Day War. Before that time they had been content with the reference "refugees." However, after the routing of the official Egyptian, Jordanian, and Syrian armies, the refugees assumed they had better take on the role of fighting for themselves, conduct their own "War of Liberation"—under the political banner "Palestinian."

Although most Palestinian refugees were still living on land which had been part of Palestine, they chose to refer to Palestine *only* as the section which had been allotted to the Jews and which consituted only one-eighth of the original mandated Palestine. And 70 percent of that one-eighth had never belonged to individual Arabs. It was public land which—after four centuries—passed from the Ottoman Turks to the British Mandatory Government which turned it over to the Israel government in 1948. Much of the 30 percent which remained had been purchased from Arab and Turkish landowners from 1880 to 1948 by the Jewish National Fund. This land too had been turned over to the Israel government in 1948.

In its Partition Resolution, the United Nations had deemed that it was not unseemly that the Jews should have 8,000 square miles, much of which they had cultivated and developed themselves, since the Arabs already had some 4,000,000 square miles, containing twelve independent states, some of which were notably underpopulated.

In any case, over three out of every five Arabs who fled from this small "Jewish section of Palestine" in 1947 and 1948 had lived in that land for less than a generation. (In a census taken by the British government in 1922, only 186,000 Arabs lived in the land which later became Israel.)

Furthermore, though some 600,000 Arabs had fled in '47 and '48 (and 20 percent of these *had* relocated), the number of "Palestinian refugees" had nonetheless since swelled to well over a million. The Arab nations had consistently demanded that *all* the Palestinian refugees *return* "as the masters of the homeland"—even though in all of recorded history from 1350 B.C. to A.D. 1948 Palestine had never for so much as one day been ruled by the Arabs of Palestine.

In speaking of the aim of the Palestine Refugee Plan on September 1, 1961, Nasser summed up the entire matter in a single sentence: "If the Arabs return to Israel, Israel will cease to exist."

The sentence was undoubtedly true.

After the '48 war, Israel took back some 40,000 to 50,000 refugees; mainly to reunite families. She released bank accounts of the Arabs who fled from the Jewish state. And she offered to pay full compensation for land and property left by the fleeing Arabs (though she particularly pointed out that hundreds of thousands of Israelis were forced to abandon their property when they were expelled from or fled from Arab countries and this would all those who claimed they have the right to return; as all those who claimed they have the right to return: as Golda put it: "This would not be getting refugees back. This is an army, bent on destroying us."

Not only has hatred of Israel been hammered into the refugees for twenty-two years, not only have many of them received training in military subversion and guerrilla warfare, but all of them want to return to an Arab state—not a Jewish nation.

A Conference of Refugees was held in Syria in 1957. A resolution was adopted: "Any discussion aimed at a solution of the Palestine problem which will not be based on ensuring the refugees' right to annihilate Israel will be regarded as a desecration of the Arab people and an act of treason."

Because many of the refugees refused to sit and wait for the Arab nations to achieve fulfillment of this resolution, they formed their own militant terrorist organizations which regarded any means as acceptable to the end of returning as masters of the homeland. If these meant exploding in midair a planeload of passengers from many lands—so be it.

Chapter 26

Perhaps never in history had so small a nation been so completely surrounded for so long a period by so many virulent enemies. But by April, 1970, it had become clear to Golda and her government that, so far as enemies went, they were now being forced into—as the vernacular went —"a whole new ball game." And one which was far more dangerous and ominous than anything they had ever been faced with before.

Russia had now sent SAM-3's into Egypt. The 3's could track the low-flying planes which the SAM-2's let through. The new combination of surface-to-air missiles—if installed along the Suez Canal—would mean that Israeli planes would no longer be able to fly the retaliatory missions which provided Israel's chief weapon against Nasser's War of Attrition.

Because the SAM-3 was the Soviets' most complicated and newest missile, only Russians were allowed at the missile sites, which were manned by 3,500 to 5,000 Soviet technicians. "Each SAM-3 site," reported a Western diplomat, "comes with Russian cooks, bottle washers, the lot." There were also some 20,000 Russian troops, and over 3,000 Soviet instructors stationed in Egypt. A British visitor reported that Cairo was beginning to look "like Moscow on the Nile. My God, even the shopkeepers assume you speak Russian!"

With the advent of the SAM-3's, Egyptian morale soared to its highest point in months. And Israeli morale sank low. Israel's only defense against the SAMs was to try to bomb out the sites before the missiles themselves were installed. These missions often proved suicidal, for Israeli pilots had to face both the missiles and MIGs. Then Golda received word that Israeli pilots had shot down four MIGs (Soviet planes)—with Russian pilots in them. It was decided not to mention the matter at the moment because, as Golda put it, "We don't want to go to war with the Russians."

Israelis feared that Soviet pilots might be all too anxious to acquire some combat experience. And that Russia might be using the Middle East as a testing ground for her latest equipment.

As the crisis deepened, Golda's day grew longer and longer. It seemed years since the relatively quiet time after the national elections when she had worked a normal twelve- or fourteen-hour day. Yet, it had been a mere eight months ago.

Golda's personal assistant, Mrs. Lou Kaddar, described one of these typical "easy days."

"She gets up at seven. The cleaning woman, Zahava, comes at seven thirty and makes breakfast for Golda and me. I arrive around eight o'clock. We have fruit juice, eggs, *pita* [Arab bread] with cottage cheese or honey, and one or two cups of coffee. Zahava goes about her cleaning while we eat, in the kitchen. Golda reads the morning paper. I always bring the appointment book and remind her about the happenings of the day.

"After breakfast we leave for the office. One of the bodyguards opens the car door for us (because they see us as mothers and grandmothers, not because they see Golda as the Prime Minister). Golda now has four or five bodyguards—and she finds this very hard to get used to.

"We drive to the Prime Minister's office, where the morning is usually taken up by meetings with Cabinet ministers, correspondents, visiting foreign dignitaries. If possible, Golda goes home for lunch. I usually join her. And, while we eat, in the kitchen, Zahava generally washes the pots, while Lea, the cook, chats to us about her family, her son, her problems. We go back to the office for more meetings until seven at night.

"Then Golda often returns home and—since Lea leaves at three thirty—Golda warms up the dinner the cook has left for her. She eats alone, unless, of course, someone drops in—which often happens. In the evenings, she may go out to speak. Or she works at home, going over papers, cables, letters, taking phone calls from various Cabinet members. (She has three separate phones on her desk.) She goes to bed around midnight."

Golda's political adviser, Simcha Dinitz, described a typical "crisis day." This particular day occurred at the start of the so-called Rogers crisis. The U.S. Secretary of State, William Rogers, had proposed, publicly, that Egypt and Israel declare a cease-fire as a forerunner to peace talks to be held under the auspices of United Nations' mediator Gunnar Jarring. Egypt had already agreed to the cease-fire and the talks. Israel was yet to be heard from.

On the face of it, here was the opportunity for which Golda had pleaded throughout her long political career. She had often declared, "We say 'Peace,' and the echo comes back from the other side, 'War.'" Now the Egyptians were actually agreeing to a truce to be followed by peace talks.

But what were Nasser's true motives? That was the question which threatened to tear Golda's government apart. Many members of the Knesset were convinced that Nasser's cease-fire offer was a trick and a trap. For the past three months the Israeli Air Force had bombed the Egyptian missile sites daily—some pilots flying as many as five missions a day. By doing so, they were effectively thwarting all Egyptian and Russian efforts to move SAM batteries into the critical zone 18 miles or closer to the canal. The opponents to the Rogers peace initiative held that the cease-fire would give Egypt and Russia opportunity to install an integrated and virtually impenetrable SAM mission system which would not only prevent any effective retaliation raids by the Israeli Air Force but would act as cover for Egyptian forces crossing the Suez Canal on their way to a new war with Israel.

Why, the opponents to the Rogers peace initiative asked, could the peace talks not proceed without a cease-fire, which, after all, was being done in the case of Vietnam? In this way, if Nasser was sincere about at last wanting peace, he would have ample chance to prove it. And Israel would not risk her national security, which, in this case, could be synonymous with national survival.

The United States, however, did not take to this suggestion. Indeed, they put the most telling type of pressure upon Golda and her government to accept the cease-fire plan. It was intimated that the delivery of the ordered Phantoms might be held up. It was already evident that the United States was not rushing to fulfill any new delivery promises which may have been made to Golda on her "shopping trip" to Washington. And the United States had adamantly refused to allow Israel to buy replacements for any planes lost in action against Jordan or Lebanon.

Many Israelis longed for a cease-fire, believing that if the door for peace were opening even a crack, their government should take the risk of proceeding with the negotiations—though they fully realized that the slightly open door might well have a gun muzzle behind it.

Other Israelis just as firmly believed that Nasser could not be trusted. Furthermore, they resented the fact that their government had not been consulted before the Rogers peace initiative was announced. And they resented the pressure the United States was placing upon them to accept the cease-fire. "With such friends," they asked, "who needs enemies?"

The 120 members of the Knesset reflected, of course, all the diverse views of the populace regarding this desperate national dilemma.

It was against this background of the Rogers crisis that Simcha Dinitz described "the Boss's" typical crisis day. (Dinitz and Lou Kaddar, Golda's closest day-by-day associates, frequently referred to her with fondness and affection as the Boss. The Director General of her office was virtually the only person in the government who called her Prime Minister. To everyone else she was Golda or—at most—Mrs. Meir.)

Said Dinitz: "Her day actually started last night. I was with her in her kitchen sitting over formulations regarding this Rogers Crisis. She made coffee. We started our meeting at five thirty in the evening and sat till seven. Then came in Yakov Shimshon Shapiro, the Minister of Justice, and Galili, Minister Without Portfolio. (They'd been invited.) We sat together till eight thirty—when in walked the new Minister of Health and the Minister of Labor to talk about the nurses' strike. (They had *not* been invited. They were afraid if they called I'd tell them not to come. So they came.) Golda went with them into the sitting room. She backed the moves they were planning to take in that particular crisis. They left. Then she came back to us —and the international crisis—in the kitchen. When I left around ten for another meeting, she was fixing herself something to eat. (She enjoys this. It makes her feel she still has time to be a woman too.) Golda had two more meetings scheduled that night.

"I got to the office at seven thirty the next morning. Golda was already there. (She had four hours' sleep.) At eight we had a meeting with Dayan about the Rogers Crisis. At nine o'clock we had a Cabinet security meeting ——*not* about the Rogers Crisis, about all our other security crises. At eleven there was a full Cabinet meeting on the Rogers Crisis. Then we switched to regular matters: the old age bill, some land reforms. Life must go on just the same, crisis or no crisis.

"At one o'clock we came down from the Cabinet meeting to Golda's office. We ordered in some sandwiches, and while we ate we went over cables about various matters. Then Golda lay down for a few minutes. At two o'clock we went to the Knesset where there was a Party caucus meeting on the Rogers Crisis. At four thirty I went home with Golda, back to the kitchen. We had coffee and a blintz. She said, 'You haven't eaten all day.' I said, 'I ate with you at lunch.' She said, 'That's not enough for you. You don't eat enough.' And she gave me a blintz. We conferred more about the Rogers Crisis till six o'clock when I had to leave for another appointment and Golda went upstairs to pack her suitcase because at six thirty she had to drive to Tel Aviv for two more meetings.

"I met a government guest at the King David. At eight that evening I arrived at the Dan Hotel in Tel Aviv for another meeting on the crisis with government officials. Golda was already there. After that meeting we went to Golda's house for another meeting with other officials on the Rogers Crisis. It lasted till three in the morning.

"I'm averaging now around three to four hours' sleep a night. Golda gets more than that. About four to six hours. She's always telling me that I should get more sleep, that she's older than me—she's seventy-two, I'm forty-one—so she needs less sleep than I do." Dinitz smiled a little. "She's always worrying about me and everyone else she's close to. When she was Foreign Minister we went through a period of working eighteen to twenty hours a day. When that particular crisis was over I suggested she take a vacation. 'Why?' she said 'Do at me. 'So, *you* take a vacation!' she said."
you think I'm tired?' I told her, 'No, but I am.' She looked

The press gallery of the Knesset was so filled with television cables that it was impossible to move about without tripping or being entwined. There was a sibilant hum as dozens of broadcasters spoke quietly into their tape recorders describing the proceedings. Mrs. Meir seemed very small as she stood at the podium far below. It had been rumored that if the government agreed to go along with the Rogers peace initiative, the Gahal Party—the second largest vote-getter in the last election—would withdraw from the Cabinet. Would this mean the downfall of Golda's coalition?

The Prime Minister spoke with no great charge of optimism. But she stated that her government was prepared to proceed with the cease-fire and the peace talks.

At which point Menachem Begin, leader of the Gahal Party, stood up abruptly, faced the television cameras in the press gallery, and strode from the Cabinet table.

Golda went on. The government of Israel had accepted the cease-fire on the firm understanding that "Egypt and the USSR would refrain from changing the military status quo by emplacing SAMs or other new installations in an agreed zone west of the Suez Canal cease-fire line." The U.S. government had, furthermore, pledged to see to it that there would be no violations. In private assurances and in a news conference on July 31, President Nixon had told Israel it could agree to the standstill cease-fire "without fear" that it would "run the risk of having a military build-up occur" on the Egyptian side of the Suez Canal.

The Prime Minister's speech was long. It was sober. It was realistic. It concluded: "Members of the Knesset, the decision taken by the government of Israel was not an easy one. Not because we hesitated to launch a move that may bring us nearer to peace, but because of the doubts we have concerning the readiness of the Arab leaders to embark sincerely on the road to peace . . . Even so, in the past as in the present, we have felt duty-bound to examine every prospect, be it ever so slim, which could lead us to peace—to examine with fullest readiness and maximum responsibility."

Despite the walkout of the Gahal Party, the Cabinet backed the Prime Minister. And four days after, on August 8, 1970, an almost uncanny quiet spread along the length of the Suez Canal, which had for so long exploded with the sounds of shelling and bombardment. The ninety-day cease-fire had started.

That night Defense Minister Moshe Dayan toured the front in an open jeep. With him was Captain David Halevy who later reported, "The quiet along the Canal was deafening for anyone who had been there when the artillery was in full blast." At daybreak a few Egyptian soldiers bathed in the Canal and shouted, "Salaam" (peace) to Israeli soldiers who shouted back "Shalom" (peace).

Egypt and Israel had each agreed to observe a complete military standstill within a zone extending 30 miles on each side of the Canal. Jordan had also agreed to observe the cease-fire and to enter into peace negotiations.

Syria and Iraq, however, had not agreed. Nor had the Palestinian terrorists, who proclaimed that they would now intensify their military operations "until the final victory."

And they promptly made good their words by firing salvos of Russian-made Katyusha rockets from Jordan into Israel. One of the chief terrorist leaders, Yasir Arafat, announced: "We shall never lay down our arms until we reach victory."

Two weeks later Prime Minister Golda Meir issued a statement which fell like a sledgehammer of doom on the fragile hopes of her countrymen. Aerial reconnaissance photographs showed that the Egyptians had installed twelve to fifteen SAM-2 batteries in their cease-fire zone and were busy fortifying them—in flagrant violation of the agreements they had signed.

But the United States—certain that the forthcoming peace talks offered real hope for the Middle East—convinced the Israelis to proceed with the discussions. Consequently, early on Tuesday morning, August 25, Israel's United Nations Ambassador Yosef Tekoah met for an hour and a half with the United Nations' Middle East Mediator Gunnar Jarring in an office overlooking the East River. Then Mr. Jarring met separately with Jordan's Ambassador to Washington. And, in the afternoon, he met with Egypt's chief UN Delegate.

This round-robin form of negotiation was necessitated by the fact that, for years, the Arabs had refused to so much as sit in the same television studio with an Israeli. Indeed after 22 years they still refused to officially recognize the fact that the state of Israel existed. Consequently, actual face-to-face negotiations were, they insisted, out of the question.

Later that same day, Israel's Ambassador Tekoah flew home for further consultations with his government.

Defense Minister Moshe Dayan promptly threatened that he would resign from the government if the peace talks were resumed before the missile violations were rectified. Although Begin's walkout had not brought the government down, Dayan—a national hero—was so popular that his resignation would undoubtedly have caused a government crisis.

After five days of intensive debate, Dayan's position was

officially adopted. The Prime Minister announced that Israel would proceed with the peace talks just as soon as the violations were rectified and the SAM missiles removed.

The United States then acknowledged that cease-fire violations had, indeed, taken place on the Egyptian side of the Canal. The State Department had been reticent about backing up Israel's claims because, when setting up the standstill agreements, the United States had asked for, and had received, the promise of the USSR that it would not permit the Egyptians to engage in a military buildup along the Canal. Since Russia was now loudly proclaiming that no violations had taken place, the United States had been hesitant about publicly challenging Russia's word.

Golda, however, was not so shy about calling a spade a spade—or a hammer and sickle. "Our problem today is not one of confronting the Arabs," she said bluntly. "But of confronting the Soviets—because they are there in very large measure. There is no doubt," she added, "that if Nasser gets up one morning and the Russians say to him, 'This is it, we have no more arms for you,' then Nasser would have to make peace."

Nasser, however, was getting up in the morning and hearing no such thing. Instead, detailed reconnaissance photographs—released by the United States and by Israel—showed that by late September the 17 SAM-2 batteries which had existed in Egypt's standstill area before the cease-fire had now mushroomed to 40 or 50, containing 500 to 600 missile launchers. A third of the missiles were the dread SAM-3's, which had obviously been installed by the Russians since they were so top-secret that no Egyptian general was permitted to come near the compound unless the Russians had given him a special pass. In her matter-of-fact way Golda pronounced: "The SAM-3 missiles cannot be put there by the Egyptians. They were put there by the Russians. The Russians should take them away!"

The Soviet military personnel in the standstill area was now estimated at 3,000.

U.S. military experts called the newly installed missile

system "one of the best in the world." "We couldn't match it," said one Pentagon official. "We don't have the equipment."

It was, as Golda acidly pointed out, to prevent such missile emplacements that the Israeli Air Force had bombed Egyptian positions daily for the three months prior to the cease-fire. The Russians and the Egyptians had accomplished under the flag of truce what they had never been able to do with Israeli planes flying overhead.

In addition, Russian freighters were continuing to arrive in Egyptian harbors, delivering more arms. These now included the immense 203-mm artillery pieces, the largest conventional weapon in the Russian inventory, plus engineering equipment to build bridges, plus amphibious armored personnel carriers. (Since spring, the Soviets had conducted landing maneuvers with Egyptian troops.) Also installed by early September was one of Russia's newest radars—the first outside the Soviet bloc. Reaching 80,000 feet up and over 300 miles out, it covered all of Israel's air space under its ever-watchful eye.

Not only would the newly installed SAM system prevent Israeli planes from flying retaliatory raids over Egypt, but the missiles could reach from twelve to fifteen miles into the Israeli-occupied side of the Suez, thereby preventing Israeli planes from flying in their own territory. The missiles could also act as a super-effective cover for Egyptian troops crossing the Suez into Israeli-occupied Sinai.

The United States insisted that it was approaching the USSR about securing the withdrawal of the missiles. But the violations continued day after day.

Chapter 27

At the end of September, Golda flew again to the United States. Again, to see the President. This time there were no nineteen gun salutes. No formal festive dinners. This time there were only dead-serious talks. This time, as New York *Times* correspondent C. L. Sulzberger wrote: *Mrs. Meir is negotiating for Israel's existence.*

Before the cease-fire began, the United States had pledged that it would try to "rectify" any violations, including military buildups, which might occur during the ninety days. This was one reason Israel had agreed to the cease-fire. It was now quite evident, however, that the President and the State Department had scored zero on the matter of getting the missiles removed. But there was one thing the President could do. This time Golda's shopping list was longer, more comprehensive. It included sophisticated electronic equipment which might partially offset Israel's loss of advantage on the Suez front. Golda also asked for long-term loans to enable the country to pay for the new military equipment—which Israel presumably would not have needed had there been no SAM buildup.

The specific outcome of the private talks between President and Prime Minister were not disclosed. But as Golda left the White House she did not look displeased.

While Golda was still in the United States, another brewing Mid-East crisis erupted, so—after a swift three-day visit—she rushed home on a midnight plane.

233

The Palestinian terrorists were so incensed by the cease-fire that they had plotted ways to sabotage it. The twelve chief terrorist groups disagreed on many points. Some, for example, were faithful disciples of the Russian line; some were ardent advocates of the Red Chinese. They all, however, agreed on one basic principle; there must be no cease-fire. The fight against Israel must continue nonstop.

As one step toward this end, the Popular Front for the Liberation of Palestine had hijacked five international planes carrying travelers home from the Middle East. An El Al plane frustrated the plot against it—a security guard killed one terrorist and a New York City passenger tackled the girl hijacker who came aboard carrying hand grenades in her brassiere. She was imprisoned when the plane landed safely in London.

A Pan American 747 was diverted to Cairo where the passengers were forced to slide down the emergency chutes seconds before the plane was blown up. Some suffered broken hips and legs and were hospitalized.

The other three jets—a TWA, Swissair, and BOAC—were forced to land precariously in the Jordan desert. (The Swissair almost crashed into the TWA upon landing.) The kidnapped passengers were held as hostages while the Palestinian terrorists bargained with England, Switzerland, and West Germany to release Arab terrorists held prisoner for previous skyjackings.

The kidnapping of the 340 passengers and crewmen on the three jet airliners sparked a civil war in Jordan, for King Hussein—who had sat by unable or unwilling to stop the illegal actions of the terrorists—now decided to show his countrymen and the world that he was still in full control of his nation. As he announced over his short-wave radio set: "We are putting our house in order." The hijacking episode was, he said, "The shame of the Arab nation."

He sent out his army. Savage street battles raged in the capital city of Amman between the King's men and the Palestinian guerrillas. The fighting spread to other parts of Jordan. There were over 10,000 Iraqi troops in Jordan, where they had been since the days prior to the Six-Day

War. Hussein feared they would now fight on the side of the guerrillas. Then Radio Amman reported that a Syrian armored brigade had crossed into Jordan, with Soviet-built tanks.

Golda and her government watched the borders closely. They knew that both Syria and Iraq would not be averse to enlarging their own countries by taking over Jordan. Israel could not sit idly by while Communist-dominated Arab countries and terrorists overthrew Jordan's King. Both Israel and the United States hinted that they might intervene—whereupon the Syrians, after several days of fighting, turned their tanks around and fled back home. The Iraqi soldiers in Jordan refrained from entering the fray. And King Hussein's army was able to regain control of Amman and other guerrilla strongholds.

But the civil war continued. There were some 5,000 casualties. The Jordan Red Crescent (the equivalent of the American Red Cross) reported that in Amman there were "hundreds of wounded dying in the streets or in the wreckage of their homes for lack of medical care." Other reports spoke of starving civilians in the capital city.

Israel sent in donations of over 200 tons of flour, sugar and oil, dispatched to Amman in Israeli trucks, driven by Arabs, and accompanied by International Red Cross officials. Israel's Hadassah Hospital donated anesthetics. And Israel also supplied urgently needed blood plasma. Many seriously wounded Jordanians—guerrillas, army men, and civilians—never knew that they were being saved by Jewish blood.

The hijacked hostages were caught in the middle of the civil war. Unable to take care of their prisoners, the guerrillas first released Christian women and children, then many of the men. The Jewish women and children were separated, detained; later released. (Five, whom the terrorists had claimed were "Israeli women soldiers," turned out instead to be American high school and college girls and a young rabbi's wife.) The Jordanian Army meanwhile broke into a refugee camp near Amman and freed the remaining Swiss, West German, and British hostages who had been hidden there by the guerrillas. When all the hostages were on their way home, Britain, Switzerland, and West Germany released all the Arab terrorists they had held prisoner for previous hijackings.

After Jordan's civil war had raged on for nine days, Nasser and other Arab leaders worked out a compromise and a cease-fire between King Hussein and the terrorist leader, Yasir Arafat. On September 28, as Nasser stood at the airport seeing off the Arab chiefs of state, he suddenly clutched at his chest. He was rushed home. His doctor diagnosed a heart attack. Four hours later he was dead.

Golda made no official comment.

But nine months prior to Nasser's death Golda had been asked by New York *Times* correspondent James Reston: "What if President Nasser fell? Would his successor be better able to negotiate with Israel?"

Flatly Golda had replied, "He can't be worse. And he must be different. When Stalin left, it wasn't Stalin who followed."

On the morning of October 18, 1970, Israel's Prime Minister set off once more for the United States. Golda and some of her top advisers were in a Boeing 707 jet, which was escorted by four Israeli Phantom bombers. Suddenly, as the planes rose above Tel Aviv's Lydda Airport, a lumbering transport plane came hurtling straight at the Prime Minister's jet. At the last moment it veered off, narrowly missing the Phantom escorts.

An El Al pilot later reported that the transport plane had accidentally strayed into the convoy's air corridor. It had avoided collision with the Prime Minister's jet only by "a sheer miracle."

Nothing, however, was said about the matter by the Prime Minister or her party when they landed at Kennedy Airport. They drove straight to the hotel, the Waldorf Astoria. (Prior to her Prime Ministerial days Golda had generally stayed at the Essex House, in a suite which overlooked Central Park. She was fond of the hotel and its staff; she knew the elevator operators and chambermaids by name. When she switched to the Waldorf, she wrote a note of apology to the Essex House explaining that she had made the move only because the "security people" insisted she do so. The Waldorf, it seemed, was specially set up to handle security measures necessary for chiefs of state.)

This time Golda had left her shopping list behind. She had come because the United Nations was celebrating its twenty-fifth anniversary. Since Israel was the first country the United Nations had voted into existence, it was fitting that her Prime Minister should speak.

During the ten-day commemorative session, the leaders of forty-five member nations came to address the United Nations. Their members included U.S. President Richard Nixon, Britain's Prime Minister Edward Heath, Russian Foreign Minister Andrei Gromyko, and many other world figures. But somehow none caused quite the excitement, the respect, and the affection as was generally accorded to the stalwart seventy-two-year-old grandmother known to the world as Golda. In the words of American correspondent Max Lerner:

> *Who would have foreseen a quarter-century ago when the U.N. was founded that at its 25th anniversary meetings the focus of attention would be not the representatives of the great powers with all their fanfare and panoply, but the woman Prime Minister of a little nation, with a tiny territory and a population of scarcely 3 million? . . . Israel's Prime Minister was the center of attention because what happens to Israel holds the key to what may happen or not happen in resolving the global power struggle. Also, it should be added, because of the kind of person Golda Meir is.*

Golda spoke at eleven o'clock on a Wednesday morning, October 21. Her seat was far from the speaker's stand, and she walked toward it with slow and measured steps. She wore a simple blue suit and sensible black shoes. Her hair, still dark though graying at the temples, was parted in the center, and pulled back into a severe bun, a style she had worn without change since the days of her early kibbutz life in Merhavia. She seemed somehow to embody the essence of the ancient nation which had been reborn out of antiquity, and which had been fighting for its existence ever since.

Her speech was not long. Her words were firm, her voice was strong.

"Mr. President, rising now to look upon a quarter of a century in the life of the United Nations Organization, I cannot help but recall that the United Nations will always be linked, in the mind of our people, with the signal role this Organization played in the emergence of modern sovereign Israel. The Organization put the seal of international recognition upon our historic process of return, ingathering, liberation and development—and this we cannot forget. The rebirth of the State of Israel in its historic homeland . . . rectified an ancient wrong within the framework of international law and in accordance with the principles of international justice. . . .

"There can be little doubt that the supreme historic achievement of the Organization has been its role in ending the era of colonialism and inaugurating, in its stead, the age of national liberation. Close to seventy nations have gained freedom and independence. This phenomenal transition has changed the face of the globe, rectifying the historical injustice which for centuries had acknowledged national freedom for the few and denied it for the many."

She looked up from her typewritten speech, glanced around the vast hall at the delegates who sat before the nameplates of the new nations. During her ten years as Prime Minister she had visited many of them: Ghana . . . Tanzania . . . Zambia . . . She had been at Zambia's Independence Day ceremonies. . . .

Ninety percent of the world now had independent statehood. It seemed cruelly ironic that the only nation which had been forced to struggle for its very survival since its first day of birth should be the nation of the Jews. The Jews who had given the concept of nationhood to the world. The Jews who had suffered more than any other

people in the world, and who wanted nothing more than
to live in peace in the small section of their ancient homeland.

"Mr. President, the whole Middle East is a dramatic
demonstration of the emergence of peoples into national
independence. Once the domain of colonial powers, it is
today an area inhabited entirely by independent and
sovereign countries . . . Unfortunately, the Middle East
has for twenty-two years been the scene for the cynical
flouting of solemn agreements. International order, the
integrity of the United Nations itself, depend upon the
scrupulous observance of international obligations. Unless
the members of the august body respect the sanctity of
agreements, no treaties can be binding and no pacts can
be maintained. . . . Any member state that disregards
. . . agreed covenants imperils the peace as well as the
United Nations. For this reason . . . let me recall the sad
record of broken covenants in the Middle East. From
the initial violation of the Charter of the United Nations
by the concerted Arab invasion of the new state of Israel,
to the present day, the sequence of events follows the
same disastrous line of agreements made and instantly
broken.

"The Arab states violated the armistice agreements of
1949, they nullified the arrangements concluded in 1957,
they unilaterally destroyed the cease-fire resolution of
1967 by embarking on a 'war of attrition' against Israel,
and now Egypt is undermining the American peace initiative by flagrantly violating the cease-fire standstill
agreement.

"It is these violations which have halted all progress
towards peace despite Israel's earnest commitment towards its quest."

She glanced up at her granddaughter Naomi, who was
in the gallery. She had brought the girl with her on this
trip. When Naomi returned home she would go into the
Army. She was seventeen. For how many more years must
Israel continue to conscript its teen-aged girls?
Some families had already lost three generations of sol-

diers. Mrs. Chaim Sturman, for instance. Her husband—
one of the organizers of Jewish self-defense in Palestine
—had been killed by the Arabs. His son grew up an
orphan—and was killed in the War of Liberation. He left
two sons. Both had been killed in the wars which followed.
The eighty-year-old grandmother was the family's sole
survivor. Golda had been at the funeral of the last grandson. Old Mrs. Sturman stood at the grave. There were no
tears. "The Sturmans," she said, "do not weep."

But how long could Israelis go on—without weeping?

"Despite what has happened, we still trust that, for
the sake of all our peoples, the Arab leadership will join
with us one day in guiding our area from the present
turmoil to the horizons of peace. I therefore call from
this rostrum, in the presence of the representatives of the
entire community of nations, upon the leaders of the
Arab nations of the Middle East and especially upon the
new leadership of Egypt to recognize once and for all
that the future of the Middle East lies in peace and this
must be achieved by Israelis and Arabs themselves. It
will only be achieved by the building of faith and not
the breach of faith . . . by the confrontation of peace
and not of war . . .

"All of those around us, as well as Israel, have paid
the terrible price of endless warfare. Billions of dollars
have been spent on armaments instead of on war against
poverty, disease, and ignorance. There are now deserts
of death where there could be blooming fields. I say this
today not in rancor but in sorrow.

"I am convinced that all of us in the Middle East will
continue to exist as sovereign states. None of us will
leave. But we may choose whether we will continue in
the sterile course of mutual destruction, whether we will
go on hurting each other to no one's benefit, or whether
we will venture on a constructive course and build our
lands separately and together.

"For each of us to attain the best for his people, cooperation with his neighbors in the solution of regional
problems is essential. Our borders not only separate us
but are bridges between us.

"No people is an island. We are bound to each other by the problems of our region, our world. We can make of these ties a curse or a blessing.

"Each nation, each land must decide."

She walked slowly back to her seat, looking straight ahead, almost unaware, it seemed, of the thunderous applause.

What would happen now? Where would Israel go from here? One could only do as she had always done: work—and hope.

Chapter 28

It was a quiet, cool desert night in the spring of 1972. Golda was on vacation, the first she had taken in over a year. Three days at Revivim.

She'd arrived after dinner, and now, near midnight, she entered the small flat the *kibbutzniks* had built for Sarah's "mother-the-prime-minister." She unpacked, undressed slowly, washed and got into bed. The black phone on her bedtable was blessedly quiet.

Things *were* quiet. Which was why she had allowed herself these three days.

Even relations with the Arab neighbors were relatively peaceful. Egypt's President, Anwar Sadat, still insisted in vociferous speeches that he was willing to sacrifice a million Egyptian lives (at times he upped it to three million) to win the next war against Israel. Syria, Libya and Iraq were still strident in their threats to annihilate Israel.

Yet, so far, somehow, the fragile cease-fire had remained in effect for twenty-two months. And for the first time in two dozen years the dream of the great Hebrew poet Bialik seemed a reality: Israel was becoming a very normal nation.

Replete even with TV. Though Israeli television had been in existence only four years, by now half the families in Israel owned a TV set. There were many other harbingers of normalcy and relaxation. Sales of camping equipment were skyrocketing: everything from sleeping bags to ice buckets. Sailing had become such a craze that some had taken up sunrise sailing before they left for work in the morning.

And the Prime Minister had come on vacation—with three fat books.

That midnight, May 30, 1972, she settled back against the pillows and opened one of them.

The telephone rang.

Automatically, her hand went out, picked up the receiver.

It was Brigadier Israel Lior. Her military secretary.

Swiftly, in words which shook only a little, he told her about the three-minute massacre which had just taken place at Lod Airport.

Air France flight 132 had landed. Her passengers converged around conveyor belt Number 3 waiting for their luggage. Three Japanese passengers retrieved their suitcases, opened them, took out automatic rifles. And started shooting. First they killed all passengers who stood nearby. Then their bullets sprayed through the crowded hall. The terminal—well named. Hall of bullets, screaming, blood, agony, and death.

In three minutes twenty-three people were slain. Including a man Golda knew well, Dr. Aharon Katzir, one of Israel's most brilliant and beloved scientists, a man respected throughout the world for his work in underdeveloped countries. He had been murdered in front of his wife who came to greet him at the airport. The dead also included twelve Puerto Ricans who had come on a pilgrimage to the Holy Land.

Eighty were wounded. They were being rushed to Shiba Hospital.

One of the Japanese terrorists had been killed in a burst of fire from his companion's gun. Another had slipped in blood as he was about to hurl a grenade, and was blown to pieces by that same grenade. The third killer had been taken prisoner when he stopped to reload his automatic. His name was Kozo Okamoto. He was twenty-four years old.

Golda dressed. She left Revivim. Her car hurtled along the deserted night road. The radio was on, detailing a crescendo of horror, the description of death and the dying. After some forty-five minutes the announcement came. The three Japanese had been recruited by the Popular Front for the Liberation of Palestine. They had been trained in Lebanon. "Our purpose," said the PFLP spokesman, "was to kill as many people as possible."

The Prime Minister reached Shiba Hospital near Tel Aviv before the sun came up. Forty operations had been performed during the night on the Lod Airport victims. Five more had died. Golda visited the wounded. She spoke with the doctors. Then she left for Jerusalem.

At four o'clock in the afternoon she delivered a statement in the Knesset. Her voice trembled, with anger.

"As soon as the news of what happened broke, joy broke out in Cairo and in Beirut over the 'Great Victory.' Dozens of people were killed and scores of others wounded—and there is no end to the rejoicing. Those who were unable to stand up against us on the battlefield are great heroes at hiding explosives in planes, blowing them up in midair—as they did two years ago in the Swissair disaster. This indeed takes great courage! And if the little courage needed for that is lacking—foreigners are recruited for the purpose. *Still* the joy is great!"

She looked up. Looked out. Beyond the members of the Knesset, the packed visitors gallery, the press. How

to make them listen? How to make them hear? How to
make them act?

"Two years ago, after the Swissair disaster, I made
a statement to the Knesset in which I said, 'We
are convinced that the international community is capable
of putting an end to piracy and terrorism in the air by
taking practical steps against the terrorist organizations,
their emissaries and their accessories, and against those
Arab States whose governments supply them with arms,
funds, and refuge.' "

Again she looked up from the typewritten paper she
held. Again she repeated, like the words of a dirge, a
prayer, a plea:

"That was two years ago!
"Who can recall all those dozens of hijackings and
attempts at murder which have taken place since, not only
in our region but throughout the world? This thing has
spread like an infectious disease. . . . It is no secret that
Beirut is openly enabling the centers of the terrorist
organizations to reside in its midst. There they plot, from
there instructors set out to various countries, and from
there come the broadcasts of their 'great success.' Can
it be possible that governments, that aviation companies,
should acquiesce in this state of affairs, on the presump-
tion that they would emerge unscathed?

"Not only Israelis are the target. This has been proven
on both domestic and international flights. Yesterday it
was a group of Puerto Ricans. Twelve of them. Maybe
more. There are still seven casualties unidentified, and
we do not know who they are. This hits every one of us.
These organizations, the pioneers in murder and lawless-
ness, have placed a question mark against safety in the
air.

"We, in Israel, shall do all we possibly can to safe-
guard our planes and, indeed, they are secure. We have
taken all the necessary steps to make sure that everybody
coming to Israel or leaving Israel in our planes can fly
in safety. We shall do everything that can be done. But

I have not the slightest doubt that unless other governments and airlines will cooperate and consider this as
their concern—and not merely for our sake—the scourge
shall remain to plague all."

The Prime Minister's speech held not only a warning
for the world, but a dual remedy.

First, all airlines should at once increase their security
measures. "The Lod tragedy could have been averted,"
she said later, "if even the most elementary precautions
had been taken." The French Union of Airline Pilots
backed up her statement by its own. "Since March 21,
security measures have been softened . . . and in certain
cases cancelled . . . on planes serving the Middle East."

However, after the Lod Massacre, Air France and seven
other airlines did strengthen security measures on planes
bound for Israel.

Golda's second solution was more far-reaching. All
international airlines should ban flights to those Arab
countries which harbored and supported terrorists. The
Japanese terrorist, Kozo Okamoto, issued a statement
which further backed the Prime Minister's warning that
this scourge was not Israel's problem alone; that the existence of the Arab terrorists, their well-publicized deeds
and the destruction they wrought, acted as a magnet to
their ilk around the world.

Okamoto revealed that he and his two cohorts were
members of the United Red Army, a radical terrorist
group in Japan. They had met the Arab representatives
of the Popular Front in North Korea, had journeyed to a
terrorist base in Lebanon to spend two months training
for their attack at Lod Airport. But, said Okamoto, the
United Red Army was not interested in the Arabs, indeed
tended to scorn them. "This cooperation with the Popular
Front," he explained, "was a jumping board to propel
ourselves onto the world stage. Our other actions are
coming—and they may be in New York or Washington.
The United Red Army will slay anyone who stands on the
side of the bourgeoisie."

No international airlines cancelled flights to Arab nations. And only one government made any attempt to apply pressure on Lebanon. The United States "urged" Beirut to "take all steps necessary" to prevent future terrorist attacks on airlines.

The Japanese government sent a top-level delegation to Israel in order to express Japan's feeling of shock and distress that the murderers had been Japanese. Indeed, Japan announced she would compensate the families of the dead and injured.

But the official expressions of horror ended abruptly when several Arab nations indicated that Japan's "sympathy" could harm her interests in the Middle East. With over ninety percent of Japan's oil coming from the Middle East, she could not afford to antagonize Arab leaders.

Israel was once again left on her own so far as solutions were concerned. Her methods were simple and direct. She sent soldiers and planes to destroy terrorist bases in Lebanon.

The United Nations Security Council condemned Israel for such actions.

Syria announced that "aid to the guerrillas will continue regardless of Israeli reprisals." Other Arab countries offered like reassurances to the terrorists. All save Jordan. For King Hussein had driven the Palestinian terrorists from his Kingdom after they landed three hijacked planes in the Jordan desert in September 1970. And he had not allowed them back.

In mid-August Golda received a call from the Levenstein Hospital, a nursing home near Tel Aviv. Shana had lived there for the past four years. She'd had a heart condition. She was very feeble. But she still was—Shana. Golda had made it a point to visit her older sister every fortnight; more often, if possible.

But now, the doctor said, Shana had taken a turn for the worse.

The Prime Minister left for the hospital immediately.

Shana. Memories swarmed back. She, Goldie, a child of five, sitting on Shana's lap as her beloved older sister told her about the new movement called Political Zionism . . . told her that the words "Next Year in Jerusalem" were more than a prayer recited by Jews the world over for hundreds upon hundreds of years. . . . The words could be a reality. Something to work for. Something to live for.

Shana . . . the person who had been the single most important influence in Golda's life.

When the Prime Minister reached Levenstein Hospital, the doctor was waiting. They walked together down the hall. Shana's face always lit up when her sister entered. But this time she stared blankly, as if Golda were a stranger.

Golda now had an additional reason for dreading the sound of the black bedside phone which had shattered her sleep during so many nights. Shana's death, the doctor had told her, might come at any moment.

Two weeks later, just after dawn on September 5, the bedside phone rang. It was not the hospital. It was her military secretary, Israel Lior.

Once again he reported swiftly, clearly; once again his words left Golda shaking with anger, with despair.

At 4:20 A.M. eight Arab terrorists had scaled the six-foot chain-link fence surrounding Munich's Olympic Village. They took from their athletic bags submachine guns, pistols, hand grenades. They entered Building 31 on Connollystrasse where the Israeli Olympic team was quartered on the second floor. They knocked on a door. Israeli wrestling coach Moshe Weinberg opened it a crack; slammed it closed, shouted a warning to his roommates, who fled out the window as Weinberg, age thirty-two, father of a five-week-old son, fell dead in a burst of machine gun fire. The same scene took place at a second apartment. There, two Israelis tried to hold off the gunmen while their roommates escaped. The two now lay dead.

Eighteen Israeli sportsmen had escaped out the windows. Nine had been taken hostage. The Munich police were arriving on the scene.

When the phone call ended, Golda sat for a long moment, too shattered to move.

Presently, she lifted the black receiver; gave directions that a Cabinet meeting be called for nine o'clock.

By nine, the Munich terrorists had issued their ultimatum. Two hundred Arab terrorists now in Israeli jails must be released at once. Kozo Okamoto must also be released. Furthermore, the Arabs and their Israeli captives must be flown out of West Germany, to an Arab nation. If the demands were not met by noon, the Israeli hostages would be executed at the rate of two every hour.

The meeting held in the subterranean Cabinet Room of the Knesset was short and tense. The Ministers sent a directive to the Israeli Ambassador in Bonn. He was to inform the West German government that "The government of Israel does not enter into negotiations with the terrorists. . . . We rely on the German authorities that, in their contact with the terrorists, all will be done that is necessary to ensure the safety of the hostages."

Time ticked on towards twelve o'clock.

A hot-line was opened between Munich and Jerusalem. West German Chancellor Willy Brandt had arrived in Munich. The police were working out a plan. German officials offered themselves as replacement for the hostages. Lures of "unlimited ransom" were held out. The offers were turned down. But the noon deadline was postponed.

The Cabinet Ministers sat around a radio in the sunlit dining room of the Knesset. The terrorists issued a new deadline. By noon the Knesset was convened for an emergency session. Golda stood at the podium. She looked out at the stricken faces. She tried to keep her voice steady, but sometimes it trembled.

"To my great regret, I am again obliged to give the Knesset very grave tidings." She described the situation. She listed the names of the hostages. And she concluded, "There is nothing which underscores the heinous character of anti-Israel terrorism more aptly than this murderous deed at the Olympic Village, vitiating—as it does—the Olympic spirit which has become a token and a symbol of world-wide brotherhood between nations and races. . . ."

All countries whose representatives participate in the Olympic Games are called upon to take all necessary action for the rescue of our citizens whose life is in immediate jeopardy and to rally against lunatic acts of terrorism, abduction and blackmail which tear asunder the web of international life."

That night a plane was flown to an air base outside Munich. The eight terrorists herded their bound and blindfolded prisoners into a German army bus. They were taken by helicopter to the airfield—ringed by German sharpshooters. The field was ablaze with floodlights. Shots sounded. Lights and radio in the control tower were knocked out. For one hour shooting continued. At the end of that time, five of the terrorists had been killed. Three surrendered. Four of the Israeli hostages were burned to death when a terrorist tossed a grenade into the helicopter in which they were held. The rest of the Israeli hostages were machine gunned to death by the Arabs.

The bodies of the murdered sportsmen were flown back to Israel, all but one. The body of weightlifter David Berger, age twenty-eight, was flown to Shaker Heights, Ohio. Berger had settled in Israel in 1971. After the Olympics he planned to marry, and enter the Israeli Army. His parents had learned of his death as they watched their TV screen in Shaker Heights.

A crowd of 3000 was at Lod Airport as the pinewood coffins were brought home. Golda was not there. At midnight the black telephone on her bedtable had rung. It was Levenstein Hospital. Her sister Shana was dead.

Twelve days later there was another telephone call from Israel Lior. It concerned an Israeli diplomat stationed in London but due home in a few weeks time. Golda had met him on her last trip to London. His name was Dr. Ami Shachori.

He was at his desk, going through his morning mail. He picked up a brown envelope, postmarked Amsterdam, ripped it open. There was an explosion. Shachori staggered from the office, blood gushing from his chest, his abdomen. He shouted a warning. Then he died.

His warning was heard around the world. It saved fifty-five lives. For that week similar letter bombs, postmarked Amsterdam, were discovered and handed over to the police in Paris, Geneva, Brussels, Vienna, Jerusalem, Tel Aviv, Montreal, Ottawa, Buenos Aires, Kinshasa, New York City and forty-five other cities. Some had been sent to Israelis; some to local Jews who did business with Israel.

Some of the letter bombs were pencil shaped. Some were the size and weight of a teabag. On the twenty-third of October a letter postmarked in the West German city of Karlsruhe was addressed to Moshe Levi Simon at the Israeli Embassy in Bonn. The letter was turned over to the police, because Moshe Levi Simon was unknown at the Embassy. This letter contained cyanide which, on contact with the air, developed a lethal poison gas.

Premier Golda Meir was asked about the new terror tactics.

"First," she said, "the Arabs tried to get us out of this area by open warfare. And they failed. Then they tried to get us out by terrorism within Israel itself. And they failed. Now they try by going out and finding an Israeli—even a Jew who is not an Israeli—somewhere, anywhere, in the world. And they fail."

The next morning Golda found on her desk a report, and a memo.

The report concerned Arab tourists to Israel. The Israeli Government granted any Arab a permit to come at any time to visit relatives in the Administered Territories. During the past summer over 150,000 Arabs had come from Egypt, Saudi Arabia, Jordan, Kuwait, from virtually every Arab land to visit relatives—and then, to visit Israel. Some were Arab businessmen who took luxury tours throughout the country, staying at the best hotels. Some were university students come to spend their summer vacation with their families in Hebron, or Nablus, or Ramallah. Others came to find temporary employment in Israel.

Reading the report, Golda was reminded of a line she had read of Lincoln Steffens. *I have seen the future, and it works.* This peaceful invasion of hundreds of thousands of Arab tourists clearly showed that peaceful coexistence was perfectly possible.

Perhaps, after all, Time would lay the most permanent paving stones towards peace in the Middle East.

The memo on the Prime Minister's desk was from the Twenty-fifth Anniversary Committee. It listed some of the major events to take place during the summer of '73 when the nation celebrated its first quarter century of existence.

Opening of Independence Day Festivities, Mount Herzl Ceremonies, May 6 . . . Israeli Parade, May 7 . . . International Jewish Youth Bible Quiz, May 7 . . . The Song Festival of 5733. . . .

The Twenty-fifth Anniversary of Israel in the Jewish calendar year 5733. Each of those numbers held its own miracle. And together they held the history of the Jewish people. And the Jewish state.

For Israel was the only modern nation in the world to be reborn out of antiquity—after a struggle as dramatic as any in the Old Testament. Her citizens were the only people to have been dispersed throughout the world for almost 2000 years—and gathered together once more in their historic homeland. Her language was the only one in the world to have been resurrected from archaic prayers and religious writings—and adapted into a vibrant Twentieth Century tongue.

Perhaps, Golda reflected, considered in the light of the 5733 years on the Jewish calendar, Israel's Twenty-fifth Anniversary did not seem like such a miracle. And yet— it was. It was.

Bibliography

A Partial Listing

AGRESS, ELIYAHU, *Golda Meir: Portrait of a Prime Minister*. New York, Sabra Books, 1969.

BARATZ, JOSEPH, *A Village on the Jordan*. Tel Aviv, Ichud Habonim.

BARER, SHLOMO, *The Weekend War*. Tel Aviv, Karni Publishers, 1959.

DIMONT, MAX, *Jews, God, and History*. New York, Simon and Schuster, 1962.

EBAN, ABBA, *My People: The Story of the Jews*. New York, Random House, 1968.

FAST, HOWARD, *The Jews: Story of a People*. New York, The Dial Press, 1968.

GRUBER, RUTH, *Israel on the Seventh Day*. New York, Hill and Wang, 1968.

HERTZBERG, ARTHUR, ed., *The Zionist Idea: A Historical Analysis and Reader*. New York, Doubleday, 1959.

JOSEPH, DOV, *The Faithful City: The Siege of Jerusalem, 1948*. New York, Simon and Schuster, 1960.

KORNGOLD, SHANA, *Zikhroynes* ("Memories"). Tel Aviv, 1968 (?).

KURZMAN, DAN, *Genesis 1948: The First Arab-Israeli War*. New York, World Publishing, 1970.

LAQUEUR, WALTER, ed., *The Israel/Arab Reader: A Documentary History of the Middle East Conflict*. London, Weidenfeld and Nicolson, 1969.

LEVIN, MEYER, *The Story of Israel*. New York, G. P. Putnam's Sons, 1966.

254 GOLDA

LOWDERMILK, WALTER CLAY, *Palestine, Land of Promise.* New York, Harper and Brothers, 1944.

MEIR, GOLDA, *This Is Our Strength* (ed. Henry M. Christman). New York, Macmillan, 1962.

PERES, SHIMON, *David's Sling: The Arming of Israel.* London, Weidenfeld and Nicolson, 1969.

SHAREF, ZEEV, *Three Days.* London, W. H. Allen, 1962.

ST. JOHN, ROBERT, *Shalom Means Peace,* New York, Doubleday, 1949.

SYRKIN, MARIE, *Golda Meir, Israel's Leader.* New York, G. P. Putnam's Sons, 1969.

Three Years of Military Government, 1967–1970. Jerusalem, Coordinator of Government Operations in the Administered Territories, Ministry of Defense, 1970.

ZIFF, WILLIAM B., *The Rape of Palestine.* Toronto, Longmans, Green and Co., 1938.

Index

Palestine Refugee Plan, 220-22

Palestine Royal Commission, 79, 90

Pan-Arabic Federation, 96

Patria, SS, 108

People's Relief, 38

Peres, Shimon, 157, 164

Pineau, Christian, 158-61, 164

Pioneer Women, 63, 66

Pinsk, 1-12, 19-20, 23-24, 38

Poale Zion, 39-43, 65

Pocahontas, SS, 47, 95

Pogroms, 2, 6-8, 10, 38, 95-98, 149

Political Zionism, 247

Popular Front for the Liberation of Palestine, 216-17, 243, 245

Proclamation of Independence, Israeli, 124, 129-32, 147

Rabin, Yitzhak, 180, 185

Rechavi, Zacharia, 137, 139

Red Sea, 159, 165-66, 191

Revivim, 136-37, 153, 162, 208

Rogers, William, 225

Rogers crisis, 225-29

Roosevelt, Franklin D., 81, 83

Rothschild, Baron Edmond de, 67

Rublee, George, 86-88

Sadat, Anwar, 241

Saudi Arabia, 90, 118, 250

Shachori, Ami, 249

Shapira, Moshe, 169-70

Shapiro, Yakov Shimshon, 227

Sharett, Moshe. *See* Shertok, Moshe

Sharm el Sheikh, 164, 166, 181, 187, 191-92, 202

Sharon, Ariel, 187

Shertok, Moshe, 107, 113, 132, 135, 147

Simon, Moshe Levi, 250

Sinai Campaign, 168, 170, 178, 181, 184, 202

Sinai Peninsula, 163, 187, 191-92

Six Day War (1967), 180-90, 195, 200, 201-03, 209-10, 221, 234-35

Soviet Union. *See* Union of Soviet Socialist Republics

Steffens, Lincoln, 251

Stern, Fred, 137-38

Struma, SS, 102

Suez Canal, 98, 158-59, 163-64, 167-68, 178-80, 186, 200, 215, 225, 229-30

Syria, 66, 90, 105, 115, 117, 132, 146, 158-59, 161, 170, 180, 183, 187-88, 204, 211, 218-19, 221-22, 235, 242, 246

Tal, Israel, 186

Taylor, Myron C., 82-83

Tekoah, Yosef, 230

Tel Aviv, 49-51, 56, 72-74, 116-17, 147, 165, 183, 188-89, 202

Tran-Jordan, 61, 90, 93, 126, 218. *See also* Jordan

Truman, Harry, 132

U Thant, 180-81

Union of Soviet Socialist Republics, 113, 159-60, 163, 164, 167, 180, 186, 199-200, 204, 219, 223-24, 225, 228-29, 232, 235

United Jewish Appeal, 138

United Nations, 106, 111-14, 118, 125-26, 129, 137, 162, 165-69, 178-82, 185, 187, 192, 200, 218-21, 225, 230, 239, 246

About the Author

Peggy Mann has written some twenty books, for adults and children, including the novel *A Room in Paris* and the popular children's book, *The Street of the Flower Boxes,* which was made into a TV movie. She is currently completing a major nonfiction book on a little-known phase of Israel's history. Miss Mann has traveled extensively and made several long visits to Israel.

The author's articles and short stories have appeared in numerous national magazines, including *Harper's Bazaar, Reader's Digest, McCall's, Cosmopolitan* and *Redbook.*

In private life Peggy Mann is the wife of public relations counsel, William Houlton, and the mother of Jenny, age 10, and Betsy, age 7. The two young Houltons are actresses and appear on a daytime television series.

The Houltons live in a brownstone on Manhattan's West Side. There, Peggy Mann Houlton is often called "Mrs. Brownstone," for her work in starting the brownstone revival movement in New York City.

60

61 not refusal